Lisa Balabanlilar   tral Asian
History at Rice Uni

'Professor Lisa Balabanlilar's fluently written book on Mughal India represents a major contribution to the history of Muslim rule in the Indian subcontinent and to the study of Muslim imperial rule in the Ottoman, Safavid and Mughal empires. Her work, based on Chaghatai Turkish and Persian sources, ought to profoundly influence the future historiography of South Asia, whose scholars, with a few important exceptions, have overlooked the tenacious Turco–Mongol ligatures that tied the Mughals to their Central Asian and more particularly, Timurid inheritance. The book should also help to integrate Mughal, or Timurid–Mughal history into the broader study of the three contemporary Muslim empires, which were the legatees of Turco–Mongol and Perso–Islamic social, cultural and political traditions.'

Professor Stephen F. Dale, Department of History, Ohio State University

IMPERIAL IDENTITY IN THE MUGHAL EMPIRE

Memory and Dynastic Politics in Early Modern South and Central Asia

LISA BALABANLILAR

I.B. TAURIS
LONDON · NEW YORK

Paperback edition published in 2016 by
I.B.Tauris & Co. Ltd
London • New York
www.ibtauris.com

Copyright © 2012 Lisa Balabanlilar

The right of Lisa Balabanlilar to be identified as the author of this work has been asserted by the author in accordance with the Copyright, Designs and Patent Act 1988.

All rights reserved. Except for brief quotations in a review, this book, or any part thereof, may not be reproduced, stored in or introduced into a retrieval system, or transmitted, in any form or by any means, electronic, mechanical, photocopying, recording or otherwise, without the prior written permission of the publisher.

ISBN: 978 1 78453 128 7
eISBN: 978 0 85773 246 0

A full CIP record for this book is available from the British Library
A full CIP record for this book is available from the Library of Congress

Library of Congress catalog card: available

Typeset by Newgen Publishers, Chennai
Printed and bound by CPI Group (UK) Ltd, Croydon, CR0 4YY

CONTENTS

Genealogy of the Timurid-Mughal Dynasty of India   vii
Acknowledgements   xv
A Note on Transliteration   xvii
Maps   xviii

Introduction   1

Prologue   Timurid Political Charisma and the Ideology of Rule   7

Chapter 1   Babur and the Timurid Exile   18

Chapter 2   Dynastic Memory and the Genealogical Cult   37

Chapter 3   The Peripatetic Court and the Timurid-Mughal Landscape   71

Chapter 4   Legitimacy, Restless Princes and the Imperial Succession   100

Chapter 5   Conclusion: Imagining Kingship   140

Notes   156
Bibliography   192
Index   210

GENEALOGY OF THE TIMURID-MUGHAL DYNASTY OF INDIA*

I   Zahir al-Din Muhammad Babur, 1483–1530:

Father: Umar Shaykh, son of Sultan Abu Said Mirza, son of Sultan Muhammad, son of Miranshah, son of Timur Guregen Barlas/ Mother: Qutlugh Nigar Khanim, daughter of Yunus Khan (m. Esan Dawlat) of the Chaghatayid Khans.

Wives:

Ayshah Sultan Begim, m. 1499 (daughter of Sultan Ahmad Mirza Miranshah)
Zainab Sultan Begim, d. 1504 (daughter of Sultan Mahmud Mirza)
Ma'sumeh Begim (1) (?)
Maham Begim
Ma'sumah Begim (2), m. 1507 (daughter of Sultan Ahmed Mirza Miranshah)

---

* This genealogical chart is, of course, quite incomplete, but owes much to the on-line Mughal genealogy, prepared as an interactive excel spreadsheet, by Audrey Truschke of Columbia University: http://www.columbia.edu/itc/mealac/pritchett/00maplinks/ overview/charts/mughal_genealogy.pdf

Bibi Mubarika, the Yusufzay, "Afghani Agacheh," m. 1511
a daughter of Malik Mansour Yusufzay
Dildar Begim
Gulrukh Begim Taghai Begchik
Sayyida Afak

Children:

Humayun, 1508–1556/r. 1530–1540, 1555–1556, by Maham Begim
Askari Mirza, 1516–1558, by Gulrukh Begim
Gulbadan Begim, 1523–1603, by Dildar Begim; m. Khizr Khwaja Khan
Hindal Mirza, 1518–1551, by Dildar Begim
Kamran Mirza, 1509–1557, by Gulrukh Begim

II Humayun, "Jannat Ashyani," 1508–1556
r. 1530–1540, 1555–1556

Wives:

Hamida Banu Begim, "Maryam Makani," d. 1603
Bega (Haji) Begim
Bigeh Begim
Chand Bibi (?)
Mah-chuchak, m. 1546; d. 1564
Miveh Jan, m. 1532
Shahzade Khanim, d. of Mirza Suleyman of Badakhshan

Children:

Bakhshi Banu Begim, b. 1540, by Gunwar Bibi
Jalal al-Din Muhammad Akbar, 1542–1605; r. 1556–1605, by Hamida Banu Begim
Bahkt al-Nisa Begim, 1550–1608, by Mah-Chuchak
Mirza Muhammad Hakim, 1553/4–1585, by Mah-Chuchak

THE TIMURID-MUGHAL DYNASTY OF INDIA   IX

III   Jalal al-Din Muhammad Akbar (1542–1605;
       r. 1556–1605)

Wives:

Ruqayya Sultan (1544–1626), daughter of Hindal Mirza
Salima Sultan (1539–1611), former wife of Bairam Khan
Hira Kunwar Sahiba Harkha Bai (?), "Maryam al-Zamani,"
   (1542–1622; m. 1562)
daughter of Raja Bihari Mal of Amber; mother of Jahangir
former wife of Abdul Wasi (m. 1662)
daughter of Miran Mubarak Shah, King of Khandesh (m. 1564)
niece of Raja Kalyan Mal of Bikaner (m. 1570)
daughter of Raja Har Rai of Jaisalmer (m. 1570
daughter of Raja of Dungarpar (m. 1576)
daughter of Abdullah Khan Moghul
Bibi Daulatshah (?)

Children:

Sultan Salim Nur al-Din Jahangir, "Jannat Makani" (1569–1627;
   r. 1605–1627), by Maryam al-Zamani of Amber
Shahzada Begim (b. 1569)
Shah Murad (1570–1598)
Danyal (1572–1604)
Aram Banu Begim (d. 1624?), by Bibi Daulatshah
Shakr al-Nisa Begim (d. 1653), by Bibi Daulatshah

IV   Sultan Salim Nur al-Din Jahangir, "Jannat Makani"
      (1569–1627; r. 1605–1627)

Wives:

Shah Begim (m. 1584, d. 1605), d. of Raja Bhagwan Das [brother
   of Jahangir's mother, Maryam al-Zamani and father of Raja Man
   Singh, d. 1614]

Mihr al-Nisa/Nurjahan Begim (1577–1645; m. 1611), d. of Mirza Ghiyas Beg "I'timad al-Dawla" and Asmat Begim; sister of Abdul Hasan Asaf Khan (whose daughter Arjomand Banu Begim, 1592–1631, would marry Shah Jahan and become known as Mumtaz Mahal); mother of Ladli Begim (by her first husband, Sher Afghan Quli Khan, d. 1607), who would go on to marry Jahangir's son Shahryar.

Jagat Gosain Manmati/ Jodhi Bhai?/ "Bilqis Makani" (d. 1619), daughter of Raja Udai Singh "Mota Raja," son of Raja Mal Deo of Marwar; mother of Khurram "Shah Jahan"

Sahib Jamal, d. 1599

Children:

Sultan al-Nisa Begim, 1586–1646, by Shah Begim
Khusrau, 1587–1622, by Shah Begim
Parvez, 1589–1626, by Sahib Jamal
Bahar Banu Begim, 1590–1653, by Karamsi
Khurram Shihab al-Din Shah Jahan, 1592–1666, r. 1628–1659, by Jagat Gosain Manmati
Shahryar, 1605–1628, by unnamed concubine

V Khurram Shihab al-Din Shah Jahan, 1592–1666, r. 1628–1659

Wives:

Arjomand Banu Begim "Mumtaz Mahal," 1592–1631, m. 1612, mother of Aurangzeb
Akbarabadi Begum/Majal Izz al-Nisa Begim, d. 1677
Fatehpuri Begim
Sirhindi Begim
Bhai Lilavati, d. of Rao Sakar Singh?

Children (all by Mumtaz Mahal)

Jahanara Begim, 1614–1681
Dara Shikoh, 1615–1659

THE TIMURID-MUGHAL DYNASTY OF INDIA   XI

Shah Shuja, 1616(?)–1659
Raushanara Begim, 1617–1671
Aurangzeb Alamgir, 1618–1707, r. 1659–1707
Murad Baksh, 1619–1661
Qudaiya, 1630–1706

VI Aurangzeb Alamgir, 1618–1707, r. 1659–1707

Wives:

Dilras Banu Bagim, Rabia al-Durrani, d. 1657
Nawab Bhai Begi Saheba Rahmat al-Nisa, d. 1691, daughter of Rajah Raju of Rajauri (Kashmir), mother of Bahadur Shah
Aurangabadi Mahal, d. 1688
Udaipuri Mahal, d. 1707

Children:

Zeb al-Nisa, 1637–1702
Muhammad Sultan, 1639–1676
Zinat al-Nisa, 1643–1721
Muhammad Muazzam Bahadur Shah Alam, 1643–1712, r. 1707–1712, by Rahmat al-Nisa
Badr al-Nisa, 1647–1670
Zubdat al-Nisa Begim, 1651–1707
Muhammad Azam Shah, 1653–1707
Muhammad Akbar, 1657–1704
Mehr al-Nisa, 1661–1706
Muhammad Kam Baksh, 1667–1709, by Udaipuri Mahal

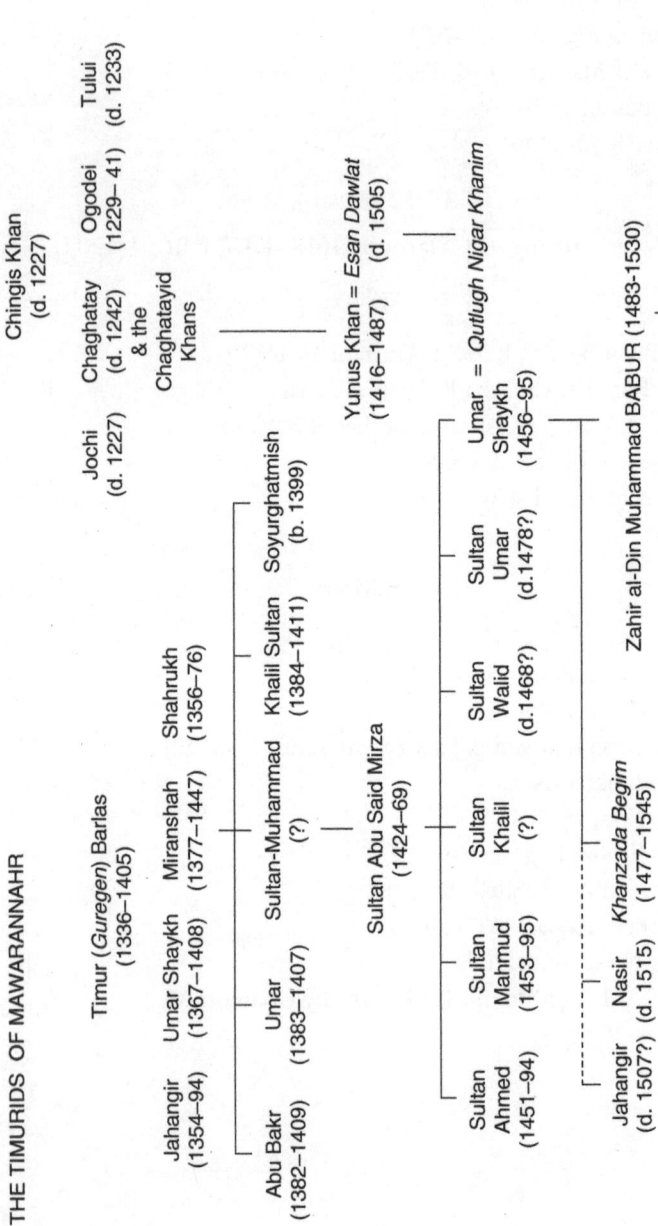

THE TIMURIDS OF MAWARANNAHR

```
                                                                    Chingis Khan
                                                                     (d. 1227)
                                        ┌──────────────┬──────────────┬──────────────┐
                                       Jochi       Chaghatay        Ogodei         Tului
                                     (d. 1227)     (d. 1242)       (1229–41)     (d. 1233)
                                                   & the
                                                 Chaghatayid
                                                    Khans
                                                        │
                                            Yunus Khan = Esan Dawlat
                                            (1416–1487)   (d. 1505)
                                                        │
                                              Umar  =  Qutlugh Nigar Khanim
                                             Shaykh
                                            (1456–95)

    Timur (Guregen) Barlas
         (1336–1405)
  ┌──────────┬──────────┬──────────┐
Jahangir  Umar Shaykh   Miranshah   Shahrukh
(1354–94) (1367–1408)  (1377–1447)  (1356–76)
                            │
       ┌────────────────────┼────────────────────┬────────────────┐
   Sultan-Muhammad      Khalil Sultan        Soyurghatmish
        (?)              (1384–1411)          (b. 1399)
         │
   Sultan Abu Said Mirza
       (1424–69)
  ┌──────────┬──────────┬──────────┐
Abu Bakr                 Umar
(1382–1409)            (1383–1407)

  ┌──────────┬──────────┬──────────┬──────────┐
Sultan    Sultan     Sultan     Sultan      Sultan
Ahmed     Mahmud     Khalil     Walid        Umar
(1451–94) (1453–95)   (?)      (d.1468?)   (d.1478?)

                    Jahangir    Nasir    Khanzada Begim
                  (d. 1507?) (d. 1515)   (1477–1545)

              Zahir al-Din Muhammad BABUR (1483-1530)

                          Continued on next page
```

THE TIMURIDS OF INDIA

Zahir al-Din Muhammad BABUR

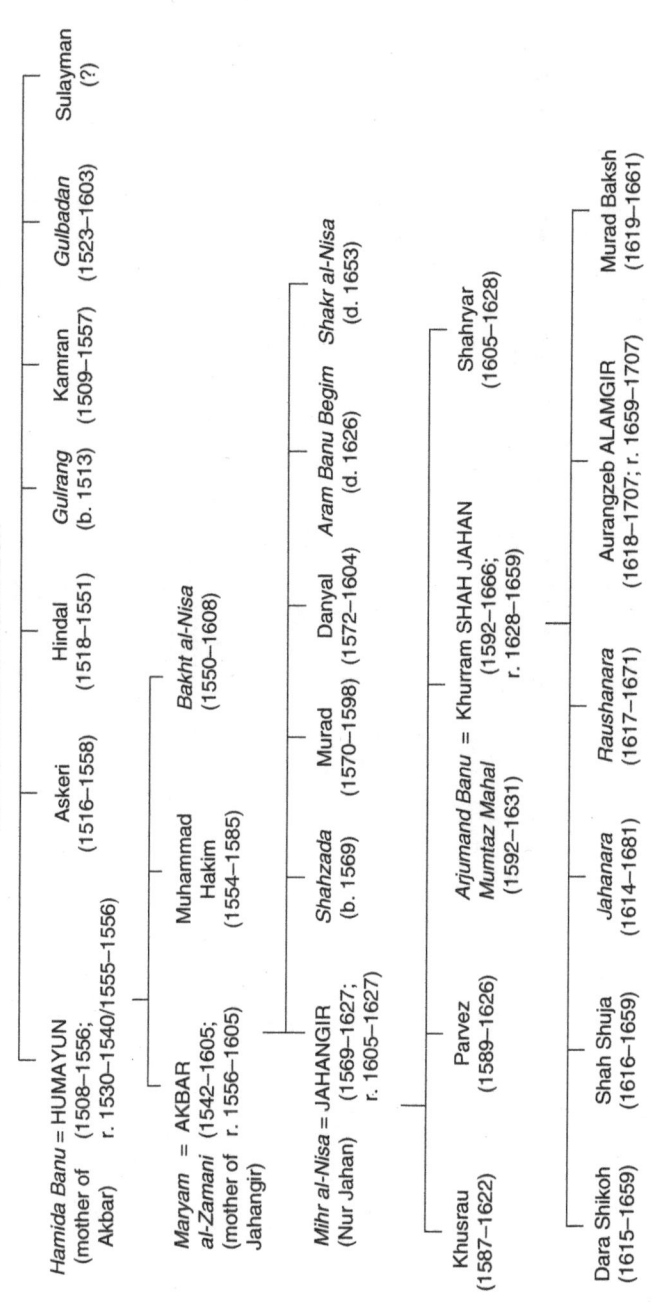

- Hamida Banu = HUMAYUN (1508–1556; r. 1530–1540/1555–1556) (mother of Akbar)
- Askeri (1516–1558)
- Hindal (1518–1551)
- Gulrang (b. 1513)
- Kamran (1509–1557)
- Gulbadan (1523–1603)
- Sulayman (?)

Children of Humayun:
- Maryam al-Zamani = AKBAR (1542–1605; r. 1556–1605) (mother of Jahangir)
- Muhammad Hakim (1554–1585)
- Bakht al-Nisa (1550–1608)

Children of Akbar:
- Mihr al-Nisa = JAHANGIR (1569–1627; r. 1605–1627) (Nur Jahan)
- Shahzada (b. 1569)
- Murad (1570–1598)
- Danyal (1572–1604)
- Aram Banu Begim (d. 1626)
- Shakr al-Nisa (d. 1653)

Children of Jahangir:
- Khusrau (1587–1622)
- Parvez (1589–1626)
- Arjumand Banu Mumtaz Mahal (1592–1631) = Khurram SHAH JAHAN (1592–1666; r. 1628–1659)
- Shahryar (1605–1628)

Children of Shah Jahan:
- Dara Shikoh (1615–1659)
- Shah Shuja (1616–1659)
- Jahanara (1614–1681)
- Raushanara (1617–1671)
- Aurangzeb ALAMGIR (1618–1707; r. 1659–1707)
- Murad Baksh (1619–1661)

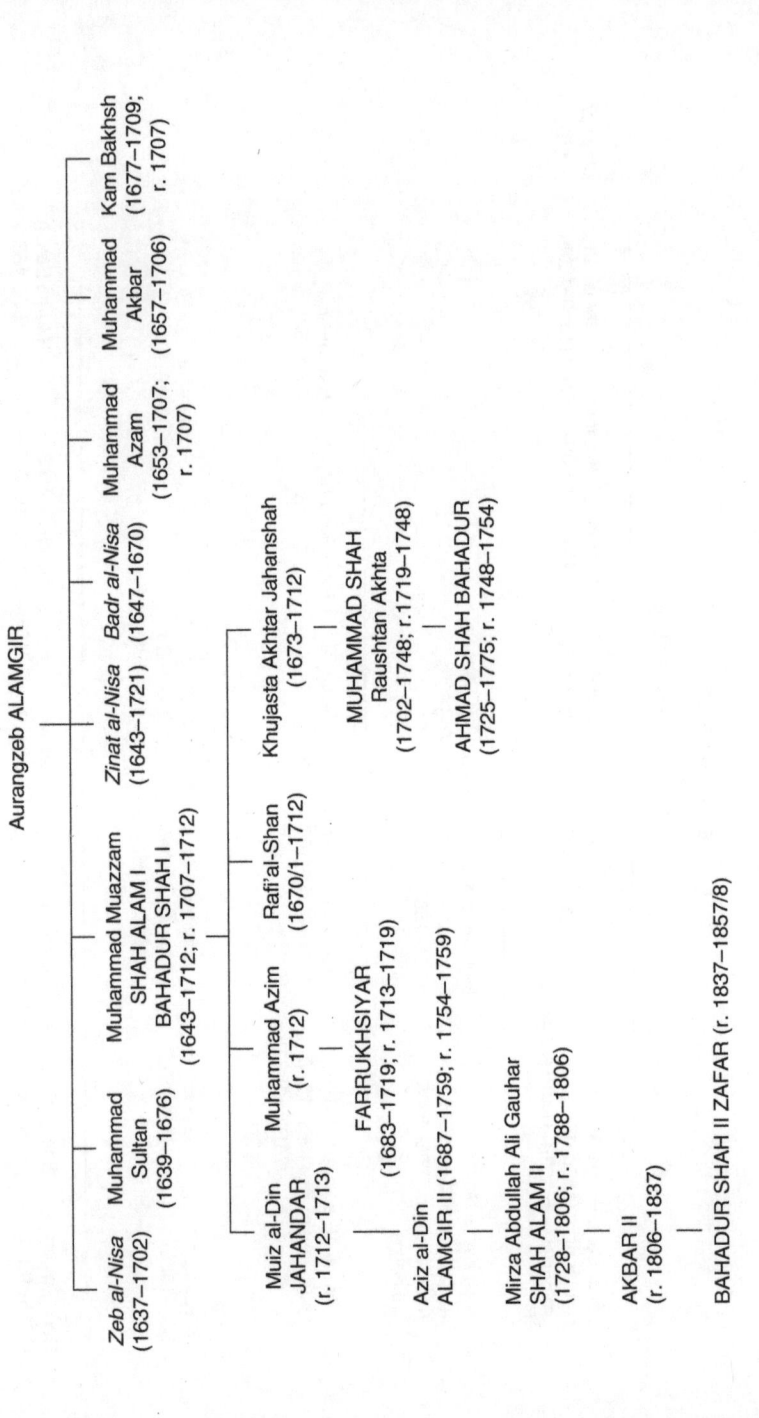

Aurangzeb ALAMGIR

- Zeb al-Nisa (1637–1702)
- Muhammad Sultan (1639–1676)
- Muhammad Muazzam SHAH ALAM I BAHADUR SHAH I (1643–1712; r. 1707–1712)
  - Muiz al-Din JAHANDAR (r. 1712–1713)
  - Muhammad Azim (r. 1712)
  - Rafi'al-Shan (1670/1–1712)
    - FARRUKHSIYAR (1683–1719; r. 1713–1719)
    - Aziz al-Din ALAMGIR II (1687–1759; r. 1754–1759)
      - Mirza Abdullah Ali Gauhar SHAH ALAM II (1728–1806; r. 1788–1806)
        - AKBAR II (r. 1806–1837)
          - BAHADUR SHAH II ZAFAR (r. 1837–1857/8)
- Zinat al-Nisa (1643–1721)
- Badr al-Nisa (1647–1670)
  - Khujasta Akhtar Jahanshah (1673–1712)
    - MUHAMMAD SHAH Raushtan Akhta (1702–1748; r.1719–1748)
      - AHMAD SHAH BAHADUR (1725–1775; r. 1748–1754)
- Muhammad Azam (1653–1707; r. 1707)
- Muhammad Akbar (1657–1706)
- Kam Bakhsh (1677–1709; r. 1707)

ACKNOWLEDGEMENTS

I would like to express my most heartfelt gratitude to Stephen F. Dale, who first introduced me to the Timurid-Mughals. Any success I might have as a scholar is due to his kind guidance and his remarkable intellectual generosity. My debt to him will be obvious to all who know his work.

Many people have had a hand in the making of this book, and I would like to thank the colleagues who offered me their invaluable time and assistance. At Rice University, my sincere thanks to Kerry Ward and Ussama Makdisi, for reading the full manuscript in its multiple iterations and offering their thoughtful criticism. To Peter C. Caldwell and Michael Maas, Paula Sanders, Lora Wildenthall, Alex Byrd, Rebecca Goetz, and Richard Smith, who patiently read various chapters and offered their insight and support, my gratitude. Warm thanks also to departmental administrator Paula Platt, for all of her advice and adept support, and to Kim Riker and Jean Niswonger, of the Rice University GIS/Data Center, for their skillful assistance in the creation of new maps. I would like to express my gratitude to the Department of History at Rice University, which offered me not only generous assistance but also, and most importantly, the support of a remarkable community of intellectually engaged and thoughtful scholars, now friends.

I would also like to warmly thank Ahmed Azfar Moin, of Southern Methodist University, for reading the manuscript and offering me the benefit of his wisdom and his encouragement. Additionally, my thanks to Jane Hathaway, of Ohio State University, for her years of academic support and warm friendship. I would like to thank Geoffrey

Parker for his encouragement and, most importantly, his wonderful intellectual curiosity. I am deeply indebted to Carter V. Findley for his early interest in my work and his years of support. Also at Ohio State, my thanks to Parvaneh Pourshariati, Farah Shadchehr, Dona Straley and Howard Crane. In gratitude for generous financial support over many years, I thank the Ohio State University Middle East Studies Center, particularly it's director, Alam Payind. My warm thanks to Richard Hermann of the Mershon Center at for International Security Studies, also at Ohio State, for making possible my early research in England and India. I would like to express my gratitude to Barbara Metcalf, Scott Levi, and Robert McChesney for their kind support in the early stages of this project. My thanks to Wheeler Thackston of Harvard University for two summers of Persian paleography on the island of Cunda, in company with the late, and much mourned, Şinasi Tekin, my teacher of Ottoman Turkish. To my early mentor, Dr. Jon Mandeville of Portland State University, who insistently set me on this path, my gratitude. I would like to thank Jerry Bentley at the Journal of World History and Charlotte de Blois at the Journal of the Royal Asiatic Society for their generous interest in my project. I also owe a real debt of gratitude to my editor at I.B.Tauris, Tomasz Hoskins, for his insights, his kindness and his support.

This book is dedicated with love and gratitude to my parents, Richard and Jocelyn Fanning, and finally, with all of my heart, this book is for my daughter, Sara Perihan.

Portions of this book have been previously published by the Journal of World History, the Journal of Asian Studies and the Journal of the Royal Asiatic Society, and are reprinted here with permission.

A NOTE ON TRANSLITERATION

Words from Persian, Arabic and Turkish have been rendered using a simplified transliteration system without diacritical marks, in the interests of keeping the text uncluttered, and generally following the conventions of the International Journal of Middle East Studies (IJMES). Transliterated words from secondary works and translations of primary sources are cited without modification, except that diacritical marks are dropped.

MAPS

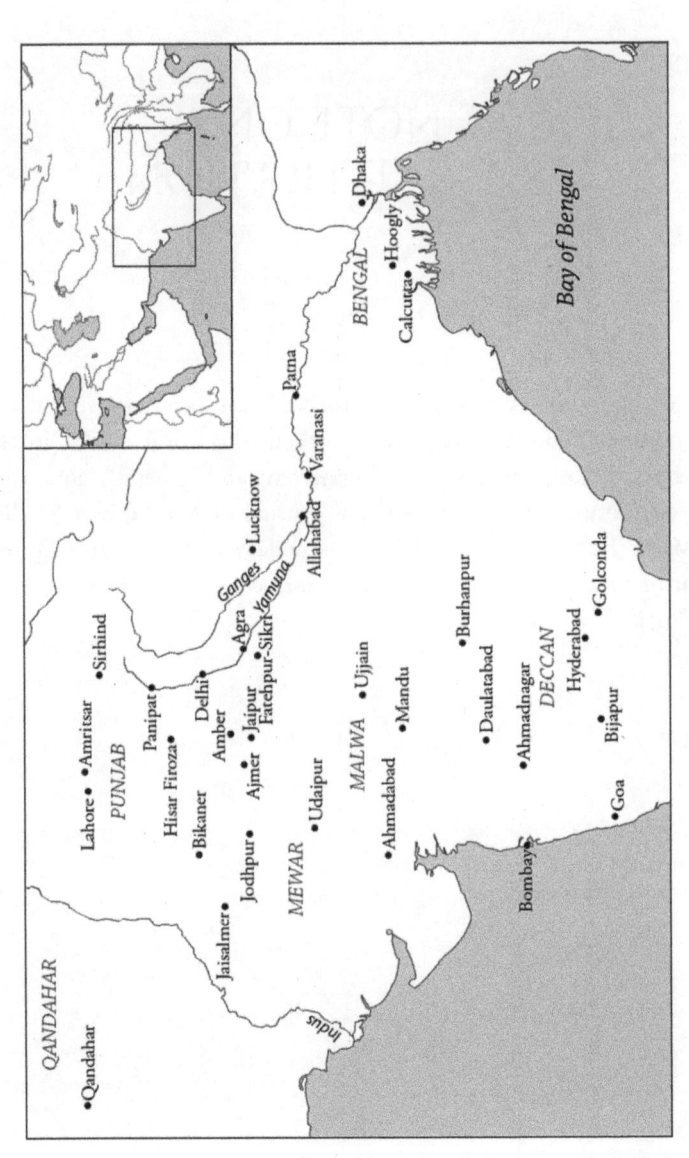

Mughal South Asia

MAPS   XIX

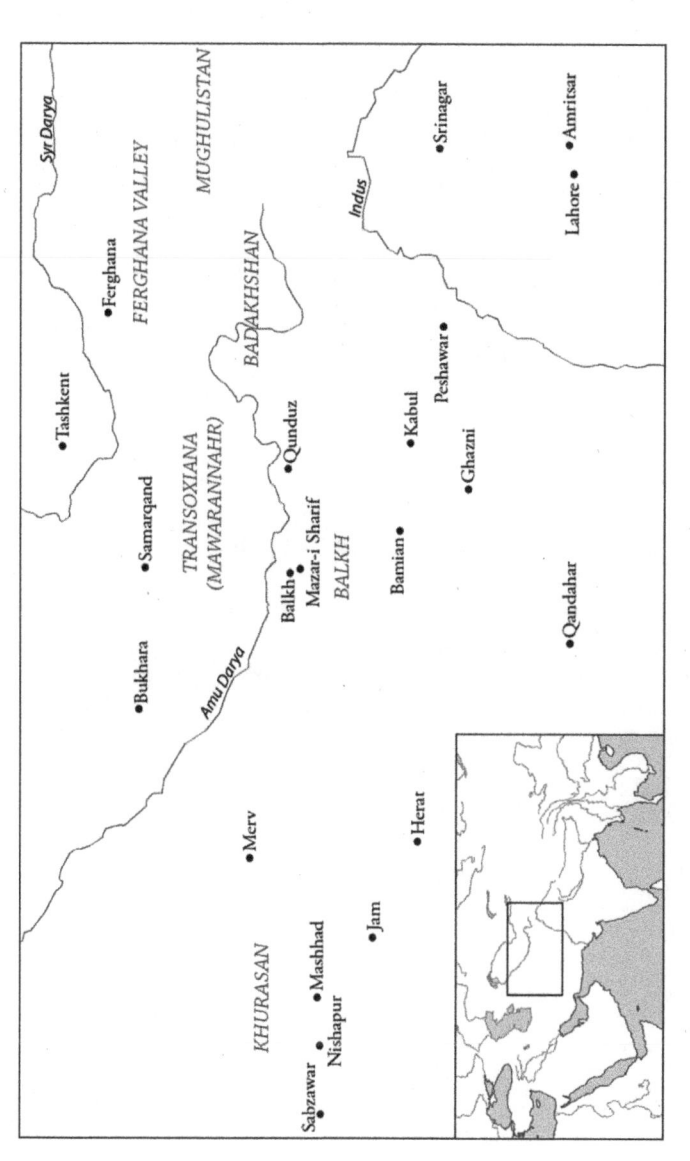

Timurid Transoxiana

INTRODUCTION

Among the most critical developments in the early modern world was the emergence of powerful Muslim empires to replace the fragmented tribal alliances and minor sultanates which had remained in the void left by Mongol failure and collapse in the central Islamic lands. These great empires: the Ottomans and Safavids, the Uzbeks and Mughals, shared Central Asian Turkic political traditions, Persianate aesthetic understandings and a vision of conquest rooted in Mongol aspirations of world empire. Their development of military and political trends, centralized bureaucratic institutions, and vital artistic and cultural expressions would have a powerful lingering global influence.

Contemporary studies of India's Mughal dynasty, however, long dominated by nationalist, sectarian and ideological agendas, typically present the Mughals as a singularly Indian phenomenon, politically and culturally isolated on the subcontinent. Blaming the Mongol invasions of the thirteenth century C.E., which 'first propelled Muslim India on its own separate path, distinct from that taken by the lands west of the Indus,'[1] modern scholarship on the Middle East and Islamic Central Asia has long marginalized Indian Islam and assigned to the Mughal emperors of the subcontinent a position on the periphery of the early modern Islamic world. Although the founders of the Mughal empire were immigrants from Central Asia, few scholars acknowledge that their strong personal and dynastic ties to that region might have relevance to our understanding of the empire.[2] Eminent scholars of the Mughals disregard their Central Asian legacy, declaring that 'the interests and future of all concerned were in India.'[3] Directly linked to the preceding nearly thousand years of Muslim colonization in India the Mughals are described as 'indisputably Indian ... emerging from the Indian historical experience.'[4] Mughal history for many scholars is considered to have begun with the eighth-century arrival of Umayyad Muslim armies of conquest and the establishment of 'Indo-Muslim rule – whether of foreign or Indian origin' over most of the subcontinent.[5]

Scholarship demanding one thousand years of Indo-Muslim continuity ignores the particular character of the Mughal Empire. The Mughal dynasts were culturally and politically distinct from the Turkish and Afghan dynasties which had preceded them as Muslim rulers of northern India. The founder of the Mughal Empire, Zahir al-Din Muhammad Babur (1483–1530), was half Turkish and half Mongol, a descendant of both Chingis Khan and Timur (Tamerlane; his descendants are known as Timurids). In the closing years of the fifteenth century, the Timurid-Mongol ruling elite of Central Asia were forced out of their ancestral homeland in Mawarannahr (Transoxiana) by an invading Uzbek Mongol tribal confederation. In the early years of the Timurid exile and displacement the young and ambitious prince Babur managed to maintain a limited royal court in Kabul, although it remained impoverished and under constant threat of invasion. Ever in search for territory and economic stability, Babur and his refugee army of Timurids and Chaghatay Mongols continued to raid south, eventually winning a decisive victory against the Afghan Lodi kings of northern India at Panipat in 1526 and establishing themselves as the new rulers of the region roughly comprising modern Afghanistan, Pakistan and parts of northern India.

A Timurid refugee at Babur's newly founded Indian court, one of many individuals in flight from the Uzbek invaders of Transoxiana, wrote, 'Babur is now, by the grace of God, seniormost among the progeny of Timur, and it is only becoming that he should so extend his patronage to all living Timurids, one of whom is the writer himself, that the lamp of the Timurid family may once again shine forth.'[6] As the writer had surmised, illuminating the 'lamp of the Timurid family' had long been Babur's objective and the dynastic ambition which drove him to conquer Hindustan would be expressed as a compulsion to re-create the Timurid Empire in South Asia. Self-consciously and formally, Babur offered his new kingdom in India, larger and wealthier than the first, as a refuge for members of the Timurid imperial family who had been forced out of their ancestral territories. His daughter, Gulbadan Begim, described Babur's efforts: 'He ordered letters sent to every direction, every quarter, every dominion, that all those attached to us shall receive our patronage, and most particularly those that had given service to our father, grandfather and forefathers ... And those who are of the lineage of Sahib Qiran [Timur] and Chingis Khan, let them set out for our court. God the most high has conferred upon us the kingdom of Hindustan, so let us see good fortune together.'[7]

Thus, with promises of sanctuary, land and wealth, he lured them south, and in response to Babur's offer of protection and fortune Central Asian refugees flocked to his Indian court. In the relative wealth and safety of their new capital cities of Agra and Delhi, the community of refugees who had suffered war and displacement were reunited, enriched and emboldened. The elaborate and distinctive understanding of culture and legacy which had been developed, at times deliberately and self-consciously, over a hundred years of Timurid rule in Central Asia, would shape the Timurid royal court in India. In exile, through manipulating their Central Asian legacy, the Timurid-Mughals manufactured an imperial identity which would provide them unity, and successfully legitimize, sustain and support their overwhelming imperial success. Dynastic reverence offered the exiles continuity and affirmed their potential for group identity and collective action, eventually producing a political legitimacy that long outlived the actual power of the Mughal kings.

The Timurid heritage is mentioned only briefly and occasionally in most studies of the Mughal court, although scholars of the Timurids have emphasized the 'profound influence' of the Timurid legacy on the Mughal dynasty and have questioned the absence of research which links them to their ancestry in Central Asia.[8] Historians of the Mughals affirm the 'traditionally neglected' Central Asian genealogy of the Mughals, calling it 'somewhat puzzling why the Mughal specialists have by and large refused, in the past few decades, to place the state they study in the larger context.'[9] This study is an effort to do just that, to re-evaluate the scholarly and intellectual isolation with which the Mughals have traditionally been treated, through an examination of their imperial court culture, in the context of their origins in Central Asia and their inheritance of a remarkably charismatic political and cultural legacy. The Mughals were the principal inheritors of the Central Asian Turco-Persian legacy of Timur: 'true Timurids who enthusiastically embraced Timurid legitimacy and consciously presided over a Timurid renaissance' on the Indian subcontinent.[10] An understanding of Mughal imperial culture must be grounded in recognition of the profound influence of their Timurid past.

Yet while Mughal loyalty to Timurid understandings developed in part because for a community of refugee elites they offered compelling and easily communicated metaphors of identity and kingship, it is not my intent to argue the existence of a monolithic Timurid identity. Identity is understood to be constructed on the basis of contingencies, as was surely true in the case of Timur's own deliberate efforts to build an imperial image and character from a widely disparate set of sources and models across the region of his conquests. For him – and equally for his descendants in India – these varied and multiple fragments were never collapsed into a static and monolithic identification.[11] As should quickly become clear, dynastic adaptation and assimilation occurred. Neither the identity of Timur's successors in Transoxiana nor theirs in India can or should be drawn as neatly undifferentiated wholes, but rather workable amalgams of dynamic local idioms of power – political, social, sacral and aesthetic. Identity for the Timurid-Mughals remained in India as it had been in Central Asia: deliberate and self-aware, at times resistant or threatened by local understandings of kingship and rule, but just as often responsive, elastic and contingent.

The Contents of This Book

Following a prologue which explores the rise of Timur and the deliberate development by his successors of a distinctive Timurid court culture in their imperial heartland, chapter one is concerned with the questions of exile and memory, examining the expulsion from Mawarannahr of the Timurid elites and highlighting the trauma of their losses. Those who responded to Babur's call to gather at his newly established court, first in Kabul, then in Agra, were the embodiment of Central Asian high culture and society; their small population movement created a powerful cultural bridge connecting the late Timurid world of Transoxiana and the Indian subcontinent. In the midst of humiliation and displacement, at their new imperial court in India, they unified around their charismatic elite lineage, guarded all the more zealously because of their deep sense of grievance.

From a narrative of loss, chapter two moves to a study of the deliberate institutionalization of a dynastic memory, in a process of 'official cultural shoring up.'[12] For the original community of Timurid refugees, and through the long generations of Mughal rule in northern India, the references to an ancestry rich in saints and heroes, and to a lost ancestral homeland, remained central to their imperial identity. The process centered on the development of what can be described as a 'genealogical cult,' driven not only by Mughal valorization of their own legacy, but supported strongly by an admiration for the Timurid heritage shared among their rivals and neighbors. Linked closely to this, the Mughals developed territorial narratives that not only tied them tightly to their ancestral homeland but also fabricated bonds of memory that justified ownership of their foreign conquest territories on the subcontinent. The development of formal memories of imperial culture and ideology created increasingly sacralized ties to ancestral virtues and values, which came to be expressed by the production of artifacts, in an outpouring of artistic and literary production in the form of memoirs, histories and dynastic portraits.

Chapter three examines the behavior of the Mughal royal court and its relationship to the imperial landscape – in particular its peripatetic quality, motivated in part as an effort to satisfy the Mughal passion for the hunt and the rather more languid pleasures of Persian-Timurid pleasure garden. Perhaps most notably, we can begin to view the sustained mobility of the imperial court as both powerful political theatre and as an effort of re-enactment and memorialization, in reference to the semi-nomadic past.

It is within this context that we can, in chapter four, move past the dynasty's deliberate and provocative evocations of identity to discuss the issues of motherhood and the charisma of the maternal lineage, dynastic and personal legitimacy, inheritance, and the always contentious imperial succession. Although it provoked devastating wars among Mughal princes in every generation, the re-enactment of traditional Turco-Mongol succession rivalries reasserted essential understandings of Timurid-Mughal loyalty and legitimacy. Based on a concept of individual right to rule and articulated by means of an ongoing disputatious discourse between father and son or between rival royal brothers, and at times cousins, the system of imperial succession remained nearly unmodified for generations, so successfully did it define the ruling family's essential sovereignty and political legitimacy.

While Mughal political power and communal unity were constructed on a discourse of loss and of loyalty to their charismatic Timurid genealogy and legacy, at times it was their deliberate inclusion of local and universal traditions of rule and legitimacy that allowed the Timurid-Mughals to construct an edifice of legitimate power that long outlasted their real ability to wage war or rule territory. The pragmatic Timurid refugees fabricated an imperial identity and a vision of kingship that was profoundly dependent on the Timurid legacy. Mughal contemporaries, such as the Ottomans and the Safavids, were equally attracted to and emulated many of the same models of ruling ethics and legitimacy; their mutuality of interests bound the pre-modern Islamic world together in a common image of kingship and rule. Yet at the Mughal court these understandings continued to develop in ways that were derivative and shared. Chapter five, emphasizing the dynamic qualities of identity and cultural memory, concludes this study with a brief examination of the evolving Mughal ideology of kingship – a compilation of understandings drawn from a wide variety of sources: the kings of Sassanid Iran and the early Islamic caliphal courts; the Mongol *ulus* and Timurid princely courts; Sultanate and indigenous Hindu royal court traditions. Expressing power and legitimacy through the wildly diverse cultures and languages of their subjects and rivals as well as their ancestors, the Mughals confirmed what military power alone could not sustain.

PROLOGUE

TIMURID POLITICAL CHARISMA AND THE IDEOLOGY OF RULE

The Mongol invasions, led by Chingis Khan (r. 1206–27) in the first half of the thirteenth century, had succeeded in creating the largest land-based empire in history, stretching from China to the Mediterranean.[1] Through personal charisma and superb military leadership, Chingis Khan altered and subordinated traditional loyalties, forming an army of perhaps seven to eight hundred thousand men organized on a decimal-based system of units from ten to ten thousand, rather than the traditional tribal groupings of the Turco-Mongol warlords.[2] Political legitimacy for Chingis Khan included the conviction that 'God had designated him [Chingis Khan] the sole legitimate ruler of the world, and that he had transmitted sovereignty to his descendants.'[3]

Under Mongol successor khans, major cities were rebuilt, commerce and agriculture were re-established and scholarly and artistic enterprises were again encouraged. The religious tolerance of the Mongols, marked 'not so much by high-mindedness as by indifference,'[4] led to the gradual adoption of regional religions; by the 1280's, the Ilkhanid Mongols of western Asia had begun converting to Islam. Persianate urban culture became hegemonic at the increasingly cultured Mongol successor courts, which oversaw the construction of mosques and madrasas, the production of literary manuscripts and miniature paintings, and the patronage of scientists, astronomers, poets and historians.[5] Each of the newly conquered Mongol territories had been carefully manned with troops and representative administrators from each of the four *uluses*,[6] so that even when political and administrative cohesion were gradually lost, Mongol conquest territories retained a measure of unity.[7] Population exchanges, shifting frontiers and the steady migration of tribes, rival princes, scholars and artists established and affirmed a degree of shared culture and common history.[8]

The lingering political magnetism of Chingis Khan was powerful enough to unite the successor khanates for forty years after his death, but eventually fraternal rivalry fragmented the empire. Although the years following his death saw the gradual breakup of the Mongol Empire into a series of smaller successor states, political legitimacy in Central Asia had become entirely tied to the contender's possession of the charismatic Chingisid lineage. The absolute consolidation of power under Chingis Khan and his immediate successors, and the cultural and scholarly achievements attained under Mongol patronage, particularly that of the Ilkhanid Mongol successor state incorporating much of the Islamic world, firmly established the Chingisid dynastic line as the most potent force in Central Asian politics. Rulership in the region was and would continue to be regularly and violently contested, but the only candidates for power were recognized princes of Chingisid lineage and no effort was made to set up an alternative ruling house.

Timur[9] (1336–1405, r. 1370–1405), a minor prince of the Turkic Barlas clan, one of the groups making up the Chaghatay ulus,[10] spent decades developing and consolidating his own power in Central Asia.[11] Although Timur had the good fortune to rise to power at a time when the Chaghatayid descendants of Chingis Khan had lost effective power in the region of Transoxiana, local understandings of political legitimacy and power required that a claimant to power attach himself to the glory and success of the Chingisid line. In developing and protecting his political viability, much of Timur's success lay in his ability to meticulously evoke Chingisid symbols and images in order to establish his claim to legitimate rule over former Mongol territories.

As a member of the Barlas tribe, Timur could be counted among the tribal aristocracy, but in assertions of political legitimacy he was unable to lay claim to a Chingisid lineage. Recognizing the power of the royal lineage, employing 'formal strategies of official modesty,' Timur did not attempt to ignore or circumvent regional requirements for rule.[12] Instead, in recompense for his own genealogical shortcomings, from the time when he took power in 1370 he did not attempt to claim the imperial title *khan*, the mark of sovereignty among the Turco-Mongol tribes, but instead enthroned a Chaghatayid puppet khan, through whom he ruled as *amir*, commander. To confirm his status, he married into the charismatic Chingisid line, taking Saray Malik Khanim, the daughter of the Chaghatayid Khan Qazan, as wife, from which point he effectively wielded the title of *Guregen*, son-in-law. As ruler, in fact if not in name, Timur married off his sons, Umar Shaykh (d. 1394), Miranshah (d. 1408) and Shahrukh (d. 1447), and grandsons Muhammad Sultan (d. 1403) and Ulugh Beg (d. 1449), to women of the Chingisid lineage, merging the two dynastic lines. Throughout his reign, even at the height of his powers, Timur continued to use *amir* and *Guregen* as his official titles on coinage and official correspondence. Furthermore, Timur (more likely his successors for him), began to use a pre-Islamic Persian title of supernatural and universalist implications: *Sahib Qiran*, Lord of the Auspicious Conjunction.[13]

Timur was highly sensitive to the potency of Chingisid references and symbols. It has been suggested that even Timur's extreme and systematic use of violence was part of a conscious effort to evoke the legacy of Chingis Khan. According to Timurid scholar Beatrice Manz, who accuses Timur of theatricality in pursuit of political legitimacy, Timur's early campaigns had been markedly less fierce than his latter.[14] Equally, the Timurid armies were not naïve nomad forces but were well acquainted with the urban and sedentary society they were, in many cases, destroying.[15] Even Timur's ruthless violence, then, may have been a carefully orchestrated and easily recognizable evocation of Chingisid power and legitimacy, manipulated and interpreted for an increasingly awed public audience, not only local but international. As a further assertion of Mongol imperial ideology, Timur claimed possession of a heavenly mandate, proven by his stunning military success, itself an easily recognizable echo of Chingis Khan's power and an affirmation of his own equally spectacular success.

However, in the years since the Chingisid Mongol expansion, conditions in Central Asia had altered. In the thirteenth century Chingis Khan had been able to wrench political legitimacy out of a combination of personal charisma, brute power and the careful manipulation of Turco-Mongol ruling custom. His overwhelming success, and the careful nurturing of his legacy by his immediate successors, had led to a near-sacralization of the Chingisid line. But by the fourteenth century there existed yet another critical source of legitimacy among the tribes of Transoxiana – Islam, filtered and interpreted through the urban Persianate tradition. Although military success and the wealth which resulted from brigandage and demands of tribute might have been sufficient to sustain a Turco-Mongol warlord, as the ruler of the Mongol conquest lands of Central Asia it was necessary for Timur to meld the region's two seemingly contradictory but equally powerful sources of legitimation: Turco-Mongol Chingisid custom and the Perso-Islamic tradition.

Himself a Muslim, as was most of the sedentary population he conquered, Timur was careful to affirm his Islamic identity within his constructions of legitimacy and right to rule. He did not hesitate to declare himself the champion of Islam, a strategy which succeeded, in part, because the majority of his followers, while retaining loyalty to Chingisid tradition, had long since converted to Islam and did not concern themselves with any ideological conflict between Mongol *yasa* and Islamic *shari'a*. Timur commissioned a number of mosques and madrasas, and offered patronage to the Yasavi order of Sufis, among other mystical orders. Memoirs attributed to Timur, most probably fallacious productions of a later period, claim that his stunning military success had been predicted by the fourteenth-century Naqshbandi sheikh Amir Kulal, who is said to have declared, 'The sovereignty of the territories of God has been bestowed on this young Turk.'[16] In exchange for his financial support of individual Sufi leaders and their *tariqats*, Timur was the recipient of their public support, which enhanced his religious prestige and affirmed his legitimacy as an Islamic king in the eyes of a public loyal to the popular religious orders.

Although there were those who objected,[17] a general comfort with the co-existence of the two law codes meant that not only did

Turco-Mongols identify as Muslims but even the Persian viziers of the Timurid princes at times found it useful to reference Chingisid law, the *yasa*.[18] According to a contemporary biographer of Timur, although many of his soldiers were Muslim, the Timurid armies remained of mixed religious loyalty, making Timur's balancing act all the more critical. 'He had in his army Turks that worshipped idols and men who worshipped fire, Persian magi, soothsayers and wicked enchanters and unbelievers.'[19] Timur's success lay in his ability to suggest and presume the viability of compromise between very different legitimizing traditions, developing them into a workable ideological fusion. Proclaiming himself a pious Muslim and defender of the faith, associating with *sayyids* (descendants of the prophet Muhammad) and respected members of the *ulama*, while remaining respectful and attentive to the legacy and tradition of Chingis Khan, Timur established a new and very powerful model of legitimation in Perso-Islamic/Turco-Mongol Central Asia which would sustain his descendants for well over a hundred years.[20]

Fabricating Legitimate Timurid Rule

Anxious to demonstrate his power, add to his glory, and establish his right to rule, Timur was personally involved in the carefully managed fabrication of his own public image. Following in the Persianate courtly tradition and that of the later Mongol Ilkhanates, Timur made a political statement from literary, artistic and architectural patronage. As the Ilkhanids had done, Timur seems likely to have established a *kitabkhana* in Samarqand, for the production of illustrated manuscripts.[21] Although he was illiterate, Timur not only spoke Chaghatay Turkish, his native language, but also Persian, the lingua franca of medieval Central Asia. Contemporary writings confirm Timur's awareness of and interest in the vast array of Persian literature in what was a highly literate milieu. 'He was constant in reading the annals and histories of the prophets of blessed memory and the exploits of kings and accounts of all those things which had formerly happened to men at home and abroad.'[22]

Timur, like Chingis Khan before him, robbed the conquered cities of his empire of their artisans and craftspeople, shipping them off as slaves through whose labors he might glorify the capital city of his Timurid empire, Samarqand. There, Timur articulated his vision of kingship and imperial identity – a Timurid glorification supported by a merger of Chingisid and Perso-Islamic imperial understandings – through the construction of vast and splendid ceremonial spaces. It is significant that Timur, who had begun his career as little more than a semi-nomadic brigand, chose to showcase his wealth and might through the extravagant development of an urban center, representing the sophisticated Persianate urban world he had so successfully conquered. In Samarqand, ringed by a series of suburbs named for the great cities conquered by Timur (including Damascus, Delhi and Tabriz), imperial aggrandizement was expressed architecturally, as massive domed structures were raised in Timur's honor.

Perhaps reflecting his *nouveau arrivé* tastes, the buildings he commissioned were massive in scale; when the madrasa being built by his chief wife began to loom over the mosque Timur was constructing exactly opposite, he had his architect killed and the mosque enlarged to throw the madrasa into shadow.[23] The mosque, which he had begun in 1399, was said to have had a Quranic verse inscribed on the portal in letters so large that they could be read from two miles away.[24] 'No head was raised above him but he brought it low and no back was stronger than his but he broke it and he was thus in all things which concerned and touched him.'[25] The degree of his personal interest in these grandiose displays of his own might and power was so great that even when he was too weak and old to stand, Timur was carried in every morning on a litter to oversee the construction of his monument.[26]

Pleasure gardens, the prerogative of Persian kingship, were designed to surround the palaces of Timur's capital city with acres of meadows, fruit trees and floral and vegetable plantings through which artificial streams ran and wild deer roamed. Awed observers describe seeing Samarqand's thirty imperial gardens filled with luxurious tents of brocade and silk, dazzlingly decorated with gemstones, gold and feathers, and 'roofs of silver and stairs to ascend and ... couches, on which they might recline ... They also showed rare treasures and hung there curtains of rare marvelous beauty.'[27] The elaborate gardens of Samarqand, their fragile and transitory nature notwithstanding, as much as any monumental structure of stone or marble played a carefully constructed role in the theatre of Timurid pageantry and courtly ceremony.[28]

The Death of Timur: Dynastic Legitimacy and the Timurid Renaissance

Carefully constructing the same kind of supra-tribal alliances established by Chingis Khan, Timur had been able to destroy his rival, the Mongol ruler Amir Husayn, and conquer Iran in a series of military campaigns from 1386 to 1388, from 1392 to 1396 and in 1399. Between 1398 and 1399 Timur led his armies into northern India where they sacked the ancient capital of Delhi. In 1400 Timur swept into the territory of the Mamluk sultanate, taking Aleppo, Hama, Baalbek and Damascus. Circling north, Timur then marched into Anatolia, where he defeated the Ottoman sultan Bayezid I at the Battle of Ankara on July 28, 1402. When he died in 1405 Timur was proceeding with a long-planned march on China, the success of which would have completed his conquest of the Mongol imperial territories.[29]

While claiming pre-eminence over his far flung conquests, he directly governed only Iran and west Central Asia, which supplied him with a comfortable tax base and manpower for his armies of conquest. In classic Turco-Mongol tradition, Timur distributed his conquest territories as appanages among his male descendants, who served as extensions of the central government, ruling provinces and leading armies at the behest of their father. After his death, in the absence of his dominating presence, however, there was immediate fragmentation, for the political autonomy of the princes had depended on the charismatic power held by the sovereign. In the void left by his death, Timur's chosen successor, a grandson, Pir Muhammad ibn Jahangir, was unable to impose control over rival brothers and cousins, for in the absence of clear authority the princes each pursued personal ambitions. In 1409, after five years of interfamilial war, Timur's third son, Shahrukh, the governor of Khurasan, declared victory and emerged as the heir to his father's empire. Forty years of relative stability followed, as Shahrukh ruled in Herat while his eldest son, Ulugh Beg, served as his deputy in Samarqand.

With Timur's death, his successors were forced to reinvent the Timurid public image and political identity, this time in order to defend dynastic, rather than personal, legitimacy.[30] Timur had so successfully melded the contradictions implicit in fourteenth-century Central Asian political legitimation that his descendants had no need to pursue the same goal; from this point forward, Timur's successors would defend and define their rulership through the personality of Timur himself. It was no longer necessary to govern behind a Chingisid puppet khan, and as for Timur's deliberately unpretentious appellation '*Guregen*,' over the years this title became a powerful and positive evocation of the hero-ancestor, Amir Timur, and no longer a mark of humility and apology for non-Chingisid rule.

Just as Timur had modeled his display of imperial identity and legitimacy in Mongol conquest territories on that previously established by Chingis Khan, Timur's descendants developed and molded Timur's identity to define and support their viability as individuals within the dynasty of Timur and within Timurid conquest territories. In the interest of maintaining their right to rule, through the manipulation of Timurid historiography and the development of a 'cult of artistic patronage,' Timur's successors artfully developed and codified Timur's imperial identity and therefore that of the entire dynastic line.[31] From this time forward it would be Timur's lineage, as much as that of Chingis Khan, which would serve to establish and confirm political legitimacy in Central Asia.

The comfort Timurids felt with their blended Turco-Mongol and Perso-Islamic cultural traditions is perhaps best illustrated by Timur's mausoleum, the *Gur-i Amir* in Samarqand, erected by Timur's grandson, Ulugh Beg. The great tombstone is inscribed with Timur's genealogy, affirming common ancestors with Chingis Khan and describing a lineage going back to the mythological Mongol ancestress, Alanqua, who was, in ancient legend, impregnated by a heavenly light. Ulugh Beg, in a classic Timurid melding of traditions, identified the paternal light as the spirit of 'one of the descendants of the prince of the Faithful Ali ibn Abu Taleb.'[32]

The Late Timurid World

In the early decades of the fifteenth century, Timur's successors found themselves in an insecure position. The lineage of the Great Amir was not sufficient to guarantee individual rival princes a political role or sustain imperial power; for that they would be required to develop legitimizing discourses of their own. Out of these conditions – the individual need of the Timurid princes to establish political legitimacy, the specific components of the imperial image already established by Timur, the inheritance of the Turco-Mongol/Perso-Islamic hybrid cultural and ideological fusion, and the fractured political situation in fifteenth-century Mawarannahr – Timur's successors developed a distinct and recognizable Timurid 'cultural personality,' a highly individual set of 'social assumptions, political and cultural values and even ... aesthetic standards.'[33] In the highly competitive, fragmented world of the Timurid princes, shared cultural values, rather than sheer military might, would establish the identity of the Timurid elite and even provide a degree of cohesion. The distinctive social and political identity developed between the death of Timur in 1405 and the Uzbek destruction of Timurid power by 1507 came to define Timurid culture across the Islamic world.

The Timurid successor kingdoms were no longer steppe regimes in the Chingisid tradition. Public displays of kinship loyalties and nomadic ideals grew less, although they never disappeared, for power remained in the hands of Turks and Mongols, admittedly increasingly sedentarized, and much of the empire's military elite continued to be drawn from traditional nomadic elements. Evocations of Chingisid tradition could always confer a degree of political support and legitimacy, for even the princes 'had memories of Timur's court; their tutelage at the hands of his queens and amirs, and the glory of his conquests instilled in many of them deep bonds with the history and traditions of the Turco-Mongol steppe, which had become tangential to their existence.'[34] Yet the new post-Timur aristocracy oriented itself, as Timur had intended, towards an urban Persianate model of kingship. His successor's decision to establish the imperial capital in the western reaches of the empire, in Herat, Khurasan's capital city and a center of Iranian culture, confirmed the dynasty's shift. Political legitimacy would remain tightly linked to the Chingisid-Timurid lineage and military tradition, yet Perso-Islamic high culture became the privileged artistic form, as unprecedented degrees of patronage at rival

Timurid princely courts quickly developed into a Timurid cultural efflorescence.

In the tradition of their ancestor Timur, the rival princes of Central Asia actively participated in the careful production of public imperial imagery designed to establish their individual legitimacy at the expense of competitors. The calculated humility of Timur, who refused the titles *khan* and *caliph*, was not a strategy which would be employed by his sons. In death, Timur's legacy would be developed and expanded to encompass the political needs of his successors. The cultural understandings of the Timurid princes developed from an education in the Islamicized Persianate tradition, in which cultivated atmosphere this Turco-Mongol military class, the descendants of nomadic and seminomadic warlords, had achieved a high degree of sophistication.

The Timurid dynastic identity and ruling ethos were further defined through an increasing emphasis on imperial patronage of the arts and the wholesale adoption of the Persian literary tradition. In a culture already heavily dominated by Iranian motifs and models 'whose conventions and connotations would be recognized by the elites of the Iranian world,' Timurid fascination with Persian forms, both literary and visual, was perhaps due in part to their value as universal symbols which marked the Timurid 'transformation from a military caste into monarchs in the Iranian Islamic mold, who recognized the necessity of cultural prowess as an ideal of rule.'[35] This was an intentionally elitist cultural movement, exclusive to the wealthy and educated, and a public demonstration of the refinement and sophistication of the individual Timurid princely courts. Although Timur and his immediate successors participated in the patronage of architects and artists, it was the later Timurid princes, firmly grounded in sophisticated urban culture and ruling independent rival courts, who became 'the leading arbiters of literary taste through the eastern Islamic world,' and were at the center of the development of a 'mature and unified Timurid art that identified and redefined the ruling house.'[36]

Their privileging of the artistic forms of Perso-Islamic high culture, and the unprecedented degree of artistic patronage at rival Timurid princely courts, produced a Timurid cultural efflorescence. The hallmark of Timurid political charisma lay not in the ability to exert military force, as had been the case with Timur himself, but in the universally recognized intellectual, cultural and aesthetic prowess of the dynasty's rival princely courts in Mawarannahr. It is difficult to exaggerate the power and influence which had by the middle of the fifteenth century accrued to the Timurid lineage and cultural personality. The emphasis on literary and artistic patronage was so profound, the cultural and aesthetic understandings so highly developed, that Timurid princely courts came to represent the enviable apex of royal court culture across the Islamic world. Contemporary Muslim dynasties such as the Ottomans, Safavids and Uzbeks expressed admiration for the Timurid courts of Mawarannahr and Khurasan, attempting to attach their own political legitimacy to a Timurid lineage while their courtiers encouraged imitation of the royal culture of the Timurid princes.

Even among the contemporary royal courts of India there was great interest in Timurid imperial culture long before the arrival of Timur's descendants, the Mughals. By the time of the Mughal conquest of northern India, the Timurid cultural personality had become recognized in disparate regions and royal courts as the unrivaled ideal, and the lineage of Timur had achieved profound charisma. Small wonder indeed that when Timur's descendants came to be driven out of their homeland and given the opportunity to construct an empire and create a royal court in India, they would rely heavily on their ancestral heritage to assert and affirm their own political legitimacy and aesthetic prowess.

CHAPTER ONE

BABUR AND THE TIMURID EXILE

Exile is strangely compelling to think about but terrible to experience. It is the unhealable rift between a human being and a native place, between the self and its true home; its essential sadness can never be surmounted. And while it is true that literature and history contain heroic, romantic, glorious, even triumphant episodes in an exile's life, these are no more than efforts to overcome the crippling sorrow of estrangement.[1]

This is a case study of the displacement, migration and survival of a particularly powerful imperial identity. For more than two hundred years of their rule in India, the Mughals adhered closely to their ancestral identity and heritage, long after they had lost their original base of power and support. Why such loyalty? It is true that by the beginning of the sixteenth century Timurid political potency had come to be broadly acknowledged and admired at rival royal courts across the Muslim world; many viewed the Timurid model as the pinnacle of imperial culture.[2] Yet more than that, the Timurid community that migrated to India had suffered the traumatic loss of political and military power, and perhaps most significantly, of homeland. In the writings of the Mughal founder, Babur, it is the language of nostalgia and exile which drives and permeates the discourse of legitimacy and rule. It would seem that the motivation behind much of the reification of a

Timurid court identity at the royal court of India was the struggle to establish a real entity to counter the sense of loss and encroaching void felt by the Timurid community in exile.[3] As a workable premise for the regeneration of identity and culture, the drama of recent territorial loss, exile and refugee status led to 'a sense of cultural urgency [in which the struggle became one] against patterns of life being forgotten and material forms erased in a rising tide of memory loss.'[4] Survival as a collective, and certainly as a dynasty, hung in the balance – the result was the conscious and concrete fabrication of an artifice, a shared bond that would hold space and community culturally together.

Babur and the Late Timurid World

Although rivalry and competition for territory raged and constant low-grade warfare marked the period, ties of blood and marriage united the mirzas and amirs of the late Timurid milieu. Zahir al-Din Muhammad Babur, born in 1487, son of a Timurid father and Chingisid mother, could claim direct family connections to all of the rulers of Central Asia as nephew, cousin, son or grandson.[5] When Babur's father died in a fall from his dovecote, leaving his twelve-year-old son to inherit the appanage of Ferghana, it was not outsiders but Babur's rapacious Timurid-Mongol uncles who posed the first and most immediate threat to the boy's inheritance. Yet while rulership in Babur's Mawarannahr was uncertain and transitory, perhaps it was the close family connections which prevented the constant military skirmishes from becoming deeply destructive. Babur's Ferghana was protected from his acquisitive uncles, although only briefly, thanks in large part to the diplomatic interventions of his grandmother and loyal counselors.

All of this was to change with the invasion of the Uzbek tribal confederation, led by Shibani Khan (1451–1510), a grandson of the Uzbek hero Abu al-Khayr, who had briefly united the tribes only a generation earlier.[6] Shibani Khan began the Uzbek invasion of Mawarannahr and Khurasan in the last decades of the fifteenth century, and by the time of his death had become known as the Great Khan, in control over most of Central Asia. In this startlingly short time he had overrun the heartland of Timurid Central Asia and put the Timurid-Chaghatay elite to flight.

Writing years later, in the comparative comfort and safety of Kabul, Babur expressed deep frustration at the Timurid lack of an effective response in defending Mawarannahr. He claimed to have tried to raise the alarm, insisting that 'an enemy like Shibaq [Shibani] Khan had arrived on the scene, and he posed a threat to Turk and Mughul [Mongol] alike. He should be dealt with now while he had not yet totally defeated the nation or grown too strong, as has been said:

> Put out a fire while you can,
> For when it blazes high it will burn the wood.
> Do not allow the enemy to string his bow
> While you can pierce him with an arrow.
>
> *Imruz bikush chu mituvan kusht*
> *atesh chu buland shud jahan sukht*
> *Makzar ki zeh kunad kaman ra*
> *dushman chu ba tir mitavan dukht.*'[7]

It is in the writings of the Timurid *fin de siècle*, that we begin to glimpse an increasing weakness and loss of military might among Timur's disunified, mutually competitive successors. Babur visited Herat between the death of its ruler, the famed Timurid prince, Sultan Husayn Bayqara, and the Uzbek takeover, and he used the device of his memoir to contrast his own passionate advocacy for the defense of the city with what he described as the effete ineptitude of the Timurid princes. Their personal discourtesies he generously blamed on hangovers rather than arrogance, but it took months for them to prepare for war.[8] By the time the princes organized their attack on the Uzbeks, the enemy had grown in size and become too dangerous for their limited forces. Within the year, in 1507, Shibani Khan's Uzbek warriors would take Herat after a completely pathetic defense by the few remaining Timurid forces in the city.

Babur, so recently in the city and therefore all the more sensitive to the loss, wrote bitterly of the failure of the Timurid princes in leaving the citadel unfortified, the army unprepared.[9] Herat, beloved capital of

Timur's son and successor Shahrukh, with its origins in ancient Persian culture, its rich dynastic history and monuments to Timurid glory, its gardens resonant with poetry and the sophisticated banter of the age's greatest intellects and artists, would remain for Babur – along with Timur's capital city of Samarqand, already lost to him twice – a symbol of Timurid imperial culture and grandeur at its most admirable pinnacle. It is no wonder that in the decades after Shibani Khan's conquest Babur would remember the great cities of Timurid Transoxiana with such nostalgia-heightened detail and remain unforgiving in his condemnation of the ineffectual response of the extended Timurid dynasty.

Even more tragic than the loss of the Timurid capitol cities, however, was the disastrous impact of war on the households of the Timurid elite. In the havoc wrought by the Uzbek invasion, made possible by the incompetence and failure of the Timurid defense, women of the Timurid royal family, bearers of both royal lineage and family honor, were either left behind in the mad rush to escape the Uzbek advance or bartered off into conquest marriages and servitude.

Describing the defense of Timurid Herat, Babur commented bitterly on the inadequate protection afforded the women and children of the Timurid princes. 'When they [the Bayqara princes of Herat] learned of it [the approach of Shibani Khan], they went to pieces and were unable to do anything – neither could they gather their men nor were they able to array their forces. Instead each set out on his own. The princes' mothers, sisters, wives and treasuries were in the Ikhtiyar al-Din Fortress, which is now known as Ala Qurghan. The princes ... could give no thought to fortifying the fortress. At such a time they left their mothers, sisters, wives and children to be taken prisoner by the Uzbek and fled ... When Shibani Khan took Herat,' mourned Babur, 'he even maltreated the prince's wives and children.'[10] The historian Khwandamir, in the more florid language of the Timurid courtier, wrote, 'The delicate beauties of the inner sanctum of inviolability were taken captive and tormented by the merciless Uzbeks, and Venuses of the chambers of chastity were left by ravaging Mughuls [Jochid Mongols and their Chaghatay allies] to wander destitute in the lanes and bazaars.'[11]

Rape as a weapon of war is understood as a form of terrorism, in which the perpetrators are driven by the desire to 'display, communicate, produce or maintain dominance.' [12] Uzbek humiliation of the Timurids was surely a factor in the performance of these conquest marriages, but perhaps even more importantly, Turco-Mongol women of royal descent traditionally supplied and supported a ruling family's political charisma. One hundred years earlier, women of the Chingisid lineage were critical figures in the legitimization of dynastic power – as illustrated by Timur's adoption of 'son-in-law' status after marrying a Chingisid princess – but by the end of the fifteenth-century the lineage of Timur had developed its own prestige. Princesses of the royal blood became valuable bargaining chips and spoils of war, not simply as victims of rape but as carriers of charismatic, legitimizing genealogies. The women of Babur's immediate family, descendants of both Chingis Khan and Timur, were no exception; eventually, over the slow decades of the Uzbek advance, his sisters, cousins and aunts would be forced into conquest marriages.

In flight from Samarqand in 1501–2, Babur had managed to take his mother with him in his desperate escape, but he claimed that Khanzada Begim, his elder sister and full sibling 'fell into Shibaq Khan's hands as we were leaving,' remaining in the city with the Uzbek conquerors.[13] Babur's daughter and cousin each described the situation differently, suggesting that Khanzada Begim was purposefully left behind for Shibani Khan as ransom, to ensure the safety of the tiny cluster of fleeing Timurids: Babur, his mother and a few women of their household.[14] Within a few days Babur's party was joined by others who had fled Samarqand, including a lady in the service of Babur's mother, Atun, who had been left behind because of a lack of mounts but, in her desperation to flee the Uzbek advance, had managed to walk from Samarqand all the way to Pishgar, on the road to Ura-Tyube.[15]

A year earlier, in July 1500, the eldest daughter of Yunus Khan and first cousin of Babur, Mihr Nigar Khanim, had been captured by Shibani Khan and forcibly married to him, 'as part of the spoils.'[16] They were divorced when Shibani Khan resolved to marry her Timurid niece, Babur's sister Khanzada; Mihr Nigar Khanim was able to eventually join Babur in Kabul.[17] Shibani Khan killed five of Sultan Mahmud's six sons but all of the daughters were kept alive, 'because of their value as wives.'[18] Qutliq Khanim, a Chaghatay Mongol, was married 'as a sequel of victory by Shaibani [Shibani] over her father.'[19] On the taking of Tashkent in 1501–2, Shibani forcibly married the Chaghatay princess Dawlat Sultan to his son Timur, by whom she had a daughter. She fled her husband in 1511 to join Babur when he took Samarqand.[20] In 1508 Rabi'a Sultan Begim, daughter of Sultan Ahmad Mirza Miranshahi, both her father and son having been murdered by Shibani Khan, was forcibly married to Jani Beg Uzbek, his cousin.[21] Sultanum Begim Miranshahi, fourth daughter of Sultan Ahmad Mirza, was married to Shibani Khan's son after her husband Ali, son of Mahmud Mirza, was killed by Shibani Khan.[22] Babur's cousin, Habiba Sultan Khanish Dughlat, full sister of the Mongol chronicler Haydar Dughlat, was taken by Shibani Khan when she was a child and remained in his household until young adulthood, when she was married to his nephew, Ubaydullah. When her Uzbek husband retreated to Turkestan in 1511, Habiba remained behind, eventually marrying a cousin.[23]

When Shibani Khan took Andijan and Akhsi, a second of Babur's sisters, Yadgar Sultan Begim, the ten-year-old daughter of the concubine Agha Sultan, 'fell to Hamza Sultan's son Abdul Latif Sultan.'[24] She eventually was able to rejoin Babur when he took Hissar from the Uzbeks and was later listed among the Timurid refugee community in Agra. During that same period yet a third of Babur's sisters, Ruqqaya Sultan Begim, daughter of Makhdum Sultan Begim (known as Qara Goz Begim) 'fell to Jani Beg Sultan,' with whom she had two or three sons, although they all died young.[25] An eyewitness to the invasion of Herat wrote that Khanzada Khanim, daughter of Ahmad Khan, was married to Muhammad Khan of the victorious Uzbeks. In this case there is a suggestion that the woman approved of her new husband, although Babur remarks with disgust that the couple did not 'wait for the prescribed passage of time,'[26] and the Mughal scholar Beveridge calls the marriage illegal.[27]

In the midst of Herat's conquest and pillage, the women of the Bayqara household were captured by the Uzbeks and taken from the town. Among them, Mihrangaz Begim, daughter of Muzaffar Husayn Mirza, was married off to Ubaydullah Sultan, after which the rest of the royal harem was returned to Herat, where the Uzbeks proceeded to rob them of their jewels.[28] Between attacks on Herat's forts, Kabuli Begim was 'given in marriage to Qambar Mirza Kukaltash and Temur Sultan took Andalib into his harem.'[29] Although not forced to marry an Uzbek husband, Khadija Begim, who had begun as a slave in the household of Sultan Abu Sa'id Mirza before becoming the influential wife of Sultan Husayn Bayqara and raised to the rank of *begim*, was turned over by the victorious Shibani Khan to the wife of her enemy, 'and he let her torment her [Khadija Begim] in every kind of way.'[30]

It is impossible to judge how many Timurid-Chaghatay noblewomen were actually forced into conquest marriages or servitude among the Uzbeks. In the case of Khanzada Khanim of Herat, Khwandamir describes an actual 'proposal' followed by the lady's acceptance and even her assurance, with witnesses, that she had been legally divorced two years earlier from her first husband Muzaffar Mirza Bayqara.[31] This cannot have been the case for many of the women, however. The sources take on an undeniably bleak tone in referring to these marriages; there is no mention of celebratory wedding parties and no effort made to explain away the nuptials as anything less than humiliation for the Timurids: defeat and loss of honor.

Padshah of Kabul

Among the women who managed to survive and escape the Uzbek taking of Samarqand, a few managed to flee to Babur in Ghari. There he was joined by 20,000 soldiers led by 'good and experienced commanders,' previously attached to Babur's enemy Khusrawshah, who had 'run off pell-mell' from the Uzbek attack on Hissar.[32] Leading this newly acquired but substantial army, Babur led his band of survivors to Kabul, which he had taken in 1504 and continued to hold as the seat of his power, surrounded by Uzbek enemy forces, for the next twenty years. Refugees fleeing the Uzbek advance trickled in, although many members of the royal Timurid and Chaghatayid families had fled into Mughulistan, Badakhshan, Iran and Ottoman Anatolia.

Further demonstrating his personal dynastic ambition and desire to 'extend his patronage to all living Timurids,' Babur encouraged their dependence on him and expressed his own hurt when relatives chose other protectors. The last of Babur's Timurid aunts, the daughter of Abu Sa'id, Payanda Sultan Begim Miranshahi, fled to Iraq at the time of the Uzbek invasion of Khurasan and 'died there in distress.'[33] Mihr Nigar Khanim, Babur's Mongol cousin, first sought refuge in Babur's Kabul but departed in 1507 to join family members on a visit to Badakhshan, in a group led by Shah Begim Badakhshi, also temporarily living in Kabul, who was hoping to claim the hereditary territory for her grandson.[34] 'It would have been more becoming,' Babur fretted, 'for her to remain with me. I was her nearest relation.' On the journey she was captured by 'one of Abu Bakr Dughlat's marauding bands' and, with the rest of her party, died of ill treatment in his prison in Kashgar.[35]

In time many more Timurids would find safe haven in Babur's outpost at Kabul, a trade center for goods from Khurasan, Iraq and Anatolia and 'the principal trade depot for Hindustan.'[36] The long-term safety of the refugees was limited by the kingdom's small size and poverty and its precarious position on the borders of Uzbek, Safavid and Afghan territory, yet there was stability there, and some comfort. Babur's days of roving brigandage were essentially over and it was in Kabul that he claimed the title *'padshah.'* There were parties in the green hills around the city, in the Timurid gardens planted not just by his ancestors but by also by Babur himself, who had inherited a love of gardens which would last his lifetime and mark all of his imperial possessions. In Kabul Babur discovered the pleasures of alcohol and drug use; he wrote a great many poems, composed his memoirs and fathered his children, including his first son, the future emperor Humayun.

Although he clearly enjoyed his role as *padshah* of Kabul, Babur was too ambitious, and too sensitive to the incessant demands of his refugee following, to remain for long in a small and somewhat insignificant province. Furthermore, the presence nearby of his Uzbek nemesis made for constant tension, pushing Babur to further conquest. 'A foreign people like the Uzbeks and an old enemy like Shibani Khan had overrun the territory held by Timur Beg's descendants ... Only I was left in Kabul. The enemy was very powerful and we were quite weak. At this point there was no way we could move far enough away from so powerful an enemy. We would have to move into either Badakhshan or Hindustan.'[37] Although Babur returned briefly to power in Samarqand, with the help of a Safavid army loaned to him by the messianic founder of the Iranian dynasty, Shah Ismail, within the year he was forced to abandon the ancestral throne, never again to march his armies north of the Oxus River. 'Leaving Samarqand and Mawarannahr to the Uzbeks and the revanchist nostalgia of his descendants,' he returned to Kabul in 1514.[38] The Uzbek tribal confederation had succeeded in routing local Timurid rulers and destroying Timurid power in Transoxiana, to emerge in their place as lords of the old and powerful capital cities of Herat, Tashkent, Bukhara and Samarqand.

Ever ambitious in the interests of empire and Timurid dynastic continuity, Babur began raiding across the Indus River by 1519, taking Lahore by 1523. Asserting ownership of the subcontinent, Babur claimed that Timur's ancestral conquest justified and legitimized his own territorial acquisitions, in that India was an integral part of the Timurid ancestral legacy. Encouraged by his success in Lahore, Babur called to the Afghan king of Delhi and Agra, Sultan Ibrahim Lodi, to surrender the properties previously taken by Timur in 1398. His demands were, unsurprisingly, rejected. Taking this refusal as justification for war, Babur attacked; his success at the battle of Panipat in 1526 established Timurid rule in India as 'an act of military imperialism legitimized by Timur's brief invasion.'[39]

It was clear from the beginning that, unlike his ancestor Timur who had in 1398 looted and laid waste to Delhi and then immediately returned to Transoxiana, Babur envisioned the establishment of permanent and entrenched Timurid rule in northern India. Having conquered for the Timurids a new capital city in Agra, with all the wealth and land available in vast India, as his daughter later recalled, Babur called for the refugees created by the Uzbek invasion of Mawarannahr to come to his new imperial court. 'He ordered letters sent to every direction, every quarter, every dominion ... God the most high has conferred upon us the kingdom of Hindustan, so let us see good fortune together.'[40] Just who was invited to participate in the re-establishment of Timurid glory is made very clear by the letter his daughter quotes: 'All those attached to us shall receive our patronage, and most particularly those that had given service to our father, grandfather and forefathers ... And those who are of the lineage of Sahib Qiran [Timur] and Chingis Khan, let them set out for our court.'[41] Almost immediately an exodus into India began and a large number of refugees managed to reach Babur's promising neo-Timurid royal court.

Who were these individuals who made their way south to find refuge in the vast, wealthy territory newly conquered by the last independent Timurid prince? Babur's daughter, the memorialist Gulbadan Begim and her foster mother, Maham Begim, left Kabul for Agra almost immediately and were among the first of Babur's female relatives to arrive. Within a few years, confirmed Gulbadan Begim, 'all the begims and khanims went, a total of ninety-six persons, and all were appointed property and a home and furnishings and gifts to their hearts' content.'[42] The ninety-six female 'stipendiaries,' recipients of Mughal imperial largesse, who arrived within those first five years of Timurid-Mughal rule in India, were all members of the extended Timurid royal family. The names cited in the sources are the names of the late Timurid Central Asian elite: Bayqara, Miranshahi, Dughlat, Barlas.

The migration to Babur's Indian court by so many members of the late Timurid courtly world, a small but significant population movement, was a matter of neither chance nor choice. Having only recently been forced out of their homeland in Transoxiana by the invading Uzbek tribal confederation, having suffered enormous loss, humiliation and indignity, they represented the last surviving remnants of the Timurid ruling elite: royal princes and princesses of Mawarannahr, Mughulistan and Khurasan, professional military men and a few stray adventurers, at least one historian, drunkards, poets and artists, sufi shaykhs, religious leaders and serving women – for whom the successful conquest of northern India was a dramatic and welcome reversal of fortune.

In This State of Exile

The particular conditions of their arrival in India had great bearing on the development of a Timurid understanding of themselves as a royal dynasty and of their new conquest territories. Babur and the tangle of Turkish and Mongol relations who followed him, however successful their migration, viewed themselves as refugees for whom the sense of loss was fresh and bitter and the riches of India not always adequate recompense. Even as early as his Kabul period, enjoying with obvious pleasure his role as 'padshah' of a stable and independent kingdom, Babur was to write, 'In this state of exile [*ghariplik*] my heart has not been gladdened. No one can be comforted at all in exile [*ghurbat*].'[43] The early Timurid reaction to the new conquest territories guided the development of the Timurid-Mughal imperial court and would remain an important and influential component of the imperial legacy. When, on defeating the Lodi kings of Delhi and Agra, Babur opened wide the gates of his new capital, drawing the displaced royals and their retinues to India with promises of territory and wealth, it was with regret, with many yearning backward glances at Transoxiana and the beloved imperial cities of Herat and Samarqand, that the Timurids trickled into India.

Timurid nostalgia could only have been heightened by the difficulties of the transition to the South Asian climate and landscape. The physical contrast to Transoxiana and Afghanistan was immediately apparent. 'It is a strange country [*gharip mamlakati*],' mused Babur, 'Compared to our country it is another world. Its mountains, rivers, forests and wildernesses, its villages and provinces, animals and plants, people and languages (*ili u tili*), even its rain and winds are all strange.' As if to more powerfully assert the foreign quality of his new dominions, he repeated: 'Once you cross the Indus, the land, water, trees, stones, people, tribes, manners and customs are all of the Hindustani style.'[44]

Babur's memoir is the only contemporary record of the first wave of the Timurid migration and our only interpreter of the Timurid response to India. At times his expressions of discomfort with the strangeness of the South Asian landscape went beyond unease, becoming an indictment of India's culture and society. He famously wrote:

> Hindustan is a place lacking grace and elegance. There is no beauty in its people, no graceful social intercourse, no respectful

mingling and exchange or coming and going, no intelligence or genius, no polite culture, no etiquette, no nobility or munificence or virile fortitude. In the arts and crafts there is no regularity or symmetry or alignment or perpendicularity. There are no good horses, no good meat, no grapes, melons or good fruits. There is no ice, no cold water, no good food or bread in the markets. There are no *hamams* and no *madrasas*. There are no candles, torches or candlesticks. Aside from the streams and still waters that flow in ravines and hollows, there are no [running] waters in their palaces or gardens, and in their buildings there is no pleasure, no fresh air, no symmetry or regularity.[45]

On what can we blame such peevish misery? There was a great deal more to Babur's outrageous comments than simple racial prejudice. Babur had already defined himself as the primary defender and passionate personal adherent of the aesthetic and social standards of late Timurid society, now lost and therefore all the more dear. Those attributes of Indian society he criticized so vehemently directly correlate to features which best represented the Timurid cultural ideal most admired by the exiled prince. It is clear that while his obsession for empire drove him, finally, to conquer foreign territories, Babur's loyalty to Timurid cultural and aesthetic understandings would prevent his finding much of value in the society and culture of Hindustan. Bemoaning the absence of courtly gatherings of the intellectual and political elites, there is very little evidence that Babur developed social ties or even regular contact with the peoples of India – Muslim or Hindu. Local laborers and soldiers joined his service but surely not his society.

In contemporary cross-disciplinary studies of refugee and exile identity, the sense of loss and displacement experienced by a community in exile is seen to enable 'the growth and development of new identities and subjectivities,' creating not only an 'unrequited desire for a lost homeland but also a 'homing desire,' a desire to reinvent and rewrite home as much as a desire to come to terms with an exile from it.'[46] Refugee populations develop a heightened sense of communal identity, and their sense of loss and displacement combine to accentuate social bonding. Among diaspora communities 'collective identities and memories of trauma are deeply intertwined ... Victims of social trauma, and their descendants, often engage in *purposeful and explicit remembering*, as a form of empowerment and identity formation.'[47] As the last independent Timurid prince, Babur used the device of his memoir to 'rewrite home,' to create a collective memory, not only of the fact of their loss but the nature of their losses. Defining and describing identity, enscribing 'who we are,' Babur proffered a deliberate alterity, 'who we are not,' for the sake of a shared essential premise that would bind the community together. Babur's personal and deeply emotional story offered a unifying, self-justifying origin narrative for his followers, the regular recountal of which would profoundly influence their descendants' performance of imperial identity, drawn as it was from the communal memories and cultural values of the Timurid refugee elite.

Abstinence and Longing

To be fair, the first months in India were extremely difficult for the Timurids and their armies. Babur would write, 'When we came to Agra it was the hot season, and all the people fled in suspicion. For ourselves and the horses neither provisions nor straw could be found. The towns had been so plundered and pillaged the people had turned to brigandage and theft. The roads could not be traveled ... That year was very hot. Men began to sicken and die ... For these reasons, most of the *begs* and worthy young men [*abdan yigitler*] lost heart [*kongul salip ediler*]. They were unwilling to stay in Hindustan and began to leave.'[48] Although Babur begged him to stay, his closest companion, Khwaja Kalan, openly appalled by the Indian climate and landscape, demanded and received permission to return to Kabul. On his departure he scrawled graffiti on the walls of his quarters in Delhi:

> If in peace and safety I cross the Indus,
> May my face turn black if I ever desire to see Hindustan again.
>
> *Eger ba-khayir u salamat guzar Sind kunam*
> *Siyah ruy shavam kar hava-yi Hind kunam.*[49]

In addition to the shared difficulties of the Timurid refugees, Babur had further, personal reasons for real misery. Perhaps just as oppressive to him as the departure of his close companions and the difficult climate and foreign customs of India, in his first year as ruler of Agra and Delhi, Babur took a vow of temperance. His renunciation of alcohol was a public sacrifice offered up in the name of religion as an effort to win the support of his wavering army.[50] Babur's strategy worked, his soldiers were heartened by his very dramatic gesture and the battle won, but at the cost of Babur's social life. His memoir to this point had been full of descriptions of Babur carousing happily and drunkenly with boon companions – how his new sobriety must have oppressed him! 'I am distraught to have given up wine,' he wrote, 'I don't know what to do and am perplexed. Everyone else is penitent and vows to sin no more, but I have made the vow and now I regret it.'[51] In a forlorn letter to his old companion Khwaja Kalan, now comfortably ensconced in Kabul, Babur queried, 'With whom do you hold parties? With whom do you drink wine?'[52] Abstention clearly heightened Babur's homesickness and fed his nostalgia – all of his losses seemed at times to merge into one, as this conquering king confirmed to his close friend, 'How can one forget the pleasures of that country [Kabul]? Especially when abstaining from drinking, how can one allow oneself to forget a licit pleasure like melons and grapes? Recently a melon was brought, and as I cut it and ate it I was oddly affected. I wept the whole time I was eating it.'[53]

Oppressed by exile, the marked contrast between his current surroundings and the home he had been driven from so reluctantly, the loss of friends, of social life and social scene, of architecture he understood and gardens which soothed and satisfied his aesthetic, Babur's stunning success must have seemed almost an enemy to him. His remarkable military achievement and the attainment of wealth and property – the very culmination of his dream to seize an empire, *mulkgirliq* – would forever keep him from returning to his beloved Kabul. In exile, the conquering king of India, while continuing to solidify his territorial claims, campaigning almost without end across the breadth of northern India, would devote much of his time to composing and arranging his memoirs, writing avid and lovingly detailed descriptions of the

Timurid cities, gardens and society he longed for. This manuscript, a prized family possession, would be read by every succeeding generation of Mughals. Babur's nostalgia for the lost Timurid heartland, his deliberate evocation of the Central Asian landscape and the Timurid princely courts, matched with his openly expressed ambivalence regarding his newly conquered territory of Hindustan, would become a central feature of the Timurid legacy, powerfully influencing his imperial descendants, enhancing their awareness of imperial identification and intensifying their efforts to affirm ancestral links in culture, ideology and territory.

The Poetry of Exile

Ambivalence was nothing new in the ancient, complex relationships of the political and cultural borderlands of Central Asia and India, and Babur's own 'conflicted feelings,' for all their fraught immediacy, have been described by modern scholars as 'typical.'[54] In the earliest days of the Ghaznavid Turkish invasion of north India the poets Firdowsi (d. 1020) and Nasir Khusraw (d. 1072), both of whom had remained unattached to any royal court and were resentful of their lack of consistent financial patronage, wrote plaintive accounts of their personal grievances, developing their sense of loss and injustice into a poetic device known as '*hasb-i-hal.*' Their writings, 'railing against fate (*ruzgar*) and society,' became a popular poetic trope in which the themes of suffering and displacement 'were taken up and put to use systematically by those poets who were exiled or imprisoned.'[55] Often the plaintive theme of loss and exile in medieval Persian poetry specifically embodied an emotional resistance to India coupled with a yearning for home in Central Asia and Iran.

> O Wind! Greet Khurasan for me.
> The learned and wise ...
> Bring me news of them ...
> Tell them the world has bent my cypress,
> This is the deceitful doing of the world ....
>
> The scorpion of exile has afflicted my heart,

> It seems no one else but lonely me on this earth.
> O, God! What does exile want from me?
> For days and nights it has attached itself to me.
> Exile has struck up a friendship with me,
> It has made me an enemy of friendship . . . .
> Exile is a taxing enemy, since it wants nothing
> From you but your country, city and home.[56]

By enhancing the foreign qualities of India, embroidering the memory of their Central Asian past, these long familiar poetic tropes may have acted as a goad to increase the Timurid exiles' longing for Samarqand and Herat. The now sober Babur would respond in similar yearning verse:

> In exile this month of abstinence ages me.
> Separated from friends, exile has affected me.
>
> I deeply desired the riches of this Indian land.
> What is the profit since this land oppresses me?
>
> Left so far from you Babur has not perished,
> Excuse me, beloved, for this, my error.
>
> *Ghurbatta ol ay hijri maini pir qilib tur*
> *Hijran bile ghurbat menka ta'sir qilib tur.*
>
> *Bu Hind yeri hasilidin kob kangul aldim*
> *Ni sud ki bu yer meini dilgir qilib tur.*
>
> *Senden bu qadr qaldi yeraq olmadi Babur*
> *Ma'zur tut ay yar ki taqsir qilib tur.*[57]

Yet for all of his misery, his nostalgia and his openly expressed longing for mountains and running streams, melons and madrasas, Babur recognized and appreciated at least some of India's charms. An amateur naturalist, Babur made careful note of the variety of exotic animals and plant life of India, in particular admiring the elephant for the load it could carry – though the ever pragmatic Babur expressed concern that elephants did indeed take a great deal to feed. As for local foods, he agreed with the poet Amir Khusraw that the mango of India was excellent, though not, Babur hastened to add, equal in flavor to the melon.[58] Ever on the lookout for an intoxicating substance, Babur tried a local date palm liquor, although he was clearly disappointed, commenting that the promised effect 'was not obvious.'[59] Babur even enjoyed the monsoon season, writing, 'The weather is unusually good when the rain ceases, so good in fact that it could not be more temperate or pleasing.' As ever, his praise is tempered with provisos, with which many visitors to monsoonal India can agree: 'The one drawback is that the air is too humid. During the monsoon, bows ... cannot be used to shoot ... Armor, books, bedding and textiles are also affected.'[60]

The seemingly limitless numbers of workmen available in India thrilled Babur, who immediately leapt into an ambitious building program. 'For every labor and every product there is an established group who have been practicing that craft or professing that trade for generations,' he exulted.[61] Comparing Timur's own construction of the great mosque in Samarqand, for which two hundred skilled stonemasons were employed (many of whom Timur had captured in his invasion of India), Babur boasted of the six hundred and eighty skilled stonemasons working on his building projects in Agra and the almost fifteen hundred more at work for him in Sikri, Bayana, Dholpur and Gwalior.[62] Above all, and most importantly, Babur was thrilled by the sheer wealth of India. 'The one nice aspect of India,' he bluntly proclaimed, 'is that it is a large country with lots of gold and silver.'[63]

His eventual answer to the taunts of the departed Khwaja Kalan was defensive, but instructive:

> Give a hundred thanks, Babur, that the Generous Pardoner of all
> Has given you Sind and Hind and a vast kingdom.
> If you cannot endure the heat and say, 'I would see the face of cold,'
> There is Ghazni.[64]

Babur wrote simply, 'Shall we return to Kabul, poverty-stricken?'

Babur and his community of exiles, for whom Samarqand had been forever removed from reach and Kabul too impoverished and vulnerable to satisfy the community of displaced Timurid royals and the ambition of their leader, remained permanently in Hindustan to build the neo-Timurid court of his and their own imagination. In the year before his death, Babur wrote to Khwaja Kalan and those Timurids who had returned to Kabul:

> O you who have gone from this country of India feeling pain and distress,
> You thought of Kabul and its wonderful climate and hotly left India.
> There you have apparently found pleasure and joy, and many good things.
> Yet we have not died, thank God, though we have suffered much pain and untold grief.
> You have no more physical distress, but then neither do we.[65]

Even his longing for Kabul's melons and grapes, the 'licit pleasures' of an abstemious king, was somewhat assuaged by agricultural experimentation. Babur's gardener, Balkhi, had been instructed to plant Afghani fruits in Babur's *Hasht Bihisht*, the Garden of the Eight Paradises, outside of Agra, successfully producing within just a few years what Babur pronounced to be 'very nice little melons and ... rather nice grapes .... I was particularly happy that melons and grapes could turn out so well in Hindustan.'[66]

Cultural Bridges and Nostalgia

Those who responded to Babur's call to gather at his court in Agra – 'those that had given service to our father, grandfather and forefathers ... And those who are of the lineage of Sahib Qiran and Chingis Khan' – were all that remained of the late Timurid world after the Uzbek onslaught; they represented the embodiment of Central Asian culture and society. It was this small migration of refugees – Babur's sisters, sons and daughters, cousins, aunts, uncles, servants, wives and even ex-wives, displaced royals and the descendants of Timur and Chingis Khan – who linked culturally the late Timurid world and the Indian subcontinent. Although their leader would die within four years of the battle of Panipat, the political, cultural and aesthetic traditions and understandings of the migrants were drawn entirely from the late Timurid milieu, and it was this worldview which would inform and guide the Mughal interpretation of courtly life in the capital cities of early modern India.

Additionally, Babur and his companions' shared sense of loss would profoundly influence subsequent generations of Timurids in India, becoming institutionalized as grievance and nostalgia through the dynasty's centuries of rule. Their carefully constructed narrative of imperial origins was founded on a communal tragedy, on the shared trauma of defeat and exile. The legacy is evident, as each succeeding generation of king carefully articulated a longing for Samarqand, the lost capital of the Timurids. More than one hundred years after Babur's success at Panipat his great-great-grandson, the Emperor Shah Jahan (r. 1627–1659), would eventually act on this ancestral grievance, gathering the armies of imperial India in what would be a failed effort to re-take Mawarannahr, a territory which had not been seen by four generations of Mughal kings, but which India's rulers continued to describe as their ancestral homeland.[67] While their sense of loss was continually affirmed and allowed to exert a profound influence on the world view of the Mughals, at the same time the reality of Indian kingship, with all of its possibilities for wealth and power and imperial reputation, won over the scions of the dynasty. For all their nostalgic yearnings, Babur and many within his exile community recognized not only the impossibility of a triumphant return to Samarqand, but also the real value of India. They chose to remain.

CHAPTER TWO

DYNASTIC MEMORY AND THE GENEALOGICAL CULT

Genealogy and the Guregeniyya

The power of a prestigious genealogy in the establishment of dynastic political rights lay in 'attention to lineages as more than family trees; they also become resources for mobilization and engagement in the present.'[1] Under the pressure of exile and trauma, to counter the sense of loss and encroaching void, it was the charisma of the Timurid genealogy that unified and mobilized Babur's refugees; it was through the manipulation of their lineage that the Timurid refugees found a workable basis for the renewal of community and political culture. In the interest of regeneration and legitimacy a veritable genealogical cult was developed among the Timurids of India.

Timur's own genealogical claims had remained, for strategic reasons, relatively modest. The overwhelming and indisputable fact of his military success not only diminished, over time, the necessity for a borrowed form of genealogical legitimacy but also allowed and encouraged his biographers to extol Timur's own antecedents. The fifteenth-century historian Dawlatshah explains that 'genealogists of the Turks say that Amir Timur Guregen's line and that of Genghis Khan met in Alanqua Khatun ... and from her sprang this noble family.'[2]

By the time of the late Timurids, however, the person of Timur had been so exalted, in part by the various histories of his reign solicited by his heirs, that the Timurid-Mughal historian Khwandamir could pretend to ignore the added value of a noble lineage, writing, 'the Sahib Qiran's person is so noble, his magnificence so great and his ambition so exalted that there is no necessity to recount his noble forefathers' excellences or to publish his mighty ancestors' virtues.' Khwandamir follows this statement, however, with an explicit rendering of Timur's lineage, again back to the mythical mother of the Mongol tribes, Alanqua, and beyond her to Japheth, the son of Noah.[3] As had occurred with Chingis Khan, Timur's own lineage became sacralized, infused with tangible political force and luster, imbuing his descendants with political authority and cultural prestige.

Recognition of Timurid Political Charisma

In the interests of his own survival and orientation, Timur had acted with great deliberation in the construction of an imperial identity, pulling from a variety of dynamic symbols and narratives of sovereignty. As for his successors in Mawarannahr, their expressions of aesthetic and political control were propagated in the interests of dynastic power at the dynamic and complex juncture of Turco-Mongol and Perso-Islamic traditions. Over time, Timurid patronage patterns and Timurid artistic and literary imagery resonated throughout the Islamic world and established an enduring historical legacy. It is this Timurid legacy that positioned the Timurid successors in India at the center of the early modern Islamic world; all of the great empires of the period, Ottoman, Safavid and Mughal, claimed some sort of Timurid inheritance – although only the Mughals were in fact genealogical descendants of Timur – which in part represented a shared aesthetic, political, and ethical vision held in common among them. It was through their publicly expressed loyalty to particularly Timurid attributes that the Mughals of India not only affirmed their right to rule as Timurid kings, but positioned themselves as important and influential members in the fraternity of powerful Islamic Turkic empires, sharing far more in common with their contemporaries, the Ottomans and Safavids, than with their Muslim predecessors on the Indian subcontinent.

Nearly universal acknowledgment of the power of Timurid dynastic legitimacy in the mobilization of contemporary political aims led rival kingdoms to link their own political pretensions to the Timurid dynasty, even long after the Timurid princes had been driven from Mawarannahr and Khurasan. In the case of Iran the transformation of Safavid political realities during the reign of Shah Abbas (r. 1588–1629), due in part to the destruction of the Turcoman ascendancy and the rise of the power of the *ulama* at the imperial center, required adjustments to Safavid legitimizing principles. In recognition of the power of Timurid connections and in an attempt to bolster Safavid political ambitions, elaborate back-stories were concocted, one of which claimed a fifteenth-century visit by Timur to the Safaviyya tariqat in Ardabil where he was said to have foreseen the rise of the Safavid dynasty. A waqf document describing an endowment by Timur in the name of the Safavid family is believed to have been forged in the court ateliers of Shah Abbas, who sent a copy of the document to the Mughal emperor Jahangir (r. 1605–1627) in order to emphasize the historical connection between the Timurid and Safavid houses.[4]

By the fourteenth century the Ottoman sultans had begun to prop up their own political legitimacy with the development of a central religious ideology and a flirtation with various origin myths which included elements of a salient genealogy. All the same, as late as the sixteenth century, the Ottoman bureaucrat and historian Mustafa Ali (1541–1600) wrote of the comparatively potent quality of Chingisid-Timurid genealogical authority.[5] His detailed discussion of the topic bespeaks a general awareness, at least among Ottoman bureaucrats and literati, of the Turco-Mongol political tradition, coupled with a defensive acceptance of the comparative weakness of Ottoman legitimizing claims. Ottoman sensitivity to the dynasty's lack of a charismatic lineage had inspired a variety of strategies to bolster genealogical and religious ideology, but addressing the Ottoman Sultan Bayezid's crushing defeat at the hands of Timur at the battle of Ankara in 1402, Mustafa Ali asserted provocatively that the title *Sahib Qiran* gave Timur's rulership universal implications, thus rendering him 'superior in status to the Sultan of Rum.' Not content to simply position Ottoman origins in the general Turco-Mongol milieu, however, Mustafa Ali eventually appropriated the more powerful genealogy, portraying the Ottomans as derived specifically from the Chingisid-Timurid line of world conquerors:

> The Timurid dynasty and Chingisid House, those sharp-headed plunderers,
> Have all been described in this volume,
> From the start of the story to its end;
> From this garden, like a moist blossom,
> Bloomed those praiseworthy ones who are the Ottoman House.[6]

As late as the eighteenth century, Nadir Shah, the Turkmen conqueror of Iran (r. 1736–47) who sacked Mughal Delhi, attached his own political legitimacy to the still charismatic Amir Timur. He claimed to have found the famed treasure of Timur while on a hunting expedition, along with an inscription that predicted his own meteoric rise to power.[7]

The Muslim courts of South Asia demonstrated their own awareness of Timurid power and political legitimacy. The sultan of the Bahmani kingdom of the Deccan, Firuz (1397–1422), who had been deeply impressed by Timur's sack of Delhi, sent ambassadors to Timur's court in Samarqand to offer homage – although his own kingdom had not been threatened by the Central Asian warriors, lying as it did far south of Timurid conquest territories. Timur graciously accepted his fealty, sent gifts, and offered Firuz the rulership of Gujarat and Malwa, although neither ruler had as yet conquered those regions.[8] 'Fancying himself playing on a larger geo-political stage than had his ancestors,' Firuz actively recruited 'Iranians or Persianized men of talent' to his Deccani court in an attempt to emulate the style of the Timurid courts.[9]

So influential had the Timurid imperial model come to be in South Asia that even non-Muslim royal courts were aware of the reputation and sought to emulate it, in much the same manner as their better known Muslim contemporaries. A fifteenth-century member of the Timurid court elite visited the southern state of Vijayanagar, noting that its Hindu kings had begun to title themselves 'sultan' (assimilated into Sanskrit as *suratrana*) and sat enthroned in a *chihil sutun*, a multi-columned Persianate hall inspired by Persepolis, rather than by traditional Hindu palace architecture based on the *mandala* design.

DYNASTIC MEMORY AND GENEALOGICAL CULT   41

The visitor was 'closely questioned about ... Samarqand, Herat and Shiraz' by the king Deva Raya II (1424–46), and noted 'an awareness of, and avid interest in, the Timurid court.'[10]

Timurid Legitimacy in India

A recent work of scholarship has asserted that Babur's entry into the particular political and military conditions of northern India in the sixteenth century required him, at the moment of geographical/political/social transition, to re-invent his original source of legitimacy.[11] Arguing that the Indo-Muslim milieu, with its long memory of Timur's violent sack of Delhi, required Babur to 'skip over' the legacy of Timur, the author suggests that Babur then replaced previously powerful Timurid idioms with more locally acceptable markers of legitimate Islamic kingship. These models include the influential legacy of Mahmud of Ghazni, the pre-Islamic warrior kings of the *Shahnama* and perhaps even that of Mehmet II, Ottoman conqueror of Istanbul, all deployed by Babur in an effort to sustain legitimacy in the new political and social context, and to present him as the ultimate ghazi authority and Islamic king.

There can be little doubt that these were deeply meaningful references, and surely Babur, an intensely literate bibliophile, would have had a detailed awareness of their power as symbols of heroic kingship. Not only would he have been attentive to the memory of Mahmud of Ghazni with whom he shared such direct geographic and historical links, but he is known to have owned an illustrated copy of the *Shahnama*, or *Book of Kings*, originally produced for Timur's grandson Muhammad Juki in 1440, now marked with Babur's seal and the date 906 AH (1501), the year he first gained the throne of Samarqand.[12]

Equally, it is clear that Babur, facing his own wavering troops on the eve of a tricky battle against a larger army, found it useful, even necessary, to evoke well-known heroic idioms in an effort to seize the moral and spiritual high ground. And so it was that in the midst of his conquest of northern India, Babur was quick to publicly align himself with the *ghazi*, holy warrior, ethos. Leading his troops against a larger and better equipped army of Hindus, Babur made a public call for spiritual help in a battle against the non-believing *kafirs*, in an effort to encourage his troops. 'Those who die,' he told them, 'are martyrs and those who kill are warriors for the faith (*olgan, shahid; olturgan, ghazi*).'[13]

The Mughal dynasts were Sunni Muslims who adhered closely to classical Persianate traditions of authority and aesthetics, as a direct inheritance from their Central Asian ancestors. Although Timur has been regularly accused, by not only his own contemporaries but by modern scholars as well, of a lack of sincerity in his religious loyalties, there is no reason to suppose that his descendants were only superficially loyal to Islam.[14] Certainly it is true that the Timurid-Mughals demonstrated a high degree of religious pragmatism and flexibility from the time of the dynasty's origins in Mawarannahr, apparent in their individual interpretations and expressions of religious identity. Like Timur and his immediate successors in Transoxiana, the Mughal emperors hovered between religious nonchalance and fervor, offering regular public gestures directed at locally popular sufi orders, the Naqshbandi in Transoxiana and the Chishtis in India, among others, which acted to affirm their Muslim credentials. It was an inherited complex of religious and ethical understandings, a stew of Perso-Islamic and Chingisid systems of morality, ethics and law that would continue to be carefully re-enacted by the Timurid émigrés on the subcontinent.

Babur's sudden expression of religious sentiment, whether or not one doubts his sincerity, was unquestionably an adept piece of political theatre. The cynicism of Babur's call to religion is apparent, perhaps even to him. '*Beg* and *noker*,[15] great and small alike, all willingly took the Qurans in their hands, and swore oaths to this effect. It was a really good plan (*tavur tadbiri idi*) and it had a good [propagandistic] effect on friend and foe (*yavuqtin yiraqtin, dust u dushman, kurkali eshitkali yahkshi buldu*).'[16] In the aftermath of victory, Babur composed a *ruba'i* to celebrate his ghazi status, although the verse has been described as 'more like a ritualistic observance or an ex post facto religious legitimation than a cry of religious triumph.'[17]

> I am become a desert wanderer for Islam,
> Having joined battle with infidels and Hindus
> I readied myself to become a martyr,
> God be thanked I am become a ghazi.

Dynastic Memory and Genealogical Cult 43

Islam ichin avara-i yazi buldum,
Kuffar u hind harbsazi buldum
Jazm aylab idim uzni shahid olmaqqa,
Amminna' lillahi ki ghazi buldum.[18]

While his pleasure in surviving as *ghazi* rather than dying a martyr, *shahid*, is understandable, it is only in the few pages dwelling on this battle and his victory that Babur conjures overt images of the Quran, and only here, in the aftermath of the battle against Rana Sanga, does he evoke the imagery of the *ghazi*.[19] Shortly after the battle of Khanua, having achieved resounding success, he began welcoming the military contributions of Hindus into his Indian army of conquest and seems to have again turned his thoughts to the conquest of territory, rather than the destruction of infidels and Hindus, *kuffar u hind.*

It is important that we recognize the value and power of multiple models of sovereignty. Kingship is performative and Babur was both intuitive and pragmatic in his willingness to employ and emote a variety of heroes, saints, and warrior kings, references to which would have been deeply meaningful to his followers and his rivals.[20] There is no reason to believe, however, that alternative models for military and political legitimacy should have ever entirely supplanted or replaced Babur's original and most potent of political/warrior models, that of his ancestor, the empire builder Timur – whose success and survival had been equally dependent on developing a workable fusion of dynamic local symbols. To do so would have been not only unnecessary but counterintuitive, for while the northern Indian memory of Timur was one of bloodshed and destruction, parts of the region were still governed by the descendants of Timurid appointees. In fact, at the time of Babur's arrival the political structures of northern Indian territories were directly tied to the historical Timurid mandate, notably Bherah, Kushab, Chenab and Chiniot.[21] Not only was legitimacy still construed locally as Timurid, but, as we have already seen, the political and cultural potency of the Timurid princely courts was recognized and celebrated in many parts of the subcontinent. Immediately after the battle of Kanauj, references to ghazi completely disappear from Babur's discourse; he and his descendants in northern India (who would, in turn, occasionally evoke their own ghazi status when politically expedient) returned to the regular use of Timurid idioms of warrior kingship as their primary source of legitimacy and strength.

The Timurid Ancestral Homeland

A component of the imperial legacy and a cultural memory installed among Babur's descendants was an awareness of the lost homeland of Mawarannahr. None of Babur's children had been born in Transoxiana, yet Samarqand and Herat remained in the Mughal imagination as the golden capital cities of a near-mythic ancestral land. Babur's descendants reiterated imperial claims to Transoxiana, confirming Mughal loyalty to the concept of an ancestral homeland, the lost patrimony of Babur and the 'hereditary dominions' of the Mughal kings.[22] Babur, in his compulsion to unite and rule Timurid Transoxiana, had made three attempts to take and hold Samarqand. When his son Humayun, with the aid of Safavid troops, returned from Iran to reclaim his patrimony, it was towards Samarqand that he first led his invading force. Only after being betrayed by his brother Kamran near Balkh in 1549 and having his army routed by the Uzbek forces did he reluctantly turn south to retake his lost empire in northern India.[23]

Akbar's biography describes imperial plans for a re-conquest of Transoxiana: 'Should the wide country of India be civilized by means of his obedient vassals he [Akbar] would proceed to Turan ... and would get possession of the lands of his ancestors. In this way the various classes of mankind would experience the joys of concord.'[24] Abu al-Fazl affirms Akbar's interest, writing in 1587 that 'his majesty has turned his attention to the conquest of Turan.'[25] The biographer removes any likelihood of a Mughal return to Transoxiana, however, by conceding that this expedition could only occur after Akbar's pacification of Hindustan and possession of the Deccan were complete.

Jahangir affirms his father's interest in the re-establishment of the Mughals in Transoxiana, declaring that 'the conquest of Transoxiana was always in the pure mind of my father, although every time he determined on it things occurred to prevent it.'[26] He goes on to describe what would ultimately remain his own unfulfilled aspiration to leave his sons as governors of the subcontinent while he himself led his armies north: 'As I had made up my mind to the conquest of Transoxiana, which was the hereditary kingdom of my ancestors, I desired to ... go myself with a valiant army in due array, with elephants of mountainous dignity and of lightning speed, and taking ample treasure with me, to undertake the conquest of my ancestral dominions.'[27]

Jahangir's son, Shah Jahan (1592–1666), did at last organize a Mughal expedition, sending his sons and 'an army of fifty thousand horse and ten thousand musketeers, rocketmen and gunners' north to conquer Balkh and Badakhshan, which 'were the hereditary territories of his House and the keys to the acquisition of Samarqand, the home and capital of his great ancestor, Timur Sahib Qiran.'[28] He too was unable to hold the region, in part because of the overextension of Mughal forces, committed as they were to the simultaneous Mughal conquest of the Deccan.[29]

Even amongst his fellow Mughals, Jahangir was remarkable for his relentless attention to dynastic lineage and the maintenance of Timurid political and cultural continuities, regularly referring in his autobiography to Transoxiana (*Turan*) as his *vilayet-i marusi*, 'hereditary territories' and *mulk-i marusi*, 'ancestral domain.'[30] In the middle of Jahangir's twenty-two year reign (r. 1605–1627) he made the lengthy nostalgic pilgrimage to Kabul, Babur's long-time capital, which he describes in his memoirs as 'our home dominions.'[31] There, Jahangir traced Babur's footsteps, visiting his favorite gardens and local views, including a particular site on the slopes of the mountains outside of the city where Babur would drink wine and write poetry, carving the words on the side of the mountain, 'The seat of the king [*takht-i padshah*], the asylum of the world, Zahir al-Din Muhammad Babur, son of 'Umar Shaykh Gurgan [*Guregen*], may God perpetuate his kingdom, 914 [1508–9].' Jahangir, in his passion for lineage, had a second platform carved next to it, along with his own name and that of their common ancestor, Timur.[32]

Visitors to Jahangir's court from Uzbek territory found themselves being intensively interviewed regarding former Timurid possessions in Mawarannahr. 'First he asked me about the condition of the mausoleum of his majesty Timur ... The emperor then asked about the color of Timur's [black jade] sepulcher.'[33] The visitor's detailed description of Timur's tomb earned him imperial gifts: a robe of honor, a 'top quality turban, and Kashmiri shawl ... a gold-embroidered robe, a sash with good golden thread,' and a horse and saddle.[34] Later, on the advice of his visitor, Jahangir set aside ten thousand rupees for 'the shrine of our great honored ancestor ... in order that that blessed station be maintained.'[35] Mughal imperial maintenance of Timur's mausoleum, the Gur-i Amir in Samarqand, would continue until the eighteenth century.

Yet the Mughals also claimed the new imperial territories in India as a legitimate portion of their Timurid inheritance. On a raiding foray into India in 1510, Babur prevented his men from pillaging Bherah by referencing Timur's conquest of northern India in 1398. 'These *vilayets* have long belonged to the Turk ... We are looking after this *vilayet* and its people. There will be no sacking or plunder (*talan u taraj*),' and repeating later, 'Because we consider the *vilayets* pacified by the Turks as ours, there was no oppression.'[36] The decision to tax Bherah, a frontier district of the Lodi sultanate, rather than loot it, has been described as 'the first phase of the foundation of the Timurid-Mughal empire of Delhi and Agra.'[37] It was as 'presumptive sultan,' a legitimate ruler in the direct line of descent from the conqueror Amir Timur Guregen, that Babur petitioned the Lodi sultans to surrender authority over those territories that had in the past 'been dependent on the Turk.'[38] Yet with the hot season upon them, Babur and his warriors returned to Kabul and the Lodi sultans immediately retook the 'Timurid' territories claimed by Babur. It was not until 1525 that Babur returned – this time determined on conquest and the 'resumption' of Timurid rule in India.

The mythology of various ancestral homelands developed in degrees and was expressed differently for those territories most valued yet permanently lost (Mawarannahr), the region which established the House of Babur and formed the springboard for success and conquest (Kabul), and finally the vast and wealthy but utterly foreign empire of India. Mughal feelings for India were mixed, as loyalty to the ancestral homeland of Mawarannahr and longing for Babur's beloved Kabul, and the initial dreadful shock of India's geography and climate, were balanced with the wealth and prestige of an outstanding Indian imperial success. The Baburi conquest would be framed as legitimate due to ancestral claims on the territory. In the minds of Babur, his forces, the refugee community and their descendants, India had been Timurid territory for a hundred and twenty-five years; it was to be expected that the last independent Timurid prince would claim his rightful inheritance.

Sahib Qiran

Timur's descendants in India never referred to themselves as Mughals, itself an Arabized Persian word for Mongol.[39] Although Babur's mother was a Chaghatay Mongol, daughter of the khan of Mughulistan, Babur and his companions identified themselves as Timurid Turks. Babur's own writings suggest a greater degree of royal authority in the pure Timurid line, dismissing the superior qualities of a Chingisid genealogy, and this in dramatic contrast to his Timurid ancestors and their loyal allegiance to Chingisid royal bloodlines.[40] For the more than two hundred and fifty years of their rule the Mughals referred to themselves as *Silsilah-i Guregen* or *Guregeniyya*, the dynasty of the son-in-law, retaining Timur's choice of imperial title as husband to a princess in the line of Chingis Khan, for their imperial dynasty in India.

Timur's ceremonial title, *Sahib Qiran*, also came to be adopted as an important dynastic reference by the Mughal kings, retaining universal applications and implications of supernatural legitimation.[41] Immediately after Timur's death, his descendants seem to have used the title opportunistically to circumvent political dependence on what was in fact a weak lineage, describing instead a degree of nobility beyond that of mundane earthly parentage. His panegyrists wrote, 'A hundred centuries of time go by before fortune hands the reins of rule to a lord of the conjunction like you,' and, 'The learned and historians are agreed that in the time of Islam, nay from Adam's era until this very moment, no lord of the conjunction of Solomonic power like Amir Timur Kuragan [Guregen] has set foot from the abyss of non-existence into the world of being.'[42] The title was used regularly to reference Timur, in support of or even replacing other titles, and came to be so powerfully identified with him that even sixteenth-century Ottoman courtiers could argue the superior political implications of Timur's title versus the pretensions to genealogical legitimacy of the Ottoman sultans.

The title remained the preferred posthumous regnal name for Timur, manipulated by future generations anxious not only to link themselves to the sacred, but also to powerfully invoke the ancestor who had established their political legitimacy had its origins. On his accession to the throne in 1605, Babur's great-grandson Jahangir expressed deepest pleasure with the chronogram composed by the courtier Maktub Khan, which described the new emperor as a second Sahib Qiran:

> King of kings Jahangir, a second Timur
> Sat in justice on the victorious throne
> Success, fortune, victory, pomp and triumph
> Are wrapped around him to serve with joy
> This is the date of his accession,
> When fortune puts its head at the feet of *sahib qiran-i sani*.[43]

Twenty-five years later, Jahangir's son, the fifth Mughal emperor, Shah Jahan (r. 1627–1659), who, unlike his father or even Timur, was actually born under the conjunction of the planets Jupiter and Venus, was inspired to permanently adopt Timur's title, inscribing *Sahib qiran-i sani*, 'the second lord of the auspicious conjunction,' on his coinage. When, in the last years of his reign, Shah Jahan was imprisoned by his rebellious sons, he appealed for help by demanding his courtiers 'march against the two undutiful sons, to inflict upon them the due reward of their misconduct,' carefully reminding them of his role not only as emperor but as the Sahib Qiran-i Sani.[44] The Qadiri sufi sheikh who served as the spiritual guide of Dara Shikoh (1615–1659), a sixth-generation Mughal prince, affirmed popular recognition of the dynasty's use of the title in describing his imperial patron: 'The first and second Sahib Qiran (*sahib qiran-i awwal u sani*), namely Amir Timur and Shah Jahan, are the kings of grandeur,' he wrote, 'while our Dara Shikoh is the Sahib Qiran of the heart (*ma sahib qiran-i dil*).'[45]

Genealogy and the Silsilahnama

In India, in the near absence of Timurid rivals, Babur's descendants were able to transform loyalty from the personal to the imperial, and yet the foundation of Mughal identity continued to be constructed and transmitted in large part through the dynasty's charismatic Timurid genealogy. Illustrated genealogical scrolls, *silsilahnamas*, produced in the Mughal workshops demonstrated Mughal claims to legitimate descent from Timur, Chingis Khan, and Alanqua, through whose impregnation by a beam of light the Mongols claimed descent. Even *silsilahnamas* produced in the Ilkhanid period were, like dynastic portraits, at a much later date amended by Timurids and Mughals to include later descendants of the House of Timur. For example, a Timurid *silsilahnama*, the *Mu'izz al-Ansab* (*The Glorifier of Genealogies*), which had been produced in 1426 by the descendants of Shahrukh, was extended in the early sixteenth century to include Badi' al-Zaman, son of Sultan Husayn Bayqara, who had been forced to flee Khurasan by the invading Uzbeks.[46] A version of the *Mu'izz al-Ansab* found its way into Mughal hands in India, where portraits were carefully added on every page to illustrate the dynastic manuscript.[47] The Mughal interest in Timurid genealogical scrolls was again displayed by the last Mughal emperor Bahadur Shah Zafar (r. 1837–58, d. 1862), in whose court ateliers a fully illustrated and versified *silsilahnama* was produced which detailed the family line from Timur to Bahadur Shah himself, with the fascinating and curious inclusion of the Afghan Sher Shah, who drove Humayun out of northern India in 1540, the Persian Shah Tahmasp Safavi (r. 1524–1576) and Nadir Shah, who had sacked Delhi a hundred years earlier, an act which may have seemed more palatable were he included henceforth as a member of the ruling dynasty.[48]

The Mughal imperial seal functioned as a very public affirmation of Mughal legitimizing genealogy, taking the form of a *silsilahnama*.[49] Babur's own ruling seal, dated to 1521/2 in the pre-Mughal Timurid era, linked the king through five lobed border panels, back to the illustrious Amir Timur.[50] Akbar's genealogical seal, called the *muhr-i muqqadas-i kalan*, the great sacred seal, was originally modeled on Babur's late Timurid version. Later modifications within

Akbar's atelier affected the seal only in form, not content; the artist, Mawlana Ali Ahmad, described 'the engraving of the seal of the just king ... on which are engraved his sublime titles and the names of his exalted ancestors as far as Amir Timur, the Lord of the (Fortunate) Conjunction.'[51]

Because of the genealogical form it had taken, additions to the seal became signifiers of legitimacy and repudiations of a contested succession. For seven months in 1658, in the midst of a violent and protracted succession dispute, the Mughal prince Murad Baksh claimed kingship and had his own name affixed in eleventh place to the imperial seal. When his brother Aurangzeb became the final victor and emperor, Murad Baksh's claims were not just refuted but rather completely ignored and Aurangzeb himself took eleventh place within the genealogical structure of the imperial seal. It was not the last time that the Mughal genealogical seal would be amended, 'striking out from the record and treating as non-existent the reigns' of defeated scions of the dynasty.[52] As a public affirmation of dynastic succession and an articulation of the Timurid genealogy upon which was so firmly anchored the basis of dynastic legitimacy, the seal remained 'one of the most important symbols of Mughal imperial authority.'[53]

For a few generations, in the reigns of Akbar and Jahangir, that seal, in miniature form, played a role in the emperor's enlistment of a small number of personal disciples. At the multi-ethnic, multi-religious royal court of Akbar, in a society of Rajput nobles, Persian intellectuals, Arab scholars, Turkish and Uzbek military men, local lineage chiefs and caste leaders, Jesuit missionaries, diplomats, mercenaries and merchants, efforts by the emperor to establish an imperial cult resulted in the creation of a body of intensely loyal courtiers in an intimate relationship with the emperor – regardless of individual religious, ethnic or hereditary service loyalties.[54] A member of the royal court described the initiation ceremony of selected disciples, in which Akbar offered each a small portrait of himself, with the dynastic genealogy displayed on the reverse: 'They looked upon it [the portrait] as the standard of loyal friendship, and the advance guard of righteousness and happiness and they put it wrapped up in a small jeweled case, on the top of their turbans.'[55]

Jahangir imitated his father's enrollment of loyal courtiers.[56] An account by Mirza Nathan, a Mughal general and author of the *Baharistan-i Ghaybi*, a history of the Mughal wars of Bengal and Orissa, describes the process by which he became a disciple of the emperor Jahangir, thereby gaining the right to wear a portrait/genealogical seal of the dynasty on his turban.[57] In the midst of a critical illness, Mirza Nathan, whose father served both Akbar and Jahangir before his death in 1612, dreamt that the emperor spoke to him: 'O, Nathan! Is this the time for the Tiger to lie down? Arise! We have granted you security from pain and trouble by our prayers ...'[58] Waking in perfect health, Mirza Nathan sent word of the dream to his commander, Islam Khan, who clearly saw it as significant. The emperor was subsequently informed and a decision made, at Islam Khan's urging, that Mirza Nathan would be 'enlisted as one of the disciples of the sublime Court.'[59]

Within the year, gifts and imperial orders were sent as usual from the imperial court to the military officers serving in the Eastern provinces. Yet while other officers received Arabian horses, a pearl studded gun, a matched pair of hunting panthers, and robes of honor, Mirza Nathan was sent, like the personal disciples of the previous emperor, 'a special portrait of his majesty.' Nathan clarified, 'If any of the servants is included among the special disciples, he is favored with a portrait adorned with a genealogical tree. Therefore on account of the many devoted services ... and the aforesaid dream about the Emperor ... he was included in the circle of his disciples.'[60]

The genealogical portrait of imperial discipleship, as in Akbar's time, was small. 'Nathan placed it on his head and honored himself by observing the formalities of obeisance and prostrations of gratitude.'[61] Although a logical extension of increasing Mughal imperial paternalism, the enlistment of personal followers hearkened back directly to Babur's recommendation that his descendants socialize intimately with the imperial retinue in order to tie them in loyalty to the throne.[62] In this case, however, the careful inclusion of the imperial genealogy served to acknowledge and confirm the disciples' loyalty not only to an individual king but to the entire Timurid dynasty.

History, Imperial Memoir and the Mughal Arts of the Book

The Chingisid courts had not previously developed a tradition of narrative court historiography, although their later incarnation in the Islamic world, the Ilkhanids, by contrast, had produced the famed Persian-language histories of Juwayni (d. 1283), Rashid al-Din (d. 1318) and Vassaf (fl. ca. 1328), which by default remain our only sources for the first century of regional Mongol rule. In the political fragmentation that followed the death of the Ilkhanid ruler Abu Sa'id Bahadur Khan in 1335, however, history writing disappeared, ultimately to be revived by Timur, who 'provided the stimulus for this development both through his general interest in history, geography and genealogy, as well as his specific desire to have his activities and achievements accurately recorded.'[63] Timur's desire to construct a legacy of his own choice and making is evidenced by his close involvement in the production of histories of his own reign; every detail of his court chronicles, most of which were composed at his instigation, was checked and cross-checked in his presence and eventually edited by Timur himself.[64]

Once in India, the production of historical chronicles, driven by the developing imperial narrative, relentlessly affirmed the legitimacy of Mughal dynastic rule. As Timur and the Timurid princes had done before them, individual Mughal kings participated fully and personally in the production of imperial narrative imagery, producing histories that were intended as dynastic affirmations and personal justifications of their inheritance of the Timurid throne.

Babur's memoir was composed both as validation of his right to rule and to serve as advice literature for his sons and future Timurid kings, but most importantly it served to construct a canonical narrative of Mughal origins. Without indulging in a great deal of personal analysis, Babur narrated his exploits, expressing grandiose imperial ambitions alongside assertions of his personal legitimacy as a Timurid prince of impeccable lineage. Although the *Baburnama* was written in Babur's Afghan and Indian territories, it was composed in Chaghatay Turkish rather than the more ubiquitous court Persian, an indication that it was directed to a Central Asian constituency, the 'legitimizing audience ... comprised of the Islamized, literate, Turki-speaking Timurid and Chaghatay Mongol elite, and beyond them the broader society of Turco-Mongol military aristocrats.'[65] A copy of the memoirs was sent back to Kabul as early as 1529, for it was primarily to the transitional post-Uzbek generation of Timurid refugee nobility that he hoped would coalesce around him, forming the crucial backbone of his new Timurid court, that Babur originally aimed his legitimizing text.

Babur's successor, Humayun retained the famed historian Ghiyas al-Din Khwandamir at his court, officially inviting him to compose a history of his rule. According to Khwandamir, Humayun explained his reasons, saying, 'It seems proper and desirable that the inventions of my auspicious mind and the improvements of my enlightened understanding should be arranged in a series and written down in order that in future ages the light of these works may shine among the people of countries near and remote.'[66]

Akbar, affirming the dynasty's imperial past and current legitimacy, requested that members of his court with personal memories of his father or grandfather record them. Babur's daughter, Gulbadan Begim, explained, 'An order was issued, 'Write down whatever you know of the doings of *Firdaus makani* and *Jannat ashyani* [Babur and Humayun].' In obedience to the royal order, I set down whatever there is that I have heard and remember.'[67] It was at Akbar's court that Gulbadan Begim composed her memoir, the *Humayunnama*; Humayun's ewer-bearer, Mihtar Jauhar Aftabchi, who had spent twenty years at the emperor's side, composed the *Tazkirat al-waqi'at*; and Bayezid Bayat wrote the *Tarikh-i Humayun*, covering the years 1542–1591.[68] In addition, Akbar commissioned dynastic histories such as the *Chingisnama* (*History of Chingis Khan*), the *Timurnama* (*History of Timur*) and the *Tarikh-i Alfi* (*History of a Thousand Years*), which asserted the dynasty's Mongol and Timurid ancestry, claiming to have 'inaugurated a new millennium' with the foundation of the South Asian Timurid empire.[69]

Akbar is the best documented of all Mughal kings, due in large part to the six volumes of personal narrative, imperial encyclopedia and ideological underpinnings for Mughal, and more particularly Akbari rule, the *Akbarnama* and *A'in-i Akbari*, written by Akbar's close friend and panegyrist, Abu al-Fazl. Abu al-Fazl exalted in Akbar's lineage, describing him as 'the glory of the House of the Guregen' (*furug-i khanadan-i Guregeni*) and 'the lamp of the illustrious house of Timur' (*chirag-i dudman-i Sahib qirani*).[70] The entire first volume is devoted to establishing Akbar's dynastic and political legitimacy, beginning with detailed descriptions of his horoscope, cautiously delineated by Abu al-Fazl for every possible component of the diverse South Asian audience, in the various Greek, Persian, Ilkhanid and Indian astrological traditions.[71] In confirmation of the continued relevance of the Mughal dynasty's Mongol-Timurid genealogy, the remainder of the volume is devoted to Akbar's dynastic lineage, beginning with the original man, Adam, through Noah and his son Japheth, for as in Timur's later genealogical charts 'the Khans of the eastern cities and of Turkestan all derive from him.'[72] Nineteen generations later, the genealogy was strategically shifted to a Mongol daughter of the lineage, Alanqua, whose miraculous pregnancy by a beam of light resulted in the birth of three sons, who would father the Mongol nobility. Abu al-Fazl, who did not invent this dynastic lineage, was quick to defend the Mongol tradition of the chaste birth – arguing against 'scientific computations' in the place of 'auspicious guidance,' he reminded the reader that Adam was born of neither father nor mother, so 'why not admit a child without the father? Especially ... in the case of Jesus and Mary.' Abu al-Fazl was not ignorant of the messianic implications when comparing the Mongol successors to Jesus, composing a simple verse: 'If you believe the tale of Mary, believe the same of Alanqua.'

A descendant of Alanqua, Qaculi Bahadur, was said to have had a miraculous dream in which a series of shining stars emerged from his breast, interpreted by his father to indicate 'seven dominant descendants bearing on their brows the diadem of primacy and the crown of rule.' An eighth star, which lighted the entire world and produced smaller stars which illuminated the universe, represented his eighth descendant, 'who would exhibit world wide sovereignty.' Although there were those who identified the first seven stars with the descendants of Qaculi Bahadur and the eighth star with Timur,

Abu al-Fazl rejected this notion, arguing that non-ruling descendants could not be counted amongst the favored kings. Rather, in Abu al-Fazl's reckoning, the very first of the stars denoting kingship represented Timur, with his celestial descendants reaching the true culmination of the prophecy in the person of Akbar.[73] He thus managed to position Akbar above even Timur, as the eighth star and 'possessor of world wide sovereignty.' In his listing of Mughal ancestry from Timur onwards, Abu al-Fazl reversed his previous pattern by 'counting backwards,' describing each new generation as ancestors of Akbar rather than descendants of great predecessors, such as Adam, Timur or Chingis Khan. With the political legitimacy of the dynasty firmly established in its descent from the greatest kings of the Islamic and Turco-Mongol worlds, the most critical aspect of Abu al-Fazl's imperial genealogy had become the placement of Akbar at the pinnacle of a long line of conquerors and kings.

Jahangir, on the other hand, followed in his great-grandfather's footsteps in composing his own memoir, the *Jahangirnama*, in what can be seen as a dynastic tradition of memoir.[74] Stylistically they are very different, reflecting among other things Babur's intrepid and unrelenting scrambling for a kingdom and Jahangir's much easier inheritance of power and enormous wealth. Yet for both kings the memoirs served the same central purpose. In composing what were intended to be public documents, Babur and Jahangir were engaged primarily in the production of politically legitimizing texts; at their core, both were the narrators of their own ambition, devoting their efforts to a delineation and explication of political and cultural legitimacy. And in both cases the origins of political power were found in the near universally acknowledged charisma of their (shared) Timurid ancestry. So while both texts describe diverse and compelling justifications for kingship – for Babur, eventual military strategic success as well as the critical ability to gather and support a loyal following; for Jahangir, the royal dispensation of justice and a divine mandate – fundamentally both place the roots of their power in their descent from Timur, through that line of fractious and contentious Timurid princes whose sole argument for control of the ancestral homeland was the possession of a powerful charismatic lineage and their sublime aesthetic vision.

Jahangir began distributing his memoir in the thirteenth year of his reign, 'to bestow on individual servants and sent to other countries to be used by rulers as guides for ruling.'[75] The first copy was given to his eldest son, Shah Jahan, with Jahangir's inscription expressing hope that 'an examination of the contents would be acceptable to God and bring praise from the people.'[76] Within the text, Jahangir interposes regular affirmations of his right to rule as 'a just and equitable monarch'[77] 'upon whose worthy form He (the Distributor of Justice) draped this *khilat* [robe of honor] ... Imperial rule has been given to this supplicant at the divine court.'[78] The memoirs do not end with the distribution of the first copies but continue through the nineteenth year of Jahangir's reign, when illness prevented him from continuing.[79] A courtier close Jahangir, Mu'tamid Khan, wrote the *Iqbalnama* in three volumes as a history of the Mughal dynasty in India: volume one contains the history of Babur's and Humayun's reigns, the second is devoted entirely to Akbar and the third volume covers Jahangir's reign. As court historian and panegyrist, Mu'tamid Khan based the final volume on Jahangir's memoir and the official interpretation of events, rendering a somewhat repetitive but appropriately laudatory account.

Shah Jahan's court produced yet another history of the reign of Jahangir, *Ma'asir-i Jahangiri* by Khwaja Kamgar Ghayrat Khan, in which Jahangir's reign is defended and Shah Jahan's behavior as the rebellious Prince Khurram is presented in a cleansed and revised version. For his own reign, Shah Jahan's courtiers produced the *Amal-i Salih*, by Muhammad Salih Kambu, the *Padshahnama*, composed by Muhammad Amin Qazwini, Abd al-Hamid Lahauri (who refers to Shah Jahan as 'that pride of the Guregen dynasty')[80] and Muhammad Wari, as well as the *Shahjahannama* by Sadiq Khan.

Shah Jahan's first historian, Qazvini, who remained at the imperial court for the first ten years of the emperor's reign, describes the emperor as being deeply involved in the process of creating an official court history, in a manner highly reminiscent of his ancestor Timur. 'Sometimes, the writer of these pages [Qazvini] enters the assembly[81] by imperial command and reports on the content of each and every narrative that has been written. If a slip in the contents or an error in the expression has occurred, His Majesty corrects it and guides this worthless speck of dust to the exalted words and pleasing turns of phrase that occur to the royal mind and the inclusion of which in this history would occasion felicity of expression, indeed which are necessary concomitants to this art. This honor lasts two or three *gharis* [about 24 minutes] or longer when there is more work.'[82]

The official court chronicle of the first ten years of rule by Aurangzeb, the last of 'the Great Mughals,' was the *Alamgirnama*, by Mirza Muhammad Kazim, son of Shah Jahan's historian Qaswini.[83] The work was originally encouraged by the emperor who, like his father Shah Jahan, demanded that the author 'submit his pages to the interested scrutiny of the emperor himself, and be guided in doubtful questions by information graciously given by the monarch respecting what account was to be rejected or admitted.'[84] In the thirty-second year of his reign, however, after hearing the author's summation of his first ten years, the emperor broke with dynastic tradition and demanded that all court history-writing cease, because 'the cultivation of his inward piety was preferable to the ostentatious display of his achievements.'[85] Not only did Aurangzeb ban court histories, he stopped the recording of most imperial transactions.

It is difficult to understand the emperor's sudden reversal of support for court history writing, but Aurangzeb's extant personal letters, composed in the last years of his reign, express deep dissatisfaction and regret for his own rulership. He wrote to his son, 'I have not been the guardian and protector of the empire. My valuable time has been passed vainly.'[86] Perhaps Aurangzeb hoped that in the absence of a historical record his failings as emperor would go unrecognized by future generations. Yet five collections of Aurangzeb's letters, including lengthy commentary on the responsibilities of the Mughal kings, were gathered and saved by members of the imperial court and the only complete chronicle of the period, the *Ma'asir-i Alamgiri* of Muhammad Saqi Mustaid Khan, written secretly throughout the author's forty years at Aurangzeb's court, was rescued from oblivion and finished under the patronage of Inayatullah Khan, *wazir* of Aurangzeb's son and successor, Bahadur Shah (r. 1707–12).

In the eighteenth century the declining Mughal court produced a surge of Timurid dynastic histories which, in an interesting twist on the late Mughal search for sources of legitimacy, emphasized the Chingisid lineage of the dynasty, including the *Tazkira-i Chaghatay* of Muhammad Hadi Kamwar Khan, recounting the history of the Mongols and developing a direct lineage from Chingis Khan to the Mughal kings, ending with the seventh year of the reign of Muhammad Shah (1724). The *Tarikh-i Chaghatay* of Muhammad Shafi Tehrani begins with the history of Babur and includes part of the reign of Muhammad Shah and the withdrawal of the post-Safavid Persian expansionist Nadir Shah in 1739. In a ravaged and desolate Delhi, the power of the Mughal kings deeply diminished by war and invasion, Muhammad Shafi described yet another dramatic reversal of Mughal imperial history writing, a reversal which not incidentally confirms the importance to the Mughals of deliberate and state-sponsored dynastic history. He writes of an imperial order issued immediately after the departure of Nadir Shah, demanding that ' "All public officers should occupy themselves in the discharge of their ordinary duties, *except the historians*. These should refrain from recording the events of my reign, for at present the record cannot be a pleasant one"... Consequently, being helpless, all the historians obeyed the royal mandate and laid down their pens.'[87]

The importance of these writings cannot be exaggerated. As intended, the Mughals' carefully controlled and deliberately manipulated dynastic regnal histories had a strong influence not only on the members of the royal court and foreign kings and courtiers, but perhaps most profoundly on succeeding generations of the dynasty. Babur carried with him everywhere a copy of Timur's *Zafarnama*, which he seems to have seen as a guide not only to kingship, but to history and geography as well.[88] Humayun also carried a copy of the *Zafarnama*, although his edition was a particularly important manuscript; it was not only memoir and guide but souvenir and nostalgia piece, having been copied at Sultan Husayn Bayqara's court in Herat by Ali Shir Nava'i and illustrated by the famed miniaturist Bihzad, both artists identified most closely with the golden age of Timurid princely patronage.[89] The *Baburnama* was translated into Persian by one of Babur's own courtiers, Shaykh Zayn, perhaps during Babur's own lifetime, although more likely at the court of his son, Humayun. The Zayn

Dynastic Memory and Genealogical Cult 59

translation was composed in 'an ornate and rhetorical style,' not at all on the model of the original, which may explain its subsequent lack of popularity.[90] It is rarely mentioned in contemporary manuscripts and only fragments of the manuscript remain. A much more successful translation of the *Baburnama*, by Abd al-Rahim Khan-i Khanan, was fantastically illustrated on four separate occasions in the court ateliers of Akbar,[91] where the *Zafarnama* and the *Chingisnama*, the *A'in-i Akbari*, and Persian literary classics were also illustrated.[92]

Gulbadan Begim's memoirs, the *Humayunnama*, were illustrated under the direction of Shah Jahan, who paid eight thousand rupees for the work and left an autograph note in the frontispiece, claiming it as a history 'which contains an abridgement of the affairs of his majesty Sahib Qiran and of his glorious descendants.' Shah Jahan is said to have particularly favored ancestral memoirs, choosing to have the *Baburnama* and Timur's *Zafarnama* read aloud to him in the evenings.[93]

Although he was familiar with them in the Persian translation, the fourth Mughal emperor, Jahangir, wrote touchingly of reading an original Turki copy of Babur's memoirs in 'entirely his own blessed handwriting ... for although I grew up in Hindustan, I am not ignorant of how to read and write Turkish.'[94] Jahangir's defensive assertion is very likely accurate, for although the court language of the Mughals was Persian, at least as late as the reign of Aurangzeb (1618–1707), at whose court the title *Chaghatay* was bestowed as a mark of imperial favor,[95] royal children were schooled in the Turkish language of their Central Asian ancestors.[96] Fulfilling Jahangir's desire that his own memoir 'be sent to other countries to be used by the rulers as guides,'[97] the *Jahangirnama* was translated into Ottoman Turkish in the eighteenth century at the imperial Ottoman court in Istanbul by order of Sultan Mustafa III.[98] In an illustration of the continued power of Mughal history writing, and the nostalgia which continued to cling to the Mughal kings, a new series of illustrations was commissioned at the Mughal court for the *Iqbalnama-i Jahangiri* as late as the nineteenth century, with the last shreds of Mughal power in imminent collapse.[99]

Just as Timur had shown great care and personal attention in the development of a legitimizing history, his descendants in Timurid

Central Asia and in India were deeply involved in producing memoirs and chronicles as an expression of dynastic identity and legitimacy. Mughal patronage of writers and historians, the establishment of sophisticated and well-populated imperial workshops and personal involvement by Mughal royals in the process illustrate imperial awareness that these writings would significantly impact perceptions of Mughal legitimacy, on an individual level as well as dynastic, within the family and the nobility, as well as internationally. Every generation of Timurid-Mughal nobility produced a body of carefully crafted legitimizing texts, defending the right of individual and, more powerfully, of dynastic rule. For successive generations of Mughals these texts served as an institutional memory, imbedded with explanations and descriptions of Timurid-Mughal cultural attributes, court traditions, understandings of law, religion and family. As the Mughal royals pored over, translated, discussed, scrawled on and cross-referenced these works, they assimilated and absorbed the sum of the dynasty's constructed imperial identity to date, that which marked and defined them, resulting in a remarkably high degree of cultural and imperial continuity for over two hundred years in Mughal India.

Painting, Portraiture and Memory

The audience for written texts is limited by levels of literacy and shared language. In the multi-lingual and only semi-literate milieu of Timur's Central Asian court, illustration had become a useful tool in the establishment of public identity.[100] A master manipulator of arts and architecture in the interests of his imperial image, employing his preferred monumental presentation, Timur had his palace walls decorated with murals illustrating imperial power and grandeur. A contemporary observer described an extensive display:

> He had depicted his assemblies and his own likeness, now smiling, now austere, and representations of his battles and sieges and his conversation with kings, amirs, lords, wise men, and magnates, and Sultans offering homage to him and bringing gifts to him from every side and his hunting nets and ambushes

Dynastic Memory and Genealogical Cult 61

and battles in India, Dasht and Persia, and how he gained victory and how his enemy was scattered and driven to flight; and the likeness of his sons and grandsons, amirs and soldiers and his public feasts and the goblets of wine and cup bearers and zither-players of his mirth and his love meetings and the concubines of his majesty and the royal wives and many other things which happened in his realms ... and therein he intended that those who knew not his affairs should see them as though present.[101]

Evidence exists of similar paintings hung in Timur's Bagh-i Shamal and Dilkushay gardens, perhaps resting near the fabulous tapestry of Sultan Bayezid, plundered from the Ottoman treasury and on public display at Timur's court.[102]

Timur's successors continued the use of wall painting as a device of imperial image making and confirmation of cultural prowess. Paintings are mentioned in the *tarabkhana* (joyhouse) of Abu Saʿid in Herat.[103] A document from the royal workshop of Baysunghur ibn Shahrukh, dated c. 1427–28, refers to a structure called the *surat khana*, or 'picture gallery,' being built on the grounds of the palace, perhaps including portrait murals.[104] No known murals matching those described in the sources now remain but related Timurid illustrations, containing similar cartouches, medallion forms, *chinoiserie*, and landscape elements, reinforce the probability of their existence at the Timurid courts of Mawarannahr and Khurasan.[105] Paintings and drawings have been identified whose large size, bold presentation and subject matter suggest that their original purpose was to serve as studies for wall paintings, and a fifteenth-century illustration in Nizami's *Haft Paykar* (Seven Portraits) shows a palace room decorated with large wall paintings of seven princesses.[106]

Babur would have seen these vast Timurid palace wall paintings when he briefly ruled Samarqand and visited Herat. Perhaps he imitated them at his own courts in Kabul and in Agra; certainly his successors employed very similar wall painting in their palaces in India. While the aniconic Ottomans shied away from large-scale portraiture, the Mughals (and to some extent the Safavids[107]) covered their palace walls with frescoes of family gatherings, most particularly, in the

Mughal case, highlighting their genealogical descent and confirming dynastic legitimacy. Many are reputed to have included family groupings, while some portrayed idealized allegorical scenes of the ruling emperor and his sons seated with their deceased royal ancestors, particularly Timur.[108]

Literary illustration had emerged in the Islamic world among the Turco-Mongol dynasties of the fourteenth century, particularly the western Iranian Jalayirids.[109] Timurid commitment to Persian literature, and their deliberate use of dynastic historiographies as a strategy to establish political legitimacy, led to the abundant production of illustrated texts, which came to be seen as 'the supreme expression of Timurid taste.'[110] The Timurids developed artistic conventions and devices which had been inherited from Turco-Mongol and Persian traditions, inspired by Chinese models and Chinese obsession with dynastic history, into a distinctive style which 'best conveyed the ideals of the dynasty,' and came to be seen as canonical by contemporary dynasties such as the Ottomans and Safavids.[111]

Beyond simple illustration, Timurid royal portraiture balanced concern for a true likeness with idealized conventions which had become codified by the fifteenth century.[112] Much of the iconography that informed Ottoman, Safavid and early Mughal works can be identified in Timurid royal portraits. An early Timurid genealogical portrait series (ca. 1405) is illustrated with three-quarter-view portraits of princes and princesses, the subject kneeling, sitting cross-legged, or sitting with one leg underneath the body, and bearing the 'insignia of royalty:' handkerchief, flower, bow, thumb ring, mace, or distinctive headgear.[113] Timurid imperial portraits were not intended solely to provide a record of distinct individuals; in addition, they stressed a common dynastic bond, while shared imperial attributes affirmed the power and legitimacy of the imperial succession.[114] Although seemingly intimate and deeply personal, the portraits can be seen as 'an official imagery of the ruling house.'[115]

There is no evidence that Babur set up imperial painting workshops in Kabul, although not to have done so would seem to be completely out of character for this ardent collector and connoisseur of literary arts. He was a covetous bibliophile – regularly quoting from the Persian literary classics, voracious in his manuscript acquisitions, despairing at their loss. Humayun was a highly literate bibliophile like his father.[116] While in exile at the Safavid royal court of Shah Tahmasp in 1544, he invited two of the most famous painters of Safavid Iran to join him when he regained the throne in India.[117] The painters, Mir Sayyid Ali and Abd al-Samad, accompanied Humayun on his reconquest of India, arriving in Kabul in 1549–50. They were joined soon after by two more Persian painters, Mir Musavvar and Dost Muhammad.[118] These artists are generally considered to have had a powerful formative influence on Mughal painting, although the canonical forms and images of late Ilkhanid painting had been the point of origin for both Persian and Timurid production, making the identification of a single original source for Mughal painting difficult, and perhaps irrelevant. Within Humayun's imperial ateliers no homogeneous style emerged in the production of what were highly standardized representations of imperial themes; certainly what should be considered the Timurid-Persianate tradition of imperial painting continued to dominate.

In comparison to the periodic iconoclasm of their contemporaries in Iran and Anatolia, imperial portraiture remained popular among the Mughals. There is a great deal of evidence to suggest that portraits of Humayun were executed during his reign. A portrait of Humayun with his son Kamran Mirza may have been produced at Kamran's court at Kabul, which would seem to indicate that Mughal princes were continuing the Ilkhanid-Timurid tradition of separate workshops at each of the princely courts.[119] The painter Abd al-Samad was commissioned in 1551 to paint a portrait of Akbar engaged in the act of painting – the emperor had reportedly received extensive training in his youth. On his accession to the Mughal throne, Akbar supported the continued imperial patronage of painters, and is quoted as saying, 'There are many who hate painting; but such men I dislike. It appears to me as if a painter had a quite peculiar means of recognizing God.'[120] He ordered Humayun's Persian painters to expand the imperial ateliers, hiring local artists using indigenous forms as well as those trained in the Timurid tradition.

The production of the royal workshops in India emphasized Mughal dynastic genealogy, imperial grandeur and religious loyalties, and explored and expanded on the images of individual kings. Akbar's original commissions from the painters of the imperial ateliers were illustrations of Persian language classics of adventure and fantasy, including the *Tutinama* (Tales of a Parrot), which may originally have been commissioned by Humayun, and a voluminous fourteen-volume *Hamzanama* (Tales of Amir Hamza) which took over fifteen years to complete and contained over fourteen hundred illustrations.[121] By the 1580's, however, Akbar had steered his workshop toward the production of illustrated dynastic histories and royal portraiture, a clear indication of their value within the imperial household. His workshops illustrated the *Timurnama* (ca. 1584), a history of Timur and his descendants including Akbar; the *Baburnama* (ca. 1589), Babur's autobiographical memoir (newly translated into court Persian from its original Turki); the *Akbarnama* (ca. 1590), the history of Akbar's own reign, carefully tracing his lineage through the Timurid line to the Mongol ancestress, Alanqua; and the *Chingisnama* (ca. 1596), a history of Chingis Khan and the Mongols, based on that of Rashid al-Din. Each of these histories was given roughly one hundred and fifty lavish color illustrations and some saw several editions with entirely new sets of illustrations.[122] In 1581–82 Akbar commissioned an illustrated history of Islam's first one thousand years, the *Tarikh-i Alfi*, which notably culminated in the reign of Akbar, ruler of the new millennium.[123]

Apart from the numbers of literary works and histories illustrated in the workshops of Akbar's court, the emperor commissioned 'an immense album,' in which were collected painted portraits of the emperor (for which he posed) and of all the nobles of the empire, so that 'those who have passed away receive new life and those who are still alive have immortality promised them,' a description which may indicate the inclusion of genealogical studies within the portfolio and most certainly affirms the real and continuing Mughal obsession with the memorialization of the dynasty and its servants.[124]

Genealogical studies were a common theme in Mughal miniature painting, particularly studies of impossibly disparate generations united in sympathetic communion, as when Shah Jahan's imperial atelier produced an allegorical scene of Timur passing an imperial crown to Babur in the presence of Humayun.[125] More daringly, the same

Dynastic Memory and Genealogical Cult 65

atelier offered the image of an improved line of succession, painting Akbar passing the crown directly to Shah Jahan, observed by a smiling, passive Jahangir. Nor were genealogical paintings of the Mughal dynasts allowed to remain static. A painting begun in the reign of Humayun, well known to modern scholars and entitled *Princes of the House of Timur*, was probably originally composed by the Persian immigrant artist Mir Sayyid Ali at some point between 1550 and 1555.[126] The king, Humayun, is seated in a pavilion, enjoying a garden party with his imperial retinue while servants carry in flasks and platters of food to the guests seated in the shade of a chenar tree. It was most likely during the reign of Jahangir, who we have already confirmed was absorbed with genealogical memorabilia and dynastic affirmations, that the original garden party painting was expanded to become a dynamic and complex genealogical study in which Humayun is joined in the garden pavilion by Akbar, holding a book, Jahangir, with his emblematic hunting falcon, and a young Shah Jahan. Hovering at the edges of the central grouping are Jahangir's elder sons, Parvez and Khusraw, although the latter is an unfinished ink sketch.[127]

At some later date, the painting was further modified. In what was surely an effort to emphasize the genealogical status of the painting, names were scrawled above the heads of the formerly anonymous figures among the garden party guests. The likenesses are vague, a great deal of over painting is evidenced, and the labeling highly suspicious, yet the painting now claims to include portraits of Babur and Umar Shaykh, Sultan Abu Sa'id and Shahrukh among other notables of the Timurid milieu. Somewhat surprisingly, the figure of Timur is not included – a large swath of the painting has deteriorated and while it is possible that this section had included an image of the dynasty's founding ancestor it seems highly unlikely that he would have been given such a marginal position. For the same reason too, the labeling of a figure as Babur is highly suspicious, positioned as he is indistinguishably in the midst of a lower grouping of Timurid princes. It is clear that the original intent of the painting was to illustrate a simple garden party scene, including Humayun's immediate retinue and anonymous courtiers. It was only much later that waves of genealogical passion converted the simple painting of a court picnic into a deliberate palimpsest on whose linen surface legitimacy and succession could be articulated and argued, and charismatic genealogical linkages affirmed.

Popular religious figures were similarly treated, and for the same purpose, to affirm political legitimacy through affiliation with local spiritual authorities. Jahangir had himself painted with a variety of holy men, with whom he described himself as being in regular contact and conversation. In particular, Akbar and Jahangir were pictured in close and affectionate communion with the Chishti Shaykh Salim, a holy man equally influential within Hindu and Muslim communities, who had prophesied the birth of Akbar's sons and next to whose *dargah* Akbar constructed his imperial capital, Fatehpur Sikri. Years later, Shah Jahan had his own portrait juxtaposed on a single page with a portrait of the (deceased) Shaykh Salim.[128] Mughal interest in the sustained ability of the Chishti order to confer legitimacy, and not incidentally link themselves to the most renowned of all Mughal kings, the original Chishti patron, Akbar, is illustrated by an allegorical portrait from the eighteenth century displaying two unidentified Mughal princes seated comfortably beside the same (by now long deceased!) Shaykh Salim Chishti, affirming continued imperial loyalty to the Chishtiyyah Sufi order even in the years of Mughal collapse.[129]

Contemporary sources confirm that the Mughal kings, like their Timurid forefathers, were extremely sensitive to the legitimizing potential of an illustrated imperial image. Like Timur, the emperors were closely and personally involved in a deliberate effort to control imperial image-making. At Akbar's court, 'the art flourishes, and many painters have obtained great reputation. The works of all painters are weekly laid before His Majesty by the *Daroghas* and the clerks; then he confers rewards according to the excellence of workmanship, or increases the monthly salaries.'[130] Considered the most deeply involved patron of all the Mughal kings, Jahangir claimed, 'I derive such enjoyment from painting and have such expertise in judging it that, even without the artist's name being mentioned, no work of past or present masters can be shown to me that I do not instantly recognize who did it.'[131]

Yet none retained tighter control over the production of imperial imagery than Shah Jahan, who visited his imperial artisans daily, offering criticism and advice.[132] The emperor's rigid court ceremonial was matched by 'his increasing formalization of the court arts, which were represented as a necessary instrument to rule.'[133] His portraits, far less evocative of the physical man than those of his predecessors, show him always in profile, almost ageless and unlined, pious and haloed, truly deserving of his regnal name, Shah Jahan, King of the World. That a critical political role had been given to the arts by the Mughal kings was clearly understood by Shah Jahan's courtiers and artisans, whose responsibility it was to articulate and promulgate the imperial image. '[Such matters] may belong [to the category] of beautiful and external things the existence of which is not so necessary [in the context] of overall rule, but they must be [present] to give full distinction and spectacular display – the more so since it becomes a matter of increase of pomp and power, magnificence and elegance ... It is evident that the increase of such things creates esteem for the ruler in the eyes [of the people] and augments their respect [for the ruler] and [their own] dignity in [their] hearts. In this form the execution of divine injunctions and prohibitions and the enforcement of divine decrees and laws, which is the ultimate aim of rulership and kingship, are carried out in a better way.'[134]

Artifacts and Memorabilia

Mughal attention to the Timurid lineage was well known, and rival rulers were quick to make use of it in diplomatic exchange. Naqshbandi ambassadors from the Uzbek courts in Herat and Samarqand carried lines of poetry penned by Babur himself, offering them as a successful entrée to Jahangir's innermost court, along with assurances of continued Naqshbandi support for 'the members of this dynasty.'[135] Jahangir extemporaneously composed a matching quatrain, 'My love for you is greater than ever, and the memory of you, O Dervish, is good fortune/ As happy as my heart is with good news of you, we are happier that your kindness is more than ever,' and sent it back to Khwaja Hashim Dahbidi in Samarqand with a thousand *mohurs*.[136]

The Emperor Jahangir was perhaps most highly susceptible among Mughal kings to dynastic memorabilia. In his third regnal year,

Jahangir was given a drinking vessel by Munis, son of Mihtar Khan, whom Jahangir describes as 'one of the old servants of this dynasty (*az ghulaman-i qadimi in dawlat*),' in that he had in the past served Humayun and Akbar. The cup had been crafted of white jade in Samarqand, ca. 1447–49, with the name of the artist's patron, Timur's grandson, Ulugh Beg Guregen, carved along the exterior rim. Jahangir had his own name and that of his father, Akbar, inscribed along the lip of the cup and described the event in his memoir.[137] When he was presented with a miscellany of Humayun's spiritual and scientific writings, he claimed to feel 'greater elation than I ever remember experiencing before ... By God, in my view no rare curiosity or precious gem could be its equal.'[138]

Diplomats returning from the Safavid court of Shah Abbas brought with them a fabulous painting of Timur pictured in battle against the last Tughluq sultan of Delhi. Portrayed were two hundred and forty 'likenesses of his glorious sons and great amirs who participated in the battle.'[139] Jahangir describes tense negotiations in which his ambassador was able 'through his auspicious ascendant' to convince Shah Abbas, who 'knew how intent we were upon rarities such as this,' to allow the picture to leave Iran for the Mughal court.[140] On the other hand, Portuguese visitors to his imperial court also offered Jahangir a portrait of Timur, painted, he was told, by a Byzantine Christian present during Timur's conquest of Ottoman Anatolia. A doubtful Jahangir felt the portrait must be a fake, for it 'bore no resemblance to his royal descendants.' He wistfully added, 'If this claim had been true, no other rarity in my possession, in my opinion, could have been better than this.'[141] In contrast Shah Jahan was quick to seize upon a so-called memoir of Timur, the *Mulfuzat-i Timuri*, which was brought to his court after having surfaced mysteriously in Yemen. Although surely a healthy skepticism was called for, Shah Jahan declared it to be indeed the writings of his illustrious ancestor and gave it a place of prominence in the imperial library.

In a period of tense haggling over control of Qandahar, the Safavid Shah Abbas sent as a gift to Jahangir a magnificent ruby which had originated in the treasury of Timur's grandson, Ulugh Beg, and was inscribed with his name, that of his father, Shahrukh, and his grandfather, Timur. 'Because it had the names of my ancestors (*nam-i ajdad-i man*) on it,' wrote Jahangir, 'I took it as an auspicious blessing.'[142] He proceeded to have his own name, Jahangir Shah ibn Akbar Shah, added to the ruby's imperial *silsilah* and presented it to his son Khurram while determinedly clinging to Qandahar, if only for a few more years.[143] When Khurram ascended to the throne as the Emperor Shah Jahan, he instructed the court ateliers to set the Ulugh Beg ruby in a fabulous, jewel-encrusted chair, which later became known as the Peacock Throne.[144] 'Among the precious stones [on the new bejeweled throne] was a ruby worth a lakh of rupees, that Shah Abbas Safavi had sent to the late emperor, on which were inscribed the names of the great Timur Sahib Qiran.'[145]

In the collapse of Mughal power in the wake of mid-eighteenth century opposition movements and invasions, there was near universal agreement among those in power 'regarding the divine right of the Timurids to rule,' and as late as the reign of the last Mughal king, Bahadur Shah II Zafar (d. 1862), hope was expressed in India's governing circles that an imperial revival could be constructed under the charismatic leadership of a Timurid descendant in order to unite the crumbling empire.[146] When, in 1857, sepoys serving in the province of Meerut rose in rebellion against British rule, they turned to the aged inhabitant of the crumbling Red Fort in Delhi to 'seek out the higher authority of the Mughal emperor.'[147] In requesting the sanction of the last Mughal king, the sepoys, who were themselves too young to have had personal experience with Mughal rule, which by that time had long been limited to Delhi and its immediate environs, managed to turn what had begun as a spontaneous local insurgency, into 'a political revolt whose legitimacy arguably transcended that of the regime it challenged.'[148] In the aftermath of the failed uprising, just prior to his capture and exile to Burma, the last emperor affirmed the centrality of the Timurid lineage to both his personal and imperial identity. 'Now it seems that I and my line are destined to be ruined,' he said. 'The name of the Timurid Emperors is still alive, but soon that name will be destroyed and forgotten.'[149] 'Now there is not a shadow of a doubt that of the great House of Timur I am the last to be seated in the throne of India. The lamp of Mughal domination is fast burning out.'[150]

Nineteenth-century European visitors to Bahadur Shah's salon were titillated by the stark contrast offered by the obvious decay of the mid-nineteenth century Mughal court, ruled by a 'poor old man who can only put up with ceremony by means of opium' and the power of his lineage and legacy: 'this old man ... on the throne of Delhi ... was a descendant of Tamerlane,' a French journalist wrote.[151] Others suggested guilt by lineage: the judge advocate general presiding over Bahadur Shah's 'mutiny' trial made a point of assigning responsibility to 'the last king of the imperial house of Taimur [who] was an accomplice in this villainy.'[152] After the death of the last Mughal emperor in Burmese exile, the British rulers of India were aware that Timurid charisma lingered on, rejecting requests by his few remaining descendants to construct an imperial tomb for the last Timurid king, in part, it was admitted, to avoid the shrine's emergence as a centerpiece of nostalgia and political unrest.[153]

CHAPTER THREE

THE PERIPATETIC COURT AND THE TIMURID-MUGHAL LANDSCAPE

The Nomadic Court

Like the Timurids before them, and most other early-modern ruling houses, the Mughals displayed their imperial power through the construction of massive urban architectural projects: most famously, the cities of Fatehpur Sikri and Shahjahanabad. Yet while the Mughals were not immune to the impulse to build, no Mughal city, no matter how splendid, innovative, accessible or enlightened, remained the imperial center for long. Through generations of Mughal rule in India, the political relevance of Mughal imperial cities continued to be very limited; it was physical mobility which remained at the center of Mughal imperial court life and, for much of the Mughal period, the imperial court was encapsulated in the physical presence of the king. For all their careful construction of massive architectural landmarks and capital cities, built in the interests of aggrandizement of the Mughal imperium, the Mughal emperors of India were and remained determinedly mobile kings, inspiring contemporary historians to describe their imperial court culture as 'peripatetic.'[1]

There was, of course, dynastic precedent for Mughal mobility. The royal courts of Timur and his immediate successors were often determinedly transient; it has been suggested that this mobility should be attributed to their ancestry and even be considered a 'transitional phase' between the true nomadism of their Central Asian ancestors and sedentary life.[2] Yet if this were true it was a transitional phase of enormous duration, for mobility remained a key feature of royal court culture through the reigns of Timur, Babur, and all of the 'Great' Mughals, lasting into the eighteenth century – until the collapse of Mughal imperial fortunes quite literally immobilized the dynasty.

It is important to differentiate between the very different forms of nomadic mobility. The distant ancestors of the Timurid-Mughals had engaged in transhumance but from the time of their earliest imperial successes in Central Asia their movements came to be directed less by pastoral herding and more often by a life of warring and raiding. Timurid mobility, in other words, was almost entirely necessitated by near-constant military campaigning. In their turn, the first two emperors of Mughal India, Babur and Humayun, lived the lives of mobile warring chieftains, completely lacking the stable courts of other emperors. In search of booty or in flight from invading Uzbeks, Afghans or rapacious Mongol and Timurid relatives, throughout their lifetimes both lost and gained kingdoms with remarkable frequency and were at regular intervals completely homeless. At one point Babur had but a single tent to his name, in which he housed his intrepid mother, who, as he wrote, remained with him 'through much of my vagabondage and the interregnum (*qazaqliqlarda u fatratlarda*).'[3] This, then, was the nomadic mobility of neither choice nor pleasure but that which was demanded by a life of constant warfare and regular exile.

Having inherited Babur's reluctantly founded kingdom in India, his successors remained relentlessly expansionist and therefore understandably mobile, but now the traveling imperial camp (*ordu-i humayun* or *urdu-i mu'alla*) served as the capital of a prosperous empire. The Mughal court progress, remarkable for its size and grandeur, was openly recognized by contemporaries as having Central Asian antecedents: 'This is indeed slow and solemn marching,' wrote a witness, 'what we here call *a la Mongole*.'[4] Moving ponderously through imperial territories, matching duplicate imperial camps leapfrogged across each other's path, housing the emperor and his enormous retinue on alternate nights. 'There is something very striking and magnificent in these royal quarters, and that is that this vast assemblage of red tents [the traditional color of the imperial tents of Timur, this was a jealously guarded marker of royal status amongst the Mughals], placed in the center of a numerous army, produces a brilliant effect.'[5] Erected at every three hundred paces were long poles, each bearing a red standard and a Mongol *tugh*, the traditional yak or horse tail marker of the Central Asian Turco-Mongol nobility, delightfully described by a European visitor to the Mughal imperial encampment as having the 'appearance of so many periwigs,' and, not incidentally, serving as a useful directional marker when an unaccustomed visitor became, invariably, lost in the vast assemblage of the Mughal camp.[6]

The emperor was protected by a personal body guard of eight thousand horsemen on either side, followed by perhaps 100,000 horsemen, more than 250,000 animals (including horses, mules, elephants, camels and oxen) and up to 500,000 persons, in a procession stretching for a mile and a half.[7] Since such a huge concentration of humans and animals could not long sustain itself, either by carrying its own provisions or by living off the country, the emperor carried a large part of the imperial treasure and arranged for bankers traveling with the army to transfer revenues from outlying territories to the royal camp, allowing his troops to buy the food they needed from the merchants and camp followers who set up bazaars – a single vast 'principal bazaar' ran through the whole extent of the army, crossed by a series of smaller royal bazaars.[8] As many as two hundred and fifty bazaars were assembled within the great traveling camp at every halt.[9]

Manning these traveling bazaars were the tradesmen of the capital cities who, bereft of the patronage of the royal family and nobles, were thereby forced to accompany the royal progress. With the departure of the imperial court, the city's merchants, laborers, prostitutes and pickpockets all were compelled to follow, and 'take with them, like … gypsies, the whole of their families, goods and chattels … The whole population of Delhi, the capital city, is in fact collected in the camp,' wrote a European visitor to Aurangzeb's court, 'because deriving its employment and maintenance from the court and army, it has no alternative but to follow them in their march or perish from want during their absence.'[10] 'All I can confidently assert,' he added, 'is that the multitude is prodigious and almost incredible.'[11]

As the empire grew in size and complexity, the Mughal kings continued to retain their peripatetic royal court as a classic Turco-Mongol strategy for political control and centralization, a reminder and a threat of imperial power and dynastic control. Wavering loyalties in far-flung provinces could be bolstered, and thoughts of rebellion quenched, by the public spectacle of the mobile Mughal court, a vast and vivid illustration of Mughal power. As pure political theatre, the grandeur on display and the sheer volume of the imperial retinue – the tens of thousands of military men marching in rank after rank, countless camp followers, horses and livestock, bullock carts loaded with artillery and supplies, dozens of elephants hung with tapestry, 'lions and rhinoceroses, brought merely for parade,' Bengal buffaloes and tame antelopes, birds of prey and hunting cheetahs, wheeled along in carts and wearing golden collars – had a staggering affect on bystanders.[12] A merchant described the massive migration of the Shah Jahan's royal court progress. 'All the face of the earth, so far as we could see, was covered with people ... All this moving in one, on so many huge elephants, seemed like a fleet of ships with flags and streamers ... so that all together it made a most majestical warlike and delightsome sight.'[13]

Not incidentally, the absence of a single capital city in which Mughal imperial identity would be centered and deeply invested, in the sense that Istanbul had long served as the undisputed center of Ottoman power, reduced Mughal military vulnerability.[14] Even in their loyal adherence to Turco-Mongol laws of succession which asserted a shared legitimacy among male members of the family and resulted in near generational wars among contestants for the throne, the control of any particular city by a rebellious prince never offered a serious threat to the sovereignty of the emperor.[15] In these frequent wars of succession and princely mutinies, the emperors' constant movement often allowed for battle to be joined at a place of the emperor's choosing rather than dangerously near the vulnerable imperial household and central treasury. Even the fabulous Fatehpur Sikri remained the Mughal's imperial capital for only fourteen years, before the restless king of India shifted his court to Lahore and eventually back to Agra.[16] The peripatetic court so successfully served these expansionist emperors that there was no incentive to forgo the life of elegant tents and well-provided caravans.

Life in a Garden

The mobility of the Mughal royal court was reinforced by the dynasty's inherited cultural affinity for a life lived out of doors in a natural setting – or at least in a carefully modified and artfully constructed natural setting. Gardens have been the topic of many studies of Timurid-Mughal patronage and aesthetic vision. The classical Timurid garden of the Mughal ancestors in Central Asia has been described as 'the pinnacle of the art of garden design in medieval Iran and Central Asia,' yet arguably its real significance lay in the degree to which it resonated with political and cultural power.[17]

The origins of the Timurid-Mughal garden can be located amongst the Medes and Achaemenids, who built enclosed gardens they called *paira daeza* (meaning 'walled space' and later translated into Greek as *paradeisos*, from which we garner the word *paradise*). The gardens were integral to ancient Persian material and political culture. The classical Persian garden form was the *chahar bagh*, composed of a rectangular grid split by symmetrical waterways to form four garden areas, usually centered on a pavilion. There have been suggestions that this particular garden was based on descriptions of paradise in the Quran, but the *chahar bagh* long pre-dates the arrival of Islam. Given the landscape and climate of Iran, surely it does not take the advent of monotheism to perceive shady, cool garden spaces with geometric irrigation canals and pools of water as a vision of paradise. From their inception, these startling gardens – walled enclaves emerging suddenly in the arid high Iranian plateau, sanctuary from the scorching heat and dust – were closely tied to ideas of imperial identity and territorial ambition. While the gardens of ancient Iran must have had been linked to spiritual practice and custom as sacred spaces, the imperial garden can be seen less as a religious act than a brute assertion of power over land, finances, labor and nature itself: an affirmation of imperial legitimacy, cultural prowess, strength and sensitivity.

As an important representation of the worldview of the kings of pre-Islamic Iran, whose conventions of kingship and aesthetics had enormous influence on the Islamic world and a profound impact on Central Asian Turco-Persian culture, the *chahar bagh* came to be considered by many in Transoxiana to be the most estimable landscape form. Timur, remarkably sensitive to local markers of Islamic and Chingisid legitimacy, adopted a strategy of revival and continuation of royal rituals. In careful imitation of the attributes of power established by his most famous and politically charismatic predecessors, he masterfully employed the artfully manipulated landscape of ancient Iranian kings, recently revived by the Mongol Ilkhans.[18] As markers of central and west Asian power, thirty magnificent gardens were eventually constructed in the suburbs of Timur's capital city of Samarqand, built on the Persian/Ilkhanid imperial model. One of Timur's biographers describes the construction, on the orders of the great amir, of what may have been a classic *chahar bagh* en route from Timur's winter quarters to the capital city: 'Along the way is a mountain, approximately seven *parasangs* from Samarqand, and at the pass flows a river. When the mighty emperor reached that mountain, since his realm-adorning mind never missed an opportunity to build something in any place that was worthy of a structure, he ordered a garden laid out there in such a way that the sweet waters of the river would flow through the garden.'

> Highland and lowland, steppe and plain, were
> Turned into pleasure parks like the gardens of
> Paradise.
> Forage herbs became tulips, stones became
> Rubies and pearls, grass became elixir, and the
> Ground became gold.[19]

Notably, while formal gardens of this design had originally served in pre-Islamic Iran as private retreats for earlier Persian rulers, it suited Timur to convert them to centers of public display and court ritual. The Timurid garden was developed into a public venue for imperial performance, becoming the site of festivities and royal receptions, the center of public display and court ritual. Furthermore, having developed Samarqand into a glorious imperial capital worthy of his success, Timur rejected residential life in his own palaces, choosing instead to sojourn within his paradise gardens.

Returning to his capital between campaigns, Timur housed himself and his retinue in luxurious tent compounds in the series of thirty gardens he designed to surround the magnificent palaces he had had built – palaces which functioned more often as prisons and treasure houses than the domiciles they were designed to be.[20] The ambassador to Timur's court from King Henry III of Castille, Ruy Gonzales de Clavijo, reported that the imperial family resided in pavilions of silk and embroidered tapestry, and 'all of these enclosures aforesaid were occupied either by the wives of Timur, or by the wives of his grandsons, and these princes and princesses have their abode therein, as does also his Highness likewise, both summer and winter.'[21] Timur granted audiences in a series of classic Persian gardens, complete with artificial waterways, orchards of fruit and shade trees, raised paths, and herds of imported deer.[22] Awed observers describe seeing Samarqand's imperial gardens filled with luxurious tents of brocade and silk, dazzlingly decorated with gemstones, gold and feathers, and 'roofs of silver and stairs to ascend and ... couches on which they might recline ... They also showed rare treasures and hung there curtains of rare marvelous beauty.'[23]

This opulent presentation included overt symbols of political power: the booty from Timur's imperial conquests. Ibn Arabshah described in detail a treasured tapestry seized by the Timurids from the vanquished Ottoman sultan, Bayezid Yildirim.

> Among them [the treasures] hung a curtain of cloth taken from the treasury of Sultan Abu Yazid [Bayezid] of which each part was about ten cubits of the new measure in breadth, decorated with various pictures of herbs, buildings, and leaves, also of reptiles and with figures of birds, wild beasts and forms of old men, young men, women and children and painted inscriptions and rarities of distant countries and joyous instruments of music and rare animals exactly portrayed with different hues, of perfect beauty with limbs firmly jointed: with their mobile faces they seemed to hold secret converse with you and the fruit seemed to approach as though

bending to be plucked. This curtain was one of the wonders of the world, yet its fame is naught to the sight of it.[24]

The Timurid defeat of the Ottomans carried enormous weight in the Islamic world – as well as the West, where the European powers who had themselves been threatened by Bayezid the Thunderbolt's expansionist military successes were suitably impressed and grateful for the reprieve Timur's campaigns had offered them. The magnificent tapestry, looted from the treasury of Timur's only real political-military rival, now destroyed, was not only a treasure worthy of a great prince but, displayed in the heart of the Timurid political landscape, it became a blatant evocation of the destructive force of Timur's armies and a tangible reminder of Timurid military invincibility. In this way, the elaborate gardens of Samarqand, their fragile and transitory nature notwithstanding, as much as any monumental structure of stone or marble played a carefully constructed role in the theatre of Timurid pageantry and courtly ceremony.[25]

Late Timurid Gardens

In the later Timurid period, by the end of the fifteenth century, their far-ranging warrior heritage in seeming retreat, the descendants of Timur became resigned to living in luxurious palaces yet still they retained a passion for the outdoors, deliberately placing the princely prerogatives of hunting, poetry, parties and courtly life in the setting of the classic Perso-Timurid garden. While the *chahar bagh* was admired in fifteenth-century Central Asia for its sophisticated geometric form and physical beauty, the enormous prestige, even reverence, it acquired in the late Timurid period was due in some measure to the function of the garden as a popular site of artistic and social expression. It was the life within the garden, as much as the garden itself, which resonated in the Timurid psyche.

Inspired by the relative freedom of the gardens' open spaces, the beauty of their lush yet tightly controlled flora, the prestige of ownership, and not least the implications for membership in elite literary circles, leading personalities of Herat developed a taste for large and sophisticated classical gardens, which came to be recognized as important urban architectural landmarks. 'Timurid personal and dynastic interests ... were pursued outside the city behind garden walls, and ... the garden became a sequestered, psychologically suggestive space,'[26] notorious for aristocratic gatherings in which the writing and recitation of poetry was coupled with heavy consumption of alcohol and the use of mild intoxicants. By the time of the Uzbek rout of the Timurids, in the early years of the sixteenth century, the princely capitals of Kabul and Herat had come to rival Samarqand in the numbers and grandeur of their suburban gardens, in which the use of luxurious tents and canopies often superseded permanent construction of palaces, pavilions and kiosks.

During his three brief occupations of Samarqand and during his visit to Herat in 1506, Babur toured the cities' famed gardens (later composing a list of the Timurid landmarks he had visited, preserving an image of the Timurid golden age for his descendants' delectation), confirming his deep personal admiration for the gardens and the late Timurid social and political milieu the landscapes had come to symbolize: the premier Timurid literary-elite culture. Within a few short years, as *padshah* of the refugee Timurid community of Kabul, Babur enthusiastically threw himself into constructing his own imperial gardens, glorying in this most aristocratic of pastimes, which resonated deeply in the increasingly nostalgic Timurid psyche as a material representation of Timurid cultural supremacy and power. It was this romantic/political vision of late Timurid courtly life, exemplified by the classical garden and the life played out within it, which Babur and his descendants would attempt to reproduce in their conquered territories over two hundred and fifty years of Mughal rule in India.

For the Timurid prince, India's failings – its heat and dust, its lack of melons and madrasas – seem to have centered on and became encapsulated in the region's utter lack of a classical garden or appropriate space upon which to build one.[27] 'Everywhere I looked,' he wrote, 'was so unpleasant and unwelcoming (*karahat u nakhoshluk*) ... Because the place was so ugly and unpleasant I abandoned my dream of building a *chahar bagh*.'[28] Already homesick, he directed the women and children who had remained behind in Kabul to travel in state to 'an appropriate site,' the city's suburban Garden of the Audience Hall (*bagh-i divanhana*) to offer prostrations and give thanks, celebrating his victories in India in the manner he himself would have preferred.[29]

Babur's interest in creating a neo-Timurid royal court in his Indian territories required that it contain a succession of imperial gardens, within which social gatherings could ease the pain of exile and affirm the cultural and political power of the Timurid dynasts. So while India's perceived limitations, its lack of running water or geometric spaces, were initially disappointing, they could not suppress Babur's desire for a Timurid life lived out of doors. Life without gardens was unthinkable, and while Babur could not improve India's climate or native flora, with Timurid pragmatism and willingness to compromise, a proper garden could be constructed. 'There was nothing to do,' he wrote, 'but work with the space we had.' Based on the water supplied by a pre-existing well, Babur's first Agra garden included a bathhouse, a great courtyard and an octagonal pool, a private garden and outbuildings. 'Thus in unpleasant and unsophisticated Hindustan (*bisafa u bisiyaq Hind*), linear and geometric gardens were produced.'[30]

Trying to adapt Timurid gardens to the Indian landscape proved to be difficult, requiring engineering skill and the generous use of the seemingly limitless manpower Babur had already noted. Tons of rock and stone were moved in order to construct the terraces and high retaining walls, sometimes three meters thick, with landing platforms along the waters edge strong enough to handle the river in monsoon season. Towers were built on the four corners, to enclose wells, an imposing entrance gate was built on the riverbanks, raised paths, pavilions and stone platforms were placed throughout the garden. Beneath the walls and terraces the Mughals often built rooms with high domed ceilings – sometimes as *hamams*, or baths, for as Babur wrote, 'These three things oppressed us in Hindustan: one was the heat, another the fierce wind and yet another, the dust. Against all three things alike, the bath is a protection, for in it, one knows nought of dust and wind. In the hot weather, the *hamam* is so cool, one feels almost cold.'[31]

An Afghan historian of the Sur dynasty described Babur's first garden, writing, 'And in the second year of his reign [in India] *Hazrat Giti Sitani* [Babur] laid out a garden without equal [the *bagh-i binazir*] on the banks of the Yamuna. And it was the first example of a plan with walkways in Hindustan ... And on the pattern of this garden Mirza Kamran [Babur's second son] made another garden at Lahore.'[32] As his son's example indicates, Babur was not the only Timurid who re-created in India the classic *baghs* of Transoxiana. Babur encouraged his followers to build garden after garden, relishing his right and ability to impose these powerful cultural-political icons across conquered northern India. An observer wrote: 'urged on ... consequent upon conquest, the king issued his commands and conveyed that, in the shortest time in all the great cities, gardens and orchards be laid out.'[33] 'All who had acquired lands on the [Yamuna] river,' Babur noted, listing his Turkish companions by name, 'also built geometric and beautifully planned gardens and pools.' Babur assured his readers of the originality of the Timurid garden in India, adding, 'Since the people of India had never seen such fashioned and symmetrical places, they nicknamed the side of the Yamuna on which these constructions stood, *Kabul*.'[34]

Babur's claims that India lacked gardens prior to the arrival of the Timurid ignored the existence of the lovely imperial Lodi gardens in Delhi and Agra, among others. It would seem that Babur, 'blinkered by his famous nostalgia and by his adherence to Timurid garden ideals,' ignored and discredited those gardens built by his predecessors because, first of all, they were not his own, but also and most tellingly, because they did not follow the classical Timurid model which spoke to him and his followers so profoundly of power and prestige.[35] And although certainly not all of the Timurid-Mughal gardens of India were constructed in the classical form, the chahar bagh remained a favored cultural icon, having come to symbolize all that the Timurid refugees had lost and were attempting to replicate on what was unfamiliar foreign soil. Imposing his will on the recalcitrant Indian landscape, Babur was to order a garden built in every place he conquered, a tradition maintained by many of his descendants, who continued to glorify landscape over urban spaces. As Stephen Dale has written, the Mughal's conquest of India, in contrast to their Ottoman contemporaries to the west, 'came to be expressed hardly at all in religious monuments but pervasively as the imperialism of landscape architecture, the civilized ideal of the Timurid period.'[36]

Almost one hundred years after Babur and his soldiers began to landscape the banks of the Yamuna River, the emperor Jahangir affirmed the continued importance of the Timurid garden to the Mughal dynasty. On a nostalgic journey, a veritable pilgrimage, to Babur's former capital, just as Babur had wandered through the Timurid gardens of Herat and Samarqand, Jahangir reverently toured Kabul's gardens: the *Shahr Ara* (Adornment of the City); the *Mahtab* (Moonlight); the *Orta* (Central); another garden nearby which had been built by Jahangir's grandmother, the *Suratkhana*; and the largest garden in Kabul, simply known as the *Chaharbagh*, writing afterwards, 'I don't recollect that I ever walked so much.'[37] Jahangir spent much of his time in Kabul at the *Shahr Ara Bagh*, which he claimed was so delicate 'that to put a shod foot on its surface would be tasteless and unnatural.'[38] Under its cherry trees he conversed with his companions and the ladies of his court and organized noodle-cooking sessions, archery contests and dances for Kabul's students. Spying 'an excellent piece of ground' nearby, he purchased it from the owners and ordered the construction of yet another garden, with a 'beauty and elegance that would have no equal in all the world. I named it *Jahanara*, Adornment of the World.'[39]

By the mid-seventeenth century, the beloved Mughal province of Kashmir is said to have contained a total of seven hundred and seventy-seven Mughal gardens, including the prototype for Lahore's famed garden, *Shalimar*.[40] Lahore, considered the second city of the empire and a favorite location for the mobile Mughal court, due in large part to its mild climate and relatively close proximity to critically important Mughal political/social nodes, such as Kashmir and Kabul, came to contain fifty Mughal gardens, many in the classic Timurid style, one of which, the circular *Gul Bagh* (Rose Garden), was perhaps the largest garden in the world, completely surrounding the city with a five-mile belt of planned landscaping. So many gardeners and craftspeople were required for the development and upkeep of Lahore's Mughal gardens that entire 'satellite settlements' were constructed near the gardens to house the population of laborers, such as the communities of Baghanpura, Begimpura and Shahdara.[41] In recognition of the construction of the Shalimar Bagh, called by Shah Jahan *Farah Baksh*

(Garden of Delight) and *Faiz Baksh* (Garden of Bounty)[42] and built by him at a cost of six lakhs of rupees,[43] a chronogram was composed:

> When Shah Jahan, the King Defender of the Faith, laid out the Shalimar in becoming style, I asked the date of the foundation from the doorkeeper of Paradise. He answered saying, 'This is the example of the highest Paradise.'[44]

In contrast to the highly symbolic Timurid garden, Mughal architecture was often manipulated to deliberately evoke the imperial legacy of the Timurid past, while convincingly asserting an authentic convergence with the vernacular traditions of the Mughals' conquest territories. Mughal imperial architecture was adaptable and multivalent in its language – at once evoking Timurid and Persian precedents yet evolving interpretations and syntheses of indigenous and imported design characteristics.

It has been argued that the physical structure of Humayun's tomb, built in 1574, the first of the Mughal garden-tombs and considered the most influential Mughal architectural effort in India, was intended as an illustration and affirmation of the Mughal genealogical legacy.[45] The same can be applied to many Mughal construction projects. Described as 'an architectural manifesto,'[46] Humayun's tomb was carefully and self-consciously constructed as an imperial conceit linking Akbar, the reigning monarch, with the architecture of his Timurid forefathers, while the indigenous construction materials (particularly the ubiquitous red sandstone) and the motif of the roofline *chatris* made a public statement that linked the emperor to his Indian empire. In this way 'past and present are united in a single building that is at once Timurid and Mughal, and thus Humayun is positioned as both descendant of Timur and progenitor of Akbar.'[47]

Akbar's imperial capital city was built thirty-five kilometers from Agra at Sikri, the home of the renowned mystic Shaykh Salim, whom Akbar publicly venerated.[48] Positioning his new imperial center, renamed *Fatehpur Sikri* (Sikri, the Place of Victory), in close proximity to the shrine of the exceptionally popular shaykh, whose following was very nearly as much Hindu as Muslim, Akbar very openly co-opted an acclaimed public source of religious charisma and legitimacy. The very architecture of Akbar's city, a wildly original amalgam of Perso-Timurid and indigenous/local design features, demonstrated a deliberate convergence of Mughal political authority by affirming both the historical legacy of the dynasty and imperial loyalty to the disparate social and political realities of rule on the subcontinent. The political use of architecture was a strategy that had been employed by generations of Timurids; their Mughal descendants showed no hesitation in appropriating and manipulating local and traditional architectural motifs and materials in the pursuit of an imperial image which could affirm their unassailable political lineage in a style acceptable to the diverse population of their new empire. In contrast, the classical Mughal garden tradition, which was confronted by no recognizably comparable, competing, entrenched landscaping tradition on the subcontinent, and which was, perhaps most significantly, seen by Babur and his founding community as the most evocative symbol of the late-Timurid court culture, remained relatively undisturbed as an affirmation of Mughal imperialist ambitions and a remnant of an unreconstructed Timurid aesthetic in India.

The Hunt

In addition to offering the Mughals a natural landscape within which to demonstrate loyalty to their Timurid legacy, the regular movements of the royal court offered the nobility the opportunity to satisfy their passion for the hunt, which some did almost daily. Totaling up the game killed from the age of twelve through his eleventh regnal year, at the age of fifty, Jahangir listed 28, 532 animals 'killed in my presence,' including mountain goat, sheep and deer, wolves, wild fox and boar, pigeons, hawks, pelicans, a total of eighty-six lions, 3, 473 crows and ten crocodiles.[49]

This passion for hunting found near universal justification at the Timurid-Mughal court as a royal duty, an act of arbitration between the ruler and the forces of nature that only the king was competent to control.[50] In the origin myths of the pre-modern world it is the model rulers and cultural heroes who hold the wild in check, allowing the land to be cultivated and agriculture to flourish; the royal hunt was seen as the first line of defense against the encroachment of a threatening nature.[51] In the ancient Indian tradition, the 'rulers had to interact with the wilderness, placate, contain and appropriate its raw power,' whereby the king gained religious merit, and the hunting ground became a ceremonial seat of royalty.[52] In Mughal India the hunt remained, just as for earlier Central Asian Turks and Mongols, a vehicle for the display of imperial dominance over nature, proof of the king's ability to tame the wild, to identify and successfully mobilize resources, to publicize his superior administrative skills, and an open-air theatre in which bravery could be publicly tested and appreciated.

Anxious to portray his constant hunting trips as a 'disinterested service to his subjects,' Jahangir extolled his own role as imperial exterminator, describing explicit invitations from his subjects to have the emperor rid them of a tiger or lion which threatened their village. Jahangir's beloved wife Nur Jahan, an active political player at the Mughal court who has often been described as a wily pre-emptor of imperial power, must have horrified her critics when she too took on the role of imperial hunter and protector of the people. Yet when near the end of his reign Jahangir was briefly taken hostage by a disgruntled noble, Mahabat Khan, it was, of all his following, his wife Nur Jahan who attempted a rescue. Her reputation as a highly skilled hunter preceded her and caused a 'disruption and agitation [among her enemies] on account of the fiery shots of the queen's gun, which could overthrow even lions.'[53]

Apart from the justification of public service, hunting served personal and political purposes. Shah Jahan fled plague-ridden Akbarabad and spent his time waiting for the disease to leave the region while hunting across the countryside.[54] Jahangir used the hunt as an excuse to leave the palace during the bustling preparations for Nauroz and in order to avoid onerous court duties, 'because his Councell desired to be at rest.'[55] On a particular occasion, Aurangzeb went hunting in order to avoid the palace on a day when his own son was to be poisoned on his orders. He returned from the hunt that evening, to hear the report of his son's death and 'pretend to cry.'[56]

The Mongol *qamargha*, the ring-hunt, remained a favored hunting tradition of the Timurid-Mughals of India, not only for the number of game killed but because the large number of participants required for the hunt's success created an opportunity to prepare and practice for a military campaign.[57] Strategically organized hunting trips offered the Mughal kings their best excuse for well-armed and warlike excursions — what began under the guise of a hunting trip could suddenly be transformed into a military campaign. During Akbar's 1564 campaign against Malwa, the emperor and his retinue of thousands presented their errand as a seemingly peaceful hunting excursion but, as the enormous imperial cavalcade edged closer to the enemy fortress, it quickly shifted into a military operation, flaring up into a menacing affirmation of might and of central control. On the subsequent collapse of local resistance, Akbar's forces returned to their interrupted 'hunt.' Of course, the opposite could also occur — without loss of face a military campaign could subside into an innocent royal outing. In 1617, the not usually very predatory emperor Jahangir moved his enormous imperial camp towards the Deccan in an attempt to intimidate local rulers into submission. When his advisors warned him that the Deccanis did not seem liable to back down and had, in fact, 'attended the borders with fifty-thousand horse resolved to fight,' they advised the emperor to avoid the humiliation of public defeat and 'convert [his approach] into a hunting journey.'[58]

Even during the time of the ascetic emperor Aurangzeb, the imperial hunt was a flamboyant show of wealth, power and control, involving at times the entire imperial court progress and its accompanying military units. Witnesses make it clear that the peripatetic quality of the royal court seamlessly converged with the movements of the vast imperial hunt. 'I could never conceive of how the *Great Mogol* could hunt with an army of one hundred thousand men; but ... he may be said to hunt with two hundred thousand, or with any number of which his army may consist ... Whenever the Monarch is about to take the field, every gamekeeper near whose district the army is to pass is called upon to apprise the grand master of the Hunt of the various sorts of game under his particular charge, and of the places where they are in the greatest plenty. Sentries are then stationed at the different roads of that district to guard the tract of ground selected, which extends sometimes four or five leagues; and while the army is on the march, on one side or another so as to avoid that tract, the king enters it with as many *Omrahs* and other persons as have liberty to do so and enjoys, leisurely and uninterruptedly the sports of the field.'[59]

The massive, far-reaching *qamargha*, like the imperial court progress, and often as an extension of it, was dramatic public theatre. Large organized hunts involved a noticeable increase in ceremonial or political activity: elaborate feast were held; organizers of the hunt were recognized; individuals praised for their skill in the field – even the simple fact of their invitation to participate brought prestige and influence. The royal hunt, with its thousands or tens of thousands of participants, was invested with enormous political meaning, not least of which was the affirmation of the ruler's ability to marshal and order manpower, training men in the arts of war, and all the while positioning the ruler at the center of a display of physical prowess. The entire performance was then projected across countryside as a forceful demonstration of the king's ability and sovereignty.

The Hunting Park

In order to facilitate the hunt, and to even more profoundly affirm imperial control over the landscape, the Mughals regularly appropriated pre-existing idyllic landscapes for use as imperial hunting parks. They claimed them as crown lands, walling them off, planting orchards and arranging watercourses – just as Timur had done in Samarqand's suburban landscape[60] – and marking them with inscriptions, fountains and statuary, and claimed them as crown lands. The link to the paradise garden is explicit: in ancient Iran the hunting park is considered to have perhaps preceded the emergence of the classical paradise garden – Xenophon writes that Cyrus the Great (c. 6th c. BCE) was given by his grandfather 'all of the game in the *paradeisos*, so that he could learn to hunt.' His gardens were filled with 'all of the good and beautiful things the earth wishes to put forth,' in which he spent all of his time 'except when the season of the year prevents it.'[61]

Hunting parks served as a very specific and carefully delineated physical and natural space within which to enact the political theatre that demonstrated and proved the rulers' ability and right to impose power. Illustrating the convergence of imperial interest in hunting and the movements of the royal court, the vast territories of the imperial hunting parks could serve as camping grounds for the tent cities of the imperial progress. Built for the comfort of the royal party, the hunting parks contained palaces and pavilions where feasting and entertainments were integral components of the royal court, at rest and on the chase.

While the act of hunting had a ritual character that legitimized authority, hunting parks were the centers for intimate socializing and political networking, a controlled environment in which the hunt could be tightly organized and staged to ensure not only the safety of the royal participants but also, and perhaps most importantly, their very public success. The royal hunting park was more than a symbol of majesty – it was an exercise in sovereignty, demonstrating ownership and control over land and resources, animals and humans. At Jahangipur, one of Jahangir's 'established hunting grounds (*shikat gauhay muqarrar*),' a tower was erected over the grave of a favorite antelope, named *Hansraj*, 'the chief of the royal antelopes,' which had been tamed and was used by the king to attract wild antelope.[62] From the time of the death of *Hansraj*, all hunting of antelopes on that plain was banned, the imperial proclamation announcing that henceforth an antelope's 'flesh would be for a *kafir* like the flesh of cows and for the Muslims like the flesh of pigs,' in memory of the emperor's favored hunting companion.[63] The walled hunting parks maintained across the subcontinent by the Mughals, many having been founded centuries earlier by their Muslim and Hindu predecessors, were an opportunity to demonstrate the Mughal kings' control over the landscape they ruled, the animal life within it, and the vast human train that followed across the Indian countryside in their wake.

It is not my intention to suggest that the Mughal passion for the hunt was driven entirely by loyalty to their powerful Turco-Mongol inheritance. While the Central Asian ancestors of the Mughals are celebrated for having developed hunting, particularly the *qamargha*, into an art form, the act of pleasure hunting was a nearly universal prerogative of the pre-modern Eurasian nobility. Yet the passion for the hunt definitively marked every generation of this Timurid-Mughal dynasty. Anyone of the royal family could participate – princes were carefully trained in the hunt in order to prove their worth on the field and, it was believed, ultimately on the throne. Elite women of the Timurids and Mughals, like their female ancestors among the Turks and Mongols of Central Asia, participated fully, hunting from horseback, howdah, or from a drawn cart. It is unsurprising that when Humayun fled to an Iran still under the political control of Turcoman tribal groupings, the Safavid Shah's sister joined their hunting parties, armed and mounted. Herodotus and Xenophon had both noted that Iranian royal women historically were hunters, and among Central Asian Turks a woman had long proved herself worthy of her royal husband by riding, shooting and hunting. An Englishwoman living in India in the nineteenth century witnessed Mulka Begum, a niece of the Mughal emperor, hunting with trained cheetahs from within a covered carriage – finding a balance between love of the hunt and proper conduct.[64] In all the years of Mughal rule in India, the hunt remained just as for earlier Central Asian Turks and Mongols, a measure of men and social status, a vehicle for political reward, an infrastructure for travel and a pretext for inspection, diplomacy and military incursions. In addition, and this cannot have been lost on the politically acute Mughal dynasty, the imperial hunt was a means of creating a public image, projecting ideological concepts and demonstrating claims of legitimacy.

'Be a Friend of Wine'

Apart from the inherent value of the hunt as an opportunity for imperial theatre, the Mughal royal family and retinue valued the hunt for its atmosphere of intimacy and informality. Propriety was rarely a central concern on the hunt, and hunting parties were, in particular, notorious for their hard-drinking atmosphere. In Mughal India, as in many premodern courts across Europe and Asia, 'the chase and the party were synonymous .... the royal hunt became identified with good times, even wild times, and viewed as a large, outdoor floating party.'[65]

Mughal references to the use of intoxicants are rife. Babur's memoir lists detailed descriptions of parties, in which the Mughal founder describes drinking and drug taking to the point of physical collapse. Babur's lack of inhibition in describing his drunken escapades can perhaps be better understood in the context of his heavy-drinking ancestors. Timur's court had been known for the vast quantities of alcohol consumed, as described by the Castilian ambassador in Samarqand: 'It is the custom with the Tartars to drink their wine before eating, and they are want to partake of it so copiously and quaffing it at such frequent intervals that the men soon get very drunk. No feast we were told is considered a real festival unless the guests have drunk themselves sot ... And further he who refuses to drink must be made to drink, and this whether he will or no.'[66]

The generous use of intoxicants seems to have been a critical component of the Central Asian Timurid majlis.[67] A history of the Timurids describes the drinking of Timur's grandson Mirza Pir Muhammad ibn Jahangir, whose aspirations to power were destroyed because 'he spent most of his time quaffing fire-colored liquid and listening to the sound of the lute and harp. The enchanting voice of the harp told of the passing of his rule.'[68] Sultan Husayn Bayqara's contemporary, the Mongol Sultan Sa'id Khan, had for the sake of Islam given up the use of intoxicants, but when offered a goblet of *kumis*, the fermented mare's milk drink of the steppes, he felt it necessary to accept the generous hospitality of his hosts. In a moment Babur would have surely understood and approved, Sultan Sa'id Khan simply 'expanded his religion to allow for drinking,' proceeding to spend the next eight days in a drunken revel with his Mongol companions.[69]

Babur's father, Umar Shaykh, had been a 'great drinker.' Babur himself had carefully avoided alcohol until after his conquest of Kabul, where as padshah he indulged to real excess. Describing one drinking session, shared with his close companions, he commented with characteristic honesty, 'We drank on the boat until late that night and left the boat completely drunk [*masti tafih*] ... I didn't remember anything, but when I got to my tent I vomited a lot.'[70] The Baburnama translated and illustrated at the Mughal court of Akbar included a representation of even this drunken escapade, in an unembarrassed, even an affectionate, homage to the dynasty's founding father.

Babur' writings confirm the homo-social nature of late Timurid drinking parties. One hundred years after Clavijo had feasted and drunk alcohol with Timur's wives and daughters-in-law, Babur wrote in astonishment that a local woman had asked to be included in one of his regular gatherings. Out of curiosity, he agreed to invite her, but the experience was not a success; the woman, Hulhul Anika, became aggressive and Babur 'got rid of her by feigning drunkenness (*akhir uzumni mastliqqa salip khilas buldum*).'[71] He did not repeat the experiment.

Babur's successor and eldest son, Humayun, openly admitted to drug addiction. His sister remembered him chiding his female relatives for complaining of his unreliability: 'I am an opium eater (*man afyuni*) ... do not be angry with me.'[72] According to contemporary reports, though by no means an addict, Akbar too had been an opium user; learning of the murder of his close friend and biographer, Abu al-Fazl, Akbar 'neither shaved nor used opium' in his grief.[73] His brother, Muhammad Hakim, and all three of Akbar's sons struggled with addiction to alcohol; two sons died young of the affects of alcohol and the third, the future emperor Jahangir, was at one point imprisoned by his father in an effort to dry him out.

The effort was unsuccessful. A nineteenth-century British historian declared himself aghast at the vast amounts of alcohol and drugs consumed at Jahangir's royal court. Referring to Jahangir's memoirs, he exclaimed, 'There are as many drinking bouts noticed as in the Memoirs of Jahangir's great-grandfather Babur, and the extraordinary potations to which he [Jahangir] confesses would have shamed even that immoderate toper.'[74]

Unapologetic drug use, and only slightly embarrassed alcoholism, received regular references in Jahangir's writings. In the year 1621 the emperor regretfully recorded the death of 'an old and trusted servant,' whose sole charge at the Mughal court seems to have been the care and keeping of the imperial intoxicants. Immediately after this servant's death Jahangir appointed a new steward for opium and another for wine.[75] Jahangir openly acknowledged his struggles with alcohol, although he remained a permanent and committed drinker and drug user. His court poet composed the couplet for him, 'I have two lips, one devoted to wine and the other apologizing for drunkenness.'[76]

Babur offered posterity a political justification and defense for the ruler's participation in regular drinking and drug taking garden parties; chiding his eldest son for remaining aloof, complaining of his reluctance to drink alcohol, he directed Humayun to socialize regularly with his followers.[77] To accept a drink is an opportunity to 'participate in social networks,' and it was those networks that lay at the foundation of retinue development and maintenance among the Timurid princes.[78] For Babur, the garden party served as an effective device through which to establish personal ties with the imperial elite, affirm the loyalty of the ruler's retinue, and develop social cohesion and camaraderie.[79] At the royal court of the Safavids, whose elites shared with the Mughals a Central Asian legacy of hard, and public, drinking, 'wine was a metaphor for power' and 'royal drinking was a ritual of shared pleasure that forged bonds and cemented loyalty.'[80]

Jahangir used a similar justification in his own memoirs, describing regular wine parties (*majlis-i sharab-i tertib*) in which his courtiers were expected to drink with him, becoming 'intoxicated with the wine of loyalty' (*sharab-i marhamat*).[81] Jahangir's memoirs contain several references to 'regular Thursday night parties,' and describe court events in which 'wine bowls and intoxicants were given to whoever wished,'[82] and his servants 'made happy on goblets of joy.'[83] On the occasion of his nostalgic pilgrimage to Kabul, at which time he carved out a *takht-i padshah* (royal seat) in stone next to that of Babur, Jahangir celebrated by filling the pools with wine in order to hold 'drinking parties with his courtiers, a time honored gesture of the Muslim prince claiming here on earth the future joys of paradise.'[84] On the first Nauruz (the pre-Islamic Persian New Year) after his accession, Jahangir celebrated with 'musicians and singers of every type ... dancing gypsies and charmers of India, who could seize the hearts of angels with their blandishments.' He encouraged the revelers with a decree that 'everyone could drink whatever intoxicants or exhilarants (*makfiyat u mugirat*) he wanted without prohibition or impediment (*mana' u mani'*).'[85] As a Muslim king, anxious to support his legitimacy in public gestures of justice and ethical rule, negotiating the gray area of social and religious norms, Jahangir defended this wildly unconventional imperial proclamation by turning to the *Divan-i Hafez*. He quoted in his memoir the sufi poet best known for supporting the most audacious of misdemeanors:

> Cup bearer, brighten our goblet with the light of wine!
> Sing, minstrel, for the world is working as we desire.
>
> *Saqi, bi nur-i bada bar afruz jam-i ma*
> *Mutrib bigu ki kar jahan shud ba kam-i ma.*[86]

Foreigners soon learned that alcohol could ease their entry to the Mughal court. In 1616, the English ambassador Sir Thomas Roe offered gifts of wine to officials of state, governors, the crown prince Khurram (later Shah Jahan), even the emperor himself, in order to facilitate acquisition of trading rights. Alcohol was a marker of imperial control and power; the gift of wine could 'breach hierarchies, obtain favors and [smooth] the process of negotiation.'[87]

Yet although it was consumed openly and publicly, alcohol was an illicit pleasure. Babur, a loyal Muslim, drank not at all until established as padshah of Kabul, in the company of carousing Timurid relatives and liege men. Although a heavy drinker thereafter, Babur solemnly vowed (and acted out) temperance in front of his troops in an effort to access a new source of power, that which sprang from moral authority and spiritual purity. Even the self-admitted addict Jahangir openly discussed the moral dilemma of alcohol, seeking justification where he could in the poetry of Hafez and the legacy of Babur. As imperial imagery became more regnal and distant and dynastic dignity more imperative, references to alcohol consumption at the royal court decreased. Shah Jahan is not known to have been a social drinker; there is only a single sad reference, recorded in the *Jahangirnama* and the *Shahjahannama*, of the alcoholic king Jahangir forcing his abstemious son, the future emperor, to drink. Shah Jahan, as son of a publicly acknowledged addict, later used the opportunity of the Deccan campaign, when the prince was thirty years old, to mimic Babur's publicly pious rejection of alcohol, framing his action as an effort to draw on new spiritual and moral strength in his military campaign. Yet rumors swirled in the emperor's later years; a European observer commented that Shah Jahan had begun to drink heavily, 'turning goode fellow,' and requesting casks of grape wine from the merchant community.[88] Among the descendants of Timur there were few who escaped the scourge of alcohol and even in the dynasty's years of stability, power and wealth, their heritage and the enduring mobility of the royal court gave the emperors of India both opportunity and sanction to indulge in a perpetual garden party.

The Pursuit of Pleasure

Even in the context of his dynastic tradition of mobility and passion for the out-of-doors, the fourth Mughal emperor, Jahangir, maintained a remarkably transient royal court which traversed the empire for over half of his reign. Jahangir's court progress had a somewhat different character than those of his predecessors, for he rarely led imperial armies; often Jahangir and his large retinue followed behind armies led by his sons or, even more usually, wandered in a seemingly aimless pursuit of personal pleasure. Yet what could be described as the feckless mobility of the Jahangiri court, his obsession with the hunt, his open use of intoxicants and above all his insistence on a continual court progress, found a degree of at least grudging acceptance within the royal retinue and imperial nobility. In the twenty-two years of his rule, the only serious threats to Jahangir's sovereignty came from his restless and ambitious sons.

In those years, Jahangir spent more than half of his time away from the official capital at Agra. He led few major military campaigns and his reign was not marked by any serious accretion of territory. In contrast to his predecessors – conquest driven leaders of armies, warriors bent on domination and strategic displays of power – Jahangir often simply wandered, north in the hot season, south in the cold, comfortably combining his own minimalist interpretation of imperial duties with life in a garden setting and the pursuit of pleasure. On one occasion he remained away from his capital, then at Agra, for a total of five years and seven months while ponderously moving at an elephant's pace through the provinces of his empire. Jahangir's court wove through the Indian countryside, pausing regularly for pleasure trips to famous sights, visits to local mystics, the personal distribution of alms, dispensation of imperial justice, and the daily hunt.

A journey in his eleventh regnal year, from Ajmer to Mandu, following behind the Mughal armies, was traveled in forty-six stages over more than four months, during which, he wrote, 'the rest stops were all delightful places on the banks of ponds or irrigation canals and magnificent rivers lined with trees, greenery, and fields of blooming poppies, and not a day passed, whether we were marching or stopping, without hunting. We travelled the whole way by horseback or elephant, seeing the sights and hunting.' As if in affirmation of the dynastic passion for landscapes, the emperor added, 'The arduousness of a journey (*mishqat-i sefer*) was never apparent. It was as if we were moving from garden to garden.'[89]

Contrast this enraptured commentary to the complaints of a companion on the very same journey, Sir Thomas Roe, the first English ambassador to the Mughal court, who had attached himself to the imperial court in hopes of attaining trade concessions. In a letter to friends, Roe wrote bitterly, 'I am yet following this wandering King, over Mountagnes and through woodes, so strange and unused in ways that his own people, who almost know no other god, blaspheme his name.'[90] Roe further reviled the journey in his diary, writing: 'Wee passed thorough woodes and over montayns, torne with bushes, tyred wth the incomodotyes of an impassable way, where many Camells perished. Many departed for Agra, and all Complayned. I lost my Tentes and Cartes ... many of the kings woemen and thowsandes of Coaches, Carts and Camells lyeing in the woody Mountaynes without meate and water.'[91] He offered his reader an explanation for the emperor's bliss however, adding 'he himselfe [Jahangir] gotte bye on a small Eliphant, which beast will Clime up rockes and passe such Streightes and noe horse or beast that I know can follow him.'[92]

Although Roe was, to his relief, given permission to part ways with the king not long after, Jahangir continued his meandering journey for another few years before wending his way back to Agra. That the constant movement continued, and was seen as a trial by those forced to remain at the king's side, is confirmed by a Jesuit visitor to the royal court, in a letter composed in the year before Jahangir's death, while the court was temporarily residing in Kabul: 'My news is that I continue with this King, going about with him every year and running about through his kingdoms ... We have suffered extraordinary discomforts as the road is full of very high and very sterile mountains.'[93]

For all his justifications, more often than not Jahangir's personal itinerancy seems rarely to reflect more than his simple desire to live a life of constant movement spent in the princely pleasures of hunting, pilgrimage, garden parties and alcoholic or drug induced pleasure – yet the mobility of the Jahangiri court was not seriously criticized nor was the emperor's essential sovereignty questioned. Much of the Mughal nobility was, after all, descended of Persian or Turco-Mongol semi-nomadic warriors and empire builders, for whom the peripatetic court (even mobilized, as was Jahangir's, for the carefully justified pursuit of an endless round of hunts and drinking parties) was a well established and respected tradition. In addition, as the overlords of India, the performance of politically legitimizing actions that would resonate with the Rajput nobility and the majority Hindu population would have been of great value to the Mughal kings. In this the descendants of Timurid kings were extremely fortunate, for there existed in India ancient and respected precedent for their peripatetic court.

In Brahmanical cosmology the *mandala* design is considered the visual representation of a sanctified space, and was used as a model to articulate and define imperial territories.[94] The *Arthashastra*, a governing manual generally attributed to Kautilya, advisor of the Mauryan kings of the fourth century B.C.E., described a *raja mandala*, or circle of kingship, which articulated concentric circles of alternating political enemies and friends, spreading outward from the central kingdom.[95] In this sacred cosmology the center takes the place of the holy Mount Meru and the wheel of concentric circles is split into four quadrants, representing the four quarters of the world.[96] Although the earliest Vedic texts describe a king as 'fixed' within the broad confines of his realm, he is further advised to traverse that territory and add to it, to 'stride out unto the great quarters,' and 'let all directions call thee.'[97] This geometric-cosmology of empire required ambitious Hindu rulers to perform a near-constant perambulation of their domain, leading imperial courts on regular 'ritual journeys in which they displayed their royal power and commemorated the military campaign(s) which had established their rule.'[98]

The most famous of ritual royal court progresses across the king's territories, known as the *digvijaya* or 'conquest of the quarters,' has been described as 'the most important Indian concept with regard to sovereignty,' and 'the key event of greatest import in ancient India.'[99] Circumambulating his imperial territories, touching on and affirming the kingdom's borders, a king illustrated his own ability to centralize power in his own person through *vishva-jit* (subjugation).[100] Through the highly ritualized performance of the *digvijaya* an ambitious king would display his 'paramount overlordship ... gain the submission of neighboring rulers, or re-establish fallen or collateral lines, rather than expand the boundaries of his own territory.'[101] Regarded as an act of powerful universal implications, the *digvijaya* affirmed the legitimacy of imperial rule and the king as a *cakravartin*, a wheel turning ruler, who through conquest and alliance obliged the minor rulers of each circle to acquiesce as subordinates in his self-centered world order in an earthly hierarchy of power.[102]

Furthermore, rulers were advised to repeat the formal royal court progress annually in a ritual journey called the *vijayayatra*, the performance of which would result in the 'renewal and reconstitution of cosmos, society and kingdom.'[103] These royal progresses were in part military campaigns but by the medieval period they had become a deliberate act of political-religious theatre which continually defined and articulated territorial control and the limits of power. Rooted as they were in ancient rituals of kingship, the court progress was carefully performed at various Hindu courts across the subcontinent well into the Mughal period. In 1674 the Maratha leader Shivaji, who was to become the arch-nemesis of the Mughals in the Deccan, seems to have performed a formal ritualized *digvijaya*, at the time of his assumption of rule, most likely because in the absence of a *kshatriya* (warrior) caste lineage, Shivaji actively sought publicly accepted rituals of consecration in order to substantiate his legitimacy.[104]

We can only speculate as to the degree to which this ancient South Asian tradition of a court progress offered the Mughal kings some legitimizing resonance within the subject population, who may have seen the wanderings of Jahangir's royal court as nothing less than the appropriate actions of a legitimizing emperor. As for Jahangir's own awareness of local traditions of kingship, his writings lack any reference to them but it is noteworthy that his mother was a princess of Rajasthan, where the royal ritual of the *digvijaya* had traditionally been performed.[105] More importantly, this confluence of imperial traditions could increase a ruler's appeal across a widely diverse imperial court, which included Rajput nobles, Persian intellectuals, Turkish and Uzbek military men, local chiefs and caste leaders, and would surely have benefited the claims of the Mughal kings.

At the end of his life, Jahangir, perhaps the most restless of Mughal kings, after years of excessive drug and alcohol abuse, exhausted from the successful effort to crush yet another filial rebellion, was an invalid, too ill to walk or even to take opium, 'of which he had been fond for forty years,' managing only a few sips of wine.[106] Yet still he traveled relentlessly, turning north to his beloved Kashmir and pausing occasionally to hunt. When, in chasing a deer wounded by the emperor, one of Jahangir's foot soldiers fell from a cliff to his death, observers describe the emperor as very deeply affected: 'It was as though the angel of death had appeared in this guise to the emperor.'[107] Jahangir insisted on continuing his journey but died shortly thereafter at the age of fifty-eight, having reigned and roamed the empire for twenty-two years. The Mughal kings who followed after Jahangir continued the transient ways of their ancestors for as long as they had the economic and political power to do so, for almost another hundred years, although none before or after seems to have indulged quite so determinedly as Jahangir in a peripatetic pursuit of pleasure.

Jahangir's successor, the emperor Shah Jahan, returned to the aggressive campaigning of his ancestors – perhaps in public renunciation of his father's shiftless, restless life. Yet he was certainly no less peripatetic a king than Jahangir. His youth had been spent for the most part leading armies in the Deccan; as king he moved constantly between the imperial capitals of the north: Agra, Lahore, Kashmir and Delhi, with brief stays in Mandu, Burhanpur and Daulatabad. In the thirty years of his reign he moved the imperial court thirty-seven times.[108]

In 1682, Shah Jahan's son, the last of the 'great' Mughal emperors, Aurangzeb, pursuing the most nagging and near un-winnable of

Mughal wars of expansion against the Marathas of the Deccan, moved his entire imperial court south. Nearly emptying Delhi and condemning the vast royal household to a lengthy exile from the (then) imperial capital of Shahjahanabad, Aurangzeb and his royal court moved into a mobile tent city, complete with bazaars, cantonments, administrative offices and imperial quarters, from which the empire was ruled for the next twenty-six years. When, after the Mughal armies had successfully defeated Bijapur and Hyderabad, a court official suggested that the war in the south was finished, and requested that the royal court return to the north, the emperor answered sympathetically in verse, 'It is hard that my runaway heart longs for home, The dew has so passed away and yet it remembers the garden.'[109] He then refused the request and returned to his conquest of the Deccan.

Aurangzeb died in 1707, having never returned to the Mughal imperial capital built by his father. He left a will which contained an advisory for his descendants: 'As far as possible,' he wrote, 'the ruler of a kingdom should not spare himself from moving about; he should avoid staying in one place, which outwardly gives him repose but in effect brings on a thousand calamities and troubles.'[110] In advice to his son and successor, Bahadur Shah, Aurangzeb further confirmed, in verse, the need for constant mobility:

> It is bad for both emperors and water to remain at the same place
> The water grows putrid and the king's power slips out of his control
> In *touring* lies the honour, ease and splendor of kings ...[111]

CHAPTER FOUR

LEGITIMACY, RESTLESS PRINCES AND THE IMPERIAL SUCCESSION

Wives, Mothers and Legitimacy

Nomadic steppe cultures of Central Asia were organized around the basic clan units, patriarchal and agnatic, led by the hereditary military elite. While polygamy was practiced, sons of different wives were considered full brothers, thereby swelling the ranks of legitimate male contenders for power. This was in part because women of the family played a critical role in the establishment of Turco-Mongol dynastic legitimacy; the earliest Turkic writings from Central Asia confirm the importance of both parental genealogical lines in the establishment of royal lineage. [1]

Although sharing similar points of origin, by the fifteenth century, in contrast to the Timurid princes, the Ottomans had developed a unique set of imperial controls over marriage, inheritance and legitimacy. The dramatic differences which developed between these two Turkic dynasties are striking and instructive – while the Timurids and later Mughals retained the traditional Turco-Mongol understanding of female genealogical charisma, at the Ottoman court a woman's access to power became removed from her personal lineage, being instead inextricably linked to the birth of a male heir and the onset of post-reproductive years. The Ottoman court became so cautious in managing the integrity and autonomy of the dynasty that a system of near-anonymous maternal concubinage had replaced wives as 'bearers of the dynasty's progeny.'[2] While strategic political marriages to women of noble birth continued to take place, after Osman and Orhan virtually all Ottoman princes were born of concubine mothers. Already devoted to a policy of slave soldiers and administrators, the Ottoman system of slave mothers, to the absolute exclusion of reproduction through legal marriage, may have been driven by similar hopes of undiluted dynastic loyalty. Certainly the Ottoman policy was successful in that it prevented the development of divisive political roles among maternal relatives, as the princes' maternal identity and lineage were generally unacknowledged at the Ottoman court.[3]

Having entered the royal harem without lineage or pedigree, Ottoman mothers developed a retroactive status as the mothers of sons and as protectors of princely power. Still, real political maturity continued to be withheld from Ottoman women until the complete cessation of childbearing. It was not menopause which ended a woman's reproductive status but the birth of a son, whose training and protection then became her sole charge and responsibility. The Ottoman policy of one mother/one son guaranteed each prince a vital political alliance with the one person at court whose loyalties were personal and undiluted: his mother. As the custodians of imperial continuity, the mothers of royal sons could at times acquire great influence and power. Their power was dramatically limited by public perception – support for a woman's public display of influence could disappear rapidly if her actions seemed to be motivated by the selfish desire for acquisition of personal power rather than simply for the support and protection of her son. Ottoman imperial manipulation of female political maturity extended to the princesses of the royal house, who were prevented from displaying public power and wealth until their own post-sexual years; it has been asserted that major public works were established only by widowed princesses.[4] Women of the Ottoman court were allowed access to power only through the suppression of a reproductive role and/or the birth of a son. 'Women without sons were women without households and therefore women of no status.'[5]

In contrast, childless Timurid women were able to dramatically influence dynastic politics. The most powerful women of the Timurid period were often childless, and Beatrice Manz has suggested that 'producing a son did not markedly enhance the position of a low status woman.'[6] Neither of Timur's Chingisid wives, Saray Mulk Khanim or Tukal Khanim, had surviving children and yet their power and influence were well noted by foreign visitors to the court.[7] 'Maternity was not in itself a path to power;' it was a woman's personal qualities and pedigree that allowed her to develop a prestigious dynastic position.[8]

As we have seen, Timur and his sons and grandsons married strategically into the Chingisid family, resulting in an 'in-law dynasty,'[9] a concept so central to their imperial identity that *Guregen* [son-in-law] became the dynasty's regnal name. In the first generations after Timur's death, although the Timurid lineage had developed its own high polish of political charisma, the ability of a Timurid prince to seize power was not considered sufficient justification for him to retain it. When a new branch of the dynasty managed to wrest control, the successful claimant carefully married women of the Chingisid line, as well as the Chingisid descendants of his conquered Timurid rivals, in order to further enhance the legitimacy of his rule, as in the case of Timur's grandson Abu Sa'id (1424–1469), who seized power from the ruling lineage of Shahrukh in the 1450's, married a Chingisid wife, and assumed Timur's regnal title of *Guregen*, son-in-law.[10] Apart from the careful establishment of legitimacy through marriage into the Chingisid line, the Timurids married into the families of their followers, in order to affirm alliances or guarantee political loyalty. Even a married woman retained an independence of identity, which allowed her to express continued loyalty to her own family line. Maternal origins were reflected in the status of princes, and Timurid children were often given names from their matrilineal line, which had a permanent claim on their loyalty and critical role in shaping their identity, as well as that of their mothers.

Babur confirms the continued dynastic importance of maternal lineage, citing, for example, Firuza Begim, the mother of Sultan Husayn Bayqara, through whom Bayqara 'was a grandson of Timur Beg's grandson Sultan Husayn and of Miranshah Mirza, and was thereby noble on both sides – he was a born king' (*karimu'l tarafayn edi – asil badshah edi*).[11] It was Sultan Husayn Bayqara's double line of descent from Timur that Babur, himself half-Timurid and half-Chingisid, so admired, obviously unconcerned that this enhanced political legitimacy sprang in part from Sultan Husayn Bayqara's maternal lineage. Furthermore, as with the earlier Timurids, princely loyalties were attached to both the maternal and paternal lines; Babur's mother was of Chingisid descent and it was this relationship which allowed Babur to seek refuge with his Mongol uncles and to call on the military assistance of Mongol warriors who owed allegiance to his royal mother. 'In my mother's service,' wrote Babur, 'were fifteen hundred to two thousand from the Mongol camps (*mugul ulusi*).'[12]

Even the Timurid-Mughal practice of inter-familial adoption does not seem to have had any impact on the adoptive mother's already substantial power and influence nor on the potential political legitimacy of fostered princes. The Timurid system of fosterage has not been fully explained or explored, but it seems to have been a common custom for elite women, most often the wives of the ruler and high-ranking amirs, to take into their households the children of sisters, daughters and common wives.[13] For example, arrangements were made before his birth to have Timur's grandson Ibrahim ibn Shahrukh raised by one of Timur's wives, Tumen Agha, rather than by his natural mother; many of Timur's grandchildren were raised 'among Timur's wives.'[14] Timur's daughter-in-law, Gawarshad, wife of Shahrukh, raised her grandchildren: Ulugh Beg's son Abd al-Latif, his daughter Hasiba Sultan Khanzada and Baysunghur's son Ala al-Dawla.[15] It has been pointed out that this practice brought grandchildren into the central imperial household, where they were raised and educated together under the close watch of the ruler.[16]

According to the sources, Sultan Husayn Bayqara's wife Afaq, daughter of Abu Sa'id, had no children but 'reared and educated nine children of [Sultan Husayn Bayqara] by her own foster-sister, Baba Agacha.'[17] Habiba Sultan Khanish Dughlat, a Chaghatay cousin of Babur, married her cousin Sa'id and raised one of his children, Rashid, whose mother was a 'tribeswoman.'[18] Babur's maternal grandmother,

Isan Dawlat Khanim, raised three of her own daughters and fostered a half-sister of Babur, Yadgar, 'Souvenir,' who had been born after the death of her father.[19] Babur's daughter, Gulbadan Begim, herself was taken at age two from her mother, Babur's wife Dildar Begim, to be raised by another of Babur's wives, Maham Begim. Gulbadan's full brother, Hindal, was taken into Maham Begim's household only three days after his birth. The arrangements for the adoption had been made long in advance and were reconfirmed by the adoptive mother in a letter to Babur, then campaigning in Swat. Maham wrote to request that Babur perform 'the divination' to determine the sex of Dildar's as yet unborn child, although she confirmed that it didn't matter were it boy or girl; she would take the baby either way.[20] Still, Maham's fosterage of the children was most assuredly not an indictment of Dildar's parenting; she gave birth to three more of Babur's children and regained parenting rights to a still young Gulbadan when Maham died. Perhaps Babur's willingness to allow Maham to foster the children of her co-wife was driven by sympathy, as all of her own children had died as babies but for one, the future emperor Humayun. In any case, the custom of fostering was well-established and commonly applied. Among the later Mughals, however, foster parentage seems to have gradually fallen out of favor, perhaps due to the increasingly linear succession patterns assumed by the dynasty in India. All the same, Jahangir's memoir mentions that his half sister, Shahzada Khanim, daughter of a serving girl, was given by her father, Akbar, to be raised by Maryam Makani.[21] Hindal's daughter, Ruqayya Begim, Akbar's first wife, who had no children of her own, raised Jahangir's son, the future emperor Shah Jahan.

It has been suggested that shared parentage/fosterage was the Timurid strategy for avoiding extreme cases of advocacy by mothers on the part of their royal sons, advocacy which could be destructive to the dynasty, as can be seen in seventeenth-century Ottoman history.[22] This may explain the origins of the custom but does not address the fosterage of so many female royal children and, of course, ignores the possibility of passionate advocacy on the part of a foster mother. Nor was the custom of fosterage devoted to removing children from less well-born or incompetent mothers; none of the sources records complaints against the mothers whose children were fostered elsewhere. For example, the lineages of both Maham Begim, Gulbadan's adoptive mother, and Dildar Begim, Gulbadan's biological mother, are obscure; as the lineage of royal-born wives was carefully recorded this seems to indicate that both women were of non-royal descent. Most interestingly, while women without influence do not seem to have been able to adopt the children of others, those women who had influence did not enhance it by adopting children from within the dynasty.

Tanistry

Legitimized by both paternal and maternal lineages, the right to rule was extended to all men of the ruling elite, a Turco-Mongol ruling tradition affirmed by Chingis Khan, for whom political legitimacy had included the conviction that 'God had designated him the sole legitimate ruler of the world, and that he had transmitted sovereignty to his descendants.'[23] Significantly, all male members of the elite held the right to claim political sovereignty in a system of universal princely legitimacy, or *tanistry*.[24]

Leadership of the clan or confederation would be confirmed by acknowledgment of members of the elite, but this was often not until after an internal battle had established which of the contenders was able to wrest power and control away from his rivals. This method of establishing royal succession was marked by constant competition for power and fluid, shifting loyalties, which resulted in regular eruptions and the inevitable fragmentation of political authority. In its defense, tanistry often 'resulted in the regular re-subjugation and reintegration of clans,' affirming their social coherence among the otherwise centrifugal forces of steppe society, yet it too could operate as a centrifugal force, pushing loyalties out from the center.[25] 'In the presence of strong, charismatic leaders, such as Chingis Khan or Timur, the right to political sovereignty found expression in the practice of appanage distribution among the male descendants, the principle of seniority of succession often being observed.'[26] In their absence, however, the competition for power by any number of princes, each of whom claimed the right to rule, resulted in wars waged across the countryside.

Modern historians have suggested that later attempts by Mughal emperors in India to select their own legitimate successors were a 'truly novel and far-reaching development, which had not been contemplated before within the Timurid-Mughal context,'[27] but from the earliest years of the Timurid dynasty, favorites had been chosen, nurtured and positioned to inherit the throne, only to ultimately fall under the onslaught of rival brothers and cousins on the death of the ruler. Timur himself had chosen a successor, his grandson Pir Muhammad Jahangir, to whom he had given the governorship of northern India, but inevitably Timur's death in 1405 was followed by fifteen years of succession struggles among his sons and grandsons, all of whom were valid political candidates with independent bases of power and influence, anxious to assert their regional power. The empire Timur had partitioned among his sons fell quickly into extreme fragmentation and decentralization, as control of the political centers was contested by rival claimants.

Timur's son Shahrukh, the eventual victor in the post-Timur succession wars, had been governor of Khurasan, Sistan, and Mazandaran since 1396 and therefore had control over a large independent treasury and a stable military following. Before competing for the imperial capital, however, Shahrukh spent the first few years after Timur's death putting down local rebellions within his own province, most notably that of Sulaymanshah ibn Da'ud, a member of the Timurid royal family and recently appointed governor of Rayy and Firuskuh, who had originally been appointed *ateke* to the twenty-year-old Shahrukh and sent with him to Khurasan as advisor and guardian.

The eventual combatants were drawn not only from among the descendants of Timur, but also from Central Asia's Chingisid Mongol groups, the Chaghatays of Mawarannahr and Mughulistan and the Jochid Uzbeks of the Kipchak steppes, who, within a hundred years, would come to be led by Babur's nemesis, Shibani Khan. Timur's emphasis on maintaining a closed elite had encouraged intermarriage within and among clans, leading to 'a paradoxical situation by the turn of the fifteenth century where the most ardent of foes and the most despicable of traitors were often the closest of blood relations.'[28] Timurid scholar Maria Subtelny writes, 'It was not so much the succession of battles, victories, and defeats in themselves, as the continual political realignments among the numerous contenders for power that are such an outstanding feature of this period. Indeed, the very notions of loyalty and treason become almost impossible to define, for even personal retainers appear to have been free to leave their masters when it was expedient to do so.'[29]

Babur's family relationships reflected the complexity of intermarriage and loyalty, with the Chingisid Mongols represented on his mother's side, Timurid Turks on his father's, and Uzbeks more distantly by marriage. Ambitious and always aware of his own royal lineage and personal right to claim sovereignty, as a fifth-generation descendant of Timur, Babur spent his youth in repeated attempts to conquer the ancestral capital of the Timurids, Samarqand, and recover his lost appanage, Ferghana. His daughter later wrote of his struggle for supremacy, 'For a full eleven years in the region of Mawarannahr his wars and exertions (*jangha u tiraddudat*) against the Chaghatay and Timurid and Uzbek princes were such that the tongue of the pen is too powerless and feeble to enumerate them.'[30] The theme of his own political legitimacy runs as a constant narrative thread throughout Babur's memoir, including his insistent claims to the rulership of the lost Timurid patrimony of Samarqand and the detailing of careful negotiations determining rank and obeisance between himself and his royal Timurid cousins in Herat.

Tragically, Babur's sons inherited his ambition for, not only dynastic but also personal, sovereignty. Before his death, Babur had attempted to dispose equitably with the imperial territories, but long after Humayun had been publicly acknowledged as his successor Babur enigmatically reminded his eldest son that he had always been expected to *share* with his brother Kamran; but share what? In a vague explanation of the intended territorial division, he wrote to Humayun, 'You know that this rule has always been observed: six parts to you and five to Kamran. Always observe this rule yourself and do not break it.' He then added, 'Conduct yourself well with your younger brother. Elder brothers need to have restraint.'[31]

Yet Babur was uncomfortably aware of the weakness inherent in shared sovereignty. 'Partnership in rule,' he had written while in

Kabul, 'is a thing unheard of,'[32] and he twice quoted Saʻdi's *Gulistan* in his memoirs, *'Dah darwish dar gilimi bakhuspanad, ve du padshah dar iqlimi nakunjanad* (Ten poor men may sleep under one blanket, but two kings cannot fit into one clime).'"[33] Several other passages reflect his concern over shared power. When Babur heard that Sultan Husayn Bayqara was impressed by a companion, Muzaffar Barlas, and promised to set aside a third of their jointly conquered territory for him, he expressed confusion. 'This was a strange promise,' Babur mused, 'When one is a king, how can it be right to make a subject co-ruler?' And significantly, he added, 'One does not make such a promise to *one's own brother or son*, much less to a Beg.'[34] Yet while he so evidently appreciated the latent tensions in territorial divisions among the royal sons, Babur seemed driven to retain the traditional Timurid principle of partition of the empire, accepting individual right to rule. The degree of political autonomy he intended for his sons, however, was not clear to anyone, least of all his successor Humayun.

Training Princes to Rule: The Imperial Appanage

In affirmation of their dynastic collective sovereignty and in keeping with the traditional Mongol system of heritable divisions of imperial territory, Chingis Khan had divided his own empire among the four lineages of his sons, each of whom was assigned a provincial governorship, an *ulus* or appanage.[35] Although there were 'constant quarrels,' the Mongol Empire retained a high degree of unity and standardized administration, manning newly conquered territories with troops and representative administrators from each of the four otherwise independent *uluses*.[36] Despite the inherently fissiparous qualities of the system, it held together for another thirty years until the death of Chingis Khan's grandson, Mongke Khan, in 1259. It was then that a succession struggle between two of Mongke's brothers, eventually won by Kubilai, caused the confederation to collapse into competing Mongol khanates.

When Timur reunited large portions of the Mongol Empire, he conformed to Mongol tradition and, perhaps most importantly, asserted his descendants' collective legitimacy by partitioning his empire among his sons, assigning each an appanage to govern.[37] The princes of the Timurid-Mughal lineage represented potential rulers, and their military and political training was of necessity the most complex and multi-faceted component of their education. Concerned for the capabilities of their princely sons, the Turkish and Mongol royal families of Central Asia included them in political life from an early age. Timur's sons and grandsons were married and had begun to take an active military and political role while still in their early teens.[38] His two eldest sons, Jahangir and Umar Shaykh, had led regiments of their father's army and on their deaths, Jahangir's sons Muhammad Sultan and Pir Muhammad, and Umar Shaykh's sons Rustam and Iskandar took on important central roles in governing and expanding the empire. Nine of Timur's twenty-one *tumens* (large military units) were eventually led by his offspring.[39] Assigned in their youth to govern imperial provinces, the royal princes thereby developed such critical skills as managing a treasure, organizing a military force and representing the center in far-flung imperial provinces, although with varying degrees of autonomy. Timur's biographer wrote of the training of the Great Amir's successors, and their efforts on his behalf, 'Truly, difficult tasks had trained them and they had been fashioned by the efforts of Timur, who by their aid had opened closed doors and by their onslaughts widened narrow places and by their attacks escaped from the stress of every melee and by their constancy obtained what he needed and by their council reached the hidden treasures of his desires.'[40]

While not in complete control of a near-autonomous *ulus* as the Chingisid princes had been, each of Timur's sons was serving as governor of a Timurid province at the time of Timur's death. The Timurid princes maintained their own provincial households modeled on that of the imperial court, including viziers, scribal staffs, tax collectors, *kitabkhanas* and artisanal workshops. Upon a prince's accession to the throne, his household was expected to serve as the nucleus of his imperial household, complete with all of its established internal networks of patronage and loyalty.[41]

Timur assigned amirs, or military commanders, to the household of each of his sons, each representing a variety of tribes or interest groups, or the relatives of Timur's own closest personal followers. In this way, the amirs, carefully positioned within the princely retinues, 'were chosen to be representative of the whole ruling class,' and the armies they led 'mirrored the composition of the whole Chaghatay army.'[42] At the same time, the amirs assigned to princely courts and military units were carefully chosen allies of Timur, acting not so much as 'servitors, but as guardians or watchdogs,' restricting princely freedom of action.[43] Their close personal ties to Timur indeed acted to trump the power of their immediate leader.

Perhaps the most critical individual within the princely household was the *ateke* (also referred to as *ataliq* or *atabeg*). The office of *ateke* is a Central Asian Turkish tradition, although the particulars of the role are somewhat unclear in the sources.[44] English-language translations of Mughal manuscripts render *ateke* as either 'guardian'[45] or 'tutor,'[46] neither of which successfully describes the full range of the *ateke's* duties and powers. The *ateke* held very high status, and were often only slightly lesser members of the royal family. The Turkish etymology of the word can better suggest the significance of the office: *ata*, father, and *eke*, brother – hence, uncle, or a kind of surrogate father.[47] Alternatively, *ataliq* can be translated as 'fatherliness.'

Atekes could be assigned to a prince as both guardian and tutor, but more specifically as paternal guide and advisor. Most importantly, the *ateke* was considered to be the representative of the ruler-father, looking after the interests of the sovereign rather than those of the individual prince, a fact which could at times lead to antagonistic relationships between *atekes* and their princely wards. All princes seem to have been assigned *atekes* throughout the entire Timurid period in Mawarannahr, but whether they always retained them past their majority is unclear. In the case of very young princes it was assumed that the *ateke* would govern the province in the prince's name because, of course, legitimate sovereignty lay only within the royal dynastic line. In any case, the *ateke* was expected to acquire a great deal of power, which was often and infamously abused in the princely courts.[48]

While the princes served as provincial governors, their status remained ambiguous and their relative political autonomy was dependent on the degree of charismatic power held by the sovereign.

Under Timur the princes were treated as extensions of the imperial center, leading armies and governing at the behest of their ruler. Their assignments were occasionally rotated, based on new territorial conquest or the death of an heir, thereby preventing them from cultivating local loyalties.[49] The death of Muhammad Sultan in 1403 inspired Timur to break the empire into its final arrangement of four quarters, as had Chingis Khan, each governed by the family of one of his sons.[50]

After Timur's death, when political authority in Central Asia became fragmented, many Timurid appanages developed into independent territories with only superficial allegiance to imperial successors, for the fissiparous tendencies of the partitioning of empire could be controlled only by leadership capable of demanding complete personal loyalty. Because of his close proximity to the capital, Timur's grandson, Khalil Sultan (1384–1411), was successful in seizing Samarqand immediately after Timur's death, yet his uncles and brothers 'looked for the end of this business,' and Khalil Sultan 'became of small account, and knew that he must be buffeted on every side by the waves of contention and that the waters of the kingdom would not be clear of trouble.'[51] While the princes, their territories, treasuries, and armies were intended to be at the service of the emperor, in the absence of clear imperial authority they could emerge in support of a prince-governor, or rebellious amirs 'pursuing their own ambition,' or other charismatic contenders for power.[52]

The system of appanage assignments continued throughout the Timurid period in Mawarannahr. Babur's grandfather had split his territory into four smaller appanages, assigning one to each of his sons. When Babur's father died, the twelve-year-old inherited the paternal appanage of Ferghana, which he lost within a very few years to Uzbeks and uncles. Oddly, Babur's younger brother, Jahangir, seems to have inherited no territory at all; certainly he made regular attempts to take Ferghana for himself.

Once established in Kabul and India, Babur unhesitatingly applied the Timurid appanage system to his own sons. Shortly after his first successful campaigns into northern India, while on the road to Kabul, a letter reached Babur from Badakhshan that the governor of the province, Mirza Khan, had died, his son was too young to replace him and the Uzbeks were near. As one might expect, the solution reached by Babur was completely Timurid in character: the young son of the deceased governor would inherit his father's patrimony while the politically critical governorship of Badakhshan was handed over to Babur's eldest son, the thirteen-year-old prince Humayun.[53] A description of the preparations entailed in establishing a princely household is sadly lacking in the Mughal memoirs and chronicles, but Babur's daughter, Humayun's half-sister Gulbadan, wrote of the affectionate parents escorting their son to Badakhshan, where they 'spent several days together. The Mirza remained and my royal father and my lady came back to Kabul.'[54] Additionally, Babur writes that in Ferghana he had had an *ateke*, Shaykh Mezid Bey, with whom he had remained on very affectionate terms. All of Babur's sons were assigned *atekes* during their years in Kabul.[55]

Within the year Babur had conquered Qandahar, to which he immediately assigned his younger son, Mirza Kamran, as governor, while Babur again returned to the family in Kabul.[56] In classic Timurid tradition, therefore, Babur's conquest of India was completed while his young sons served the empire as military leaders and governors of the provinces he had accrued. At the time of Babur's death in Agra his youngest son, Hindal, was governing in Kabul. Hindal's lifelong *ateke*, Mir Hurd, on a visit to the imperial court, was at the deathbed of the ailing emperor, whose anxious questions about his distant son illustrate the lengthy separations between parent and child. 'How tall has Hindal Mirza grown?' the father asked, and, 'What is he like?'[57]

In a letter to his successor, Humayun, Babur articulated his plans for a Mongol-Timurid system of appanages, by which he seems to mean princely rule over semi-autonomous territories with one brother dominating. 'If, by God's grace and favor,' he wrote, 'Balkh and Hissar are won and subdued, let one of your men stay in Hissar and one of Kamran's in Balkh. If, by God's grace and favor, Samarqand is also subdued, you will stay there yourself and, God willing, I will make Hissar royal demesne (*khalsa*). If Kamran thinks Balkh is small, write me. God willing, I will make up the deficiency to him out of those other territories ... There were such conquests and victories while we were at Kabul that I consider Kabul my lucky piece (*shukuntu tutubtur-i min*) and have made it royal demesne. Let none of you covet it.'[58]

That the Timurid pattern of childhood governorship continued to be considered a critical component of early Mughal princely administrative and military education in India was articulated clearly in Humayun's response to his own son and successor's childhood appanage assignment. Although the captive boy prince had only just been restored to his parents after a rout of Kamran's army had left him again behind in camp, Akbar's childhood political training was immediately structured along traditional Timurid lines; the ten-year-old was assigned an administrative household and an appanage of his own to govern. On the death of his uncle Hindal 'all the servants of Mirza Hindal, together with all his jagirs, viz., Ghaznan, etc. were assigned to him [Akbar], so that, by the practice of rule, he might exhibit favor and severity in the management of men; and by administration of a part, he might become accustomed to administer the whole.'[59] Having acquired a complete household staff and the appanage of Ghazni, Akbar was then sent on to 'strengthen Kabul' and 'practice the methods of spiritual and temporal authority.'[60]

This was not intended to be a ceremonial role and it is clear that the child-governor was expected to labor at his governorship. In Kabul, the prince's newly acquired staff found it necessary to write a complaint to Humayun, which led the ruler to gently instruct and admonish his ten-year-old son for racing pigeons and watching camel fights rather than administering the territory. 'Sit not idle; 'tis not the time for play, 'tis the time for arts and for work,' he chided.[61] The combination of responsibilities described by the king illustrates clearly the continuity of values within the Timurid-Mughal dynasty, as Humayun emphasizes to his son the importance of participation in the arts as well as the labor of governance and military campaigning.

In December of 1551 Humayun determined to acquaint Akbar with his appanage in Ghazni, 'in order that his greatness be tested, that all might know his abilities, and also that he might practice the art of rule.'[62] His father assigned Khwaja Jalal al-din Mahmud to be Akbar's *ateke*, responsible for the 'general management' of Ghazni, although

Akbar was expected to participate in the governance of his province.[63] For most of the next four years, except briefly when Humayun had a hunting accident and Akbar was temporarily recalled to his father's court in Kabul, Akbar remained in his appanage at his father's command. He did, however, accompany his father on his re-conquest of Hindustan and had only recently been assigned the governorship of the Punjab at the time of his father's death in Delhi in 1555.

Humayun and the Failure of Imperial Partition

Babur died in Agra in 1530, four years after conquering northern India. While he may have had hesitations regarding the governing abilities of his eldest son, Humayun, by the time of his death Babur had publicly confirmed Humayun as his chosen successor, formally committing their Timurid kin to his care. Like his father, and in the tradition of their Timurid ancestors, Humayun continued to use his brothers as projections of the imperial center, yet the princes had little loyalty to his sovereignty. In an examination of the subsequent rebellions of Humayun's brothers, it is clear that the princes were driven and inspired by their possession of royal blood and what were, in fact, nearly independent territories. While Humayun may have imagined his brothers to be provincial administrators at the command of the imperial center, they, as governors in command of their own military forces, administrations, and treasuries, clearly thought themselves to be legitimate competitors for imperial sovereignty. In the absence of strong and charismatic central leadership, as had been evident in Timur and Babur, the system of princely appanage, coupled with a general acceptance of universal rights to sovereignty, was divisive, threatening the unity of the fledgling empire.

As Babur had requested, the *khutba* was read in Humayun's name in Delhi, Kabul, and Ghazni, affirming his role as first among equals, after which the empire was divided amongst the princes. Kamran demanded and received the lion's share, Kabul, where he began to form an autonomous regional government, most significantly striking coins and having the *khutba* read in his own name. When, pursued by his Afghan nemesis Shir Khan (later, Shah), Humayun required passage through Kabul, he politely requested entry to the region, acknowledging Kamran's near-sovereign status in Kabul with a surprising passivity, seeming to accept his brother's claims to autonomy, although Babur himself had clearly articulated Kabul's status as royal demesne. Not surprisingly, Kamran arrogantly rejected his brother's request: 'In his lifetime the Emperor *Firdaus Makani* [Babur] gave Kabul to my mother [Gulrukh Begim]. It is not right for you to go to Kabul.' Rather than face his brother's 'large following,' Humayun chose to lead his army on the more difficult march around Kabul and its environs, while bitterly commenting, 'What was the good of my courtesy (*insaniyat*) in showing kindness (*mihrbani*) and brotherliness (*biradari*) to the Mirza [Kamran], if he is now talking to me in this way?'[64]

In a migration reminiscent of his father's years of wandering, as his inheritance disintegrated all around him, Humayun led his army through the territories of Mughal princes and amirs, some of whom welcomed and fed the emperor's forces while others refused to admit them. Meanwhile his brothers conspired over imperial territory, with Askeri in his province of Ghazni and Kamran in Kabul speculating over a joint conquest of Qandahar, then held by Hindal in Humayun's name.[65] Humayun was 'stupefied and bewildered (*mutahayir u mutafakir*),' recognizing the threat to imperial unity and yet unwilling to attack his brothers.[66] Finally forced to ask his aunt Khanzada Begim to intercede on his behalf, he requested she go to the rebellious princes. 'Tell them that the Uzbegs and the Turcomans are near them, and in this current situation, it would be better to be of one mind amongst ourselves. If Mirza Kamran will agree to carry out what I have written to him, I will do those very things that his heart desires.'[67] But Kamran proceeded to besiege Qandahar and eventually was successful in having the *khutba* read there in his own name, the traditional expression of independent sovereignty.

Significantly, the rebel Kamran took on the rights and responsibilities of a Turco-Mongol khan by immediately assigning appanages to his two other brothers in the territory to which he had claimed imperial rights—Kabul, Ghazni, Qandahar, Khutlan and Badakhshan—as part of an effort to claim fraternal allegiance and co-opt his brothers' services. Mirza Askeri was given Qandahar and Mirza Hindal was given Ghazni. Hindal, however, attempted to withdraw into seclusion in Badakhshan, seemingly in repudiation of his brothers' rebellion. The appanage was removed from his control and he was captured by Kamran, remaining under guard in Kabul. Meanwhile, Humayun's eventual flight from his brother Mirza Askeri, leading a force of two thousand troops, was so frantic that his own young son, the future emperor Akbar, was left behind to be taken hostage by his uncle.

It is interesting to note that when, after a nine-year exile from his former empire, Humayun returned at the head of an army, his earliest efforts at empire-building were directed not toward his lost patrimony in northern India but in the direction of the more favored territories of Balkh and Samarqand. Here again the disloyal machinations of Kamran frustrated Humayun's attempts at conquest, until finally Humayun turned south to re-conquer Delhi. Like his father Babur, Humayun seems to have conquered the Indian territories with a degree of reluctance, viewing them as inferior to the ancestral homelands of Central Asia, although Humayun, born in Kabul, had never seen Samarqand.

As Humayun's advisors knew, the stability of his reclaimed kingdom was dependent on the destruction of Kamran, their younger brothers Askeri and Hindal having already been killed in battle, though on opposing sides of the familial conflict. Humayun's extreme reluctance to deal conclusively with the threat, perhaps as an act of filial obedience in remembering his father's injunctions to take care of his younger brother, caused a near mutiny within his immediate circle. Legal opinions were brought forward to support the execution of Kamran, but when Humayun continued to refuse, a compromise was reached. Kamran was not killed but blinded, disqualifying him for kingship, and then exiled to Mecca. With the internal threat finally removed, Humayun was able to position his son Akbar to inherit their fragile northern Indian kingdom nearly unopposed before his own accidental death in 1556.

Humayun's son Akbar was fortunate to mount the throne with almost no competition, for his uncles had at last been disposed of and his half-brother, Mirza Muhammad Hakim, was as yet too young to

Legitimacy, Restless Princes, Imperial Succession 117

contest the throne. By the time Mirza Hakim had grown to adulthood, again very much in the model of his Timurid forebears, as the near-independent governor of the appanage of Kabul, ambitious and ready to challenge the emperor for sovereignty, Akbar had become politically entrenched and was powerful enough to destroy his brother's aspirations at little risk to his own sovereignty. In the classic Timurid-Mughal pattern of familial tolerance, notable in every generation,[68] the powerful Akbar was even able to forgive his rebellious half-brother, commenting, 'Mirza Hakim is a *memorial* of the Emperor Humayun. Though he has acted ungratefully, I can be no other than forbearing. Some bold spirits asked permission to lie in ambush and put an end to that rebel. I could not consent, thinking it remote from what was befitting in his regard.'[69]

Akbar and the Princely Appanage: Timurid Traditions Transformed

It is in the upbringing of Akbar's sons that we can identify the only Mughal modifications of the traditional political and military training of princes: the disappearance of childhood appanages and a vastly accelerated rotation of princely military assignments and governorships. The sources are regrettably silent regarding these adaptations of Timurid tradition and we can only guess that Akbar was influenced by his own sudden thrust at age ten into the responsibility and isolation of the governorship of a Mughal province. Perhaps, too, the example of his father's desperate struggles to retain sovereignty made an impact on the child. Raised in part in the household of a seditious uncle, twice left behind in the confusion and terror of a military rout, Akbar was witness to the disastrous impact of imperial partition on the royal succession. While not enough to compel him to completely forgo or transform the tradition of princely training through the assignment of governorships, his childhood experiences may have influenced the emperor's decision to keep his young sons close at hand and dependent on their father.

Without explanation or much comment of any kind, the usually verbose Abu al-Fazl writes only that 'the wise sovereign kept his children under his own care and did not appoint any guardian to them, and was continually educating them in the most excellent manner of which there are few instances in ancient times.'[70] Although the princes were, as noted, assigned tutors at age four years, four months and four days, in the traditional Timurid manner, Abu al-Fazl describes their father's influence and example as the real basis of their education. Referring to Akbar's eldest son, Salim, the future emperor Jahangir, Abu al-Fazl writes, 'Constantly acquiring various outward and inward excellencies in the society of His Majesty and in the Shahinshah's entourage ... by the blessing of His Majesty's holy spirit and of his exalted attentions he [Salim] learnt the rules of justice and the cherishing of subjects and the principles of settling disputes.'[71]

Akbar's sons, Salim (1569–1627; r. 1605–1627, using the regnal name of Jahangir), Shah Murad (1570–1598) and Danyal (1572–1604), were not given appanages in their youth, signaling the permanent abandonment of this practice among the Mughals.[72] The system of *atekes* remained in place, but the *atekes* assigned to Akbar's sons seem to have operated as tutors rather than political and military mentors, and the boys remained almost exclusively in their father's household while under the training of these men.[73] The *atekes* were chosen, in classic Timurid style, for their personal loyalties to the emperor; the brothers of Akbar's own childhood *ateke* and loyal supporter, Shams al-Din Khan, served the emperor's sons; Qutb al-Din Khan became Salim's *ateke* in 1577 and Sharif Khan as Murad's in 1580.[74] Shams al-Din Khan's wife had been Akbar's wetnurse (*anaga*), which made their son, Mirza Aziz, a milk brother (*koka*) of the emperor and an important notable of the imperial court. The *atekes'* positions were not always permanent, but their high rank at court and personal loyalty to the emperor determined their choice. Danyal was assigned Sa'id Khan Chaghatay[75] as *ateke* in 1577 and then Shaykh Fayzi, a court favorite, poet and brother of Akbar's closest friend and panegyrist, Abu al-Fazl, in 1579. Salim was assigned Akbar's loyal ally, Mirza Khan Abd al-Rahim Khan-i Khanan, in 1582.

Remaining at court, without active participatory governorships, the princes were nevertheless given positions of high rank at very early ages, although their titles were merely ceremonial. For example, in 1576, Akbar gave seven-year-old Salim authority over the entire Mughal army along with the rank of commander of 10,000, while Murad was assigned the rank of 7,000 and Danyal 6,000.[76] As none within the nobility could aspire to a rank higher than 5,000, this established the princes as the elite among all Mughal nobles. When in 1580 the province of Ajmer seemed to require the presence of Mughal royalty, the child-prince Danyal was sent, accompanied by 'other intimate courtiers,' to distribute royal gifts and 'display abundant liberality' but immediately afterwards he was recalled to his father's court to offer homage.[77] In the same year, when Akbar planned a military expedition in the Punjab, eleven-year-old Salim begged to be included, and eight-year-old Danyal remained at court as the representative of imperial authority.

Nor was the status of a princely appanage ever again in doubt, as it had been at the time of Babur's death. From the time of Akbar and through the reigns of his successors, leadership roles and governorships were assigned only to adult princes, careful constant oversight was maintained by the emperor, and princely assignments were continually and regularly rotated. In an obvious effort to impose paternal control, royal sons serving their father away from the imperial court were recalled at least annually to pay homage. In exchange for their demonstrations of fealty, the giving of magnificent gifts and affirmations of loyalty and even servility, they were regularly assigned larger incomes, higher titles, and new military or governing assignments. Because princes and their enormous personal retinues were kept far more often at court than their ancestors had been, many of the great cities of the empire contained not only the imperial palace but, nearby, the only slightly less lavish palaces of the royal princes, many of which had been built at the expense of the emperor.[78]

Imperial oversight, through the unapologetic use of spies and informants, continued even when the princes were given leave to depart the imperial presence for distant assignments. In letters written to his sons, the sixth Mughal emperor, Aurangzeb, makes it clear that the sovereign received regular reports from his own agents within the princely households. He is able to comment on his sons' every appointment and make recommendations of his own; writing to his heir apparent, Shah Bahadur, 'You have appointed Aman Allah Beg, the superintendent of the artillery and of the palace, the police officer of Navah. He gave *patel*-ships to his dishonest and corrupt relatives. The oppressed cannot complain to you against his power. Alas! Alas! You should send to the province reliable and cautious reporters, and send me daily reports of the results of the orders [issued by you].'[79]

Mughal princes continued to be employed as extensions of the imperial center, but never again were they allowed to assume personal independence or autonomy. Beginning with Abu al-Fazl, the chronicles describe Mughal princes spending their entire childhood in their father's household, serving the empire as symbols of imperial might and majesty, but lacking real sources of personal authority, often well into their twenties and certainly long after their marriages.

As for the assignment of *atekes*, scholars have assumed in the past that Mughal princes outgrew their surrogate fathers as their training was completed. 'In the beginning they had an experienced officer associated with them, who trained them to deal with administrative affairs, but as soon as the training was complete, they were given independent charge.'[80] In fact, this does not accurately represent the post-Akbar period, when *atekes*, as representatives of the sovereign/father in the households of his sons, continued to be assigned to the princes well into adulthood. For example, in 1598, when Shah Murad was temporarily assigned a territory in Gujarat, his *ateke* died. The father of the then twenty-seven-year-old prince immediately appointed Mirza Yusuf Khan to be his son's new *ateke*.[81] When the more than thirty-year-old prince Khurram, entitled Shah Jahan, was leading the Mughal armies in the Deccan and required more horses, it was his *ateke*, Nazir Beg, whom he sent to the imperial court to deliver dispatches and request equine reinforcements from the emperor Jahangir.[82]

Atekes, Naukars, Allies

The power accrued by ownership of an appanage had encouraged Timurid princes to act on individual claims to sovereign legitimacy, yet the changes instituted in sixteenth-century India did not serve as a corrective. Among post-Akbar Mughal princes, none of whom were assigned childhood appanages, succession wars continued unabated. It is clear that even without the political and military independence which sprang from control of a traditional Timurid semi-autonomous governorship in the imperial provinces, the princes were so often employed as extensions of the state that by middle age they were usually experienced administrators and hardened military commanders, each possessed of a complete imperial household, positioned to command his own networks of loyalty and patronage, and confident in his individual right to rule.

With the expectation of deadly succession wars immediately following their father's death, the princes were encouraged throughout their adulthood to form strategic relationships. A contemporary witness wrote, 'When these princes once leave the paternal house, they work and scheme to make themselves friends. They write secretly to the Hindu princes and the Mahometan generals, promising them that when they become king they will raise their allowances.'[83] In the time of the young adulthood of Aurangzeb's sons, chroniclers record their constant jockeying for influence by developing relationships with influential courtiers and political allies. Each prince acted by 'softening the rigor of government against those who labored under its displeasure; thinking that thus obliged by his mediation, they would readily return his favors, by embracing his cause whenever the death of his father should give him a claim to the empire.'[84]

There is no doubt that mature Mughal princes were eager to establish alliances with influential individuals at court, powerful factions, tribal and caste leaders, political and military families, but their royal fathers participated fully in the process, carefully positioning their favorites to achieve critical alliances through the careful assignment of *atekes*, marriage partners and military companions. Timur had carefully placed each of his heirs in the path of prominent courtiers and military leaders, insisting on the formation of relationships which could, eventually, survive his own death and offer the prince a lifesaving alliance. So too in India, Mughal fathers married their sons into the families of influential and powerful amirs and allies, establishing for them a body of supporters which could come at a time of danger to the prince's aid – provided, of course, that the prince acted carefully to maintain those alliances. There were no guarantees. Shahnawaz Khan

Safavi[85] had as sons-in-law three royal Mughal brothers, the sons of Shah Jahan: Shah Shuja (1615–1659), Aurangzeb (1618–1707) and Murad Baksh (1619–1661), yet remained neutral in the early stages of the succession war which broke out among them in the 1650's. He finally joined forces with the one brother who had not married into his own family, Dara Shikoh (1615–1659), and died defending him in 1659 at the Battle of Ajmer.[86] Yet more often healthy and lifelong alliances were formed by the princes, often with the connivance of their father, and each potential ruler was backed by a powerful faction of supporters who could be trusted to support his claims to the Mughal throne. Princes even scavenged among their father's own courtiers for followers. Jahangir refers to individuals he had 'chosen and requested' from his father's service, promoting them within his personal household.[87]

While much of a prince's retinue was originally appointed by his father, for the most part the following a prince established remained with him throughout his lifetime, becoming increasingly independent of the father's wishes, and on some occasions far more loyal to the prince's survival than were the prince's own relatives. The memoirs of Jahangir affirm the increasing partisanship of the princes' *atekes* and refer regularly to the *naukar* (alternatively: *noker*) of his sons. In the Mongol period, the term *naukar* had been used to describe a military alliance and personal fealty, but over time it gradually came to imply closer ties of loyalty and service.[88] As used by Jahangir, it is a clear illustration of the independent nature and loyalty of the princely personal retinues.[89] The loyalty of a prince's allies could be powerful. In the succession war that led to Shah Jahan's deposition, when the defeated prince Murad Bakhsh was captured by his brother Aurangzeb, so concerned was the victor about the strength of his defeated brother's followers that he used four decoy elephants to confuse the prince's partisans, making it all but impossible for them to 'fall upon the *howda* in which he was confined' and rescue him.[90]

Adapted Succession Traditions Among Mughal Contemporaries

The Mughal wars of succession exploded with the pent-up force of long awaited collisions between rivals and their allies, in part because along with the diminution of princely political autonomy, the Mughal emperors of the sixteenth and seventeenth centuries achieved remarkably lengthy reigns. Akbar reigned for forty-nine years (1556–1605), Jahangir for twenty-two (1605–1627), Shah Jahan for thirty-two (1627–1659) and Aurangzeb nearly matched Akbar's forty-nine years, ruling from 1659 until 1707. These extended reigns must have increased the tension at court and tried the patience of all ambitious, highly trained Mughal princes with political aspirations. So while sixteenth-century modifications may have reduced princely access to the potential source of power that was the Timurid appanage, thereby averting declarations of territorial autonomy such as that of Humayun's rebellious brother Kamran, the princes' awareness of their own political viability, the sophistication of their personal patronage networks, and their highly developed administrative and military skills, learned in adulthood in their role as extensions of imperial power, were frustrated by heightened paternal control, even well into middle age. It is, therefore, no wonder that tensions and conflicts over sovereignty continued to rock the Mughal court.

Confronted with similar dilemmas, and sharing something of the same Turkic Central Asian origins, Mughal contemporaries, the Ottomans and Safavids, gradually modified their original succession principles dramatically. Extremely destructive succession wars marked their early centuries, such as the twenty years of divisive rivalry between Bayezid's sons in the period just after Timur's successful invasion of Anatolia in the early fifteenth century. Beginning with the reign of the Ottoman sultan Murad I (r. 1362–89) and through the beginning of the seventeenth century, Ottoman rulers destroyed any possible rivalry by executing all princes of the royal blood immediately on achieving the throne. Murad I's near-contemporary, the Ottoman poet Ahmedi, explained:

> His brothers became enemies to him
> The affairs of all of them were ended at his hands
> They were all destroyed by the sword.[91]

An attempt by Mehmed I (r. 1413–20) to divide the Ottoman Empire amongst his sons, hoping thereby to prevent war between brothers, was skillfully outmaneuvered by an influential palace faction and the subsequent succession battle raged for three years.[92] The Ottoman sultan Mehmed II (r. 1421–51) attempted to avoid these disastrous succession rivalries by making accessional fratricide an institutionalized part of the Ottoman kanun. It may be that, as conqueror of Constantinople, Mehmed II was less concerned with the dangers of adaptations to old traditions than were his predecessors. When his son Bayezid abdicated the throne, his successor, Selim, desperate to avoid threats to his authority, had not only all of his brothers but his nephews killed as well. So anxious was he to manipulate and subvert the tradition of tanistry that he eventually killed all of his own sons, leaving alive only his chosen successor, Suleyman (r. 1520–66).

Although the modified system resulted in regular bloodshed, it was understandably successful in preventing fratricidal rivalries. In addition to continuing the now-institutional accessional fratricide, Suleyman's successor Selim II (1524–74) made a further major adaptation by entirely abandoning the Central Asian system of appanages that gave the imperial princes an opportunity to develop their own households, create networks of influence and patronage, and gain political and military experience. From that time the princes would remain in the imperial household, living entirely within a suite of apartments in the rear of the harem, which came to be known as the *kafes*, the cage. Isolated from public life, the princes were not allowed to father children, establish a public identity, or develop the retinue that might support princely aspirations to the throne. Like his Ottoman contemporaries, the Persian Shah Abbas adopted a policy of accessional fratricide and instituted a Safavid *kafes*, isolating the princes in the family quarters of the imperial palace. In a desperate bid for absolute sovereignty, Abbas eventually had all of his brothers and sons killed or blinded, nearly destroying the dynasty, to be finally succeeded by a grandson.

It was in the very early seventeenth century, under the Ottoman sultan Mustafa I, that the practice of accessional fratricide lapsed, and along with it the rule that succession must run from ruler to son. Instead succession followed a simple system of seniority, sovereignty shifting to the ruler's brother, uncle, nephew, in a style reminiscent of pre-Timurid Central Asian traditions. Male members of the dynasty continued to be limited to a life within the imperial household and the dangerously empowering tradition of princely governorships was never reinstituted. Succession conflicts, and the princes at their center, henceforth remained confined within the palace.[93]

Diplomatic exchange among these contemporary Turco-Persian empires was enough to ensure that the Mughals were aware of the alterations made to Ottoman and Safavid succession patterns. Akbar and Jahangir expressed personal horror at the bloody family dramas of their rivals, even while their own destructive succession wars continued to rage across the subcontinent. For while relatively minor changes can be identified within the related Mughal institution of the princely appanage, the fundamental Timurid-Mughal succession tradition, based on a firm adherence to the principle of universal sovereignty, tanistry, remained firmly in place. Occasional attempts were made to manipulate the Mughal succession, by assigning an official successor to whom loyalty would be guaranteed, even base the inheritance of power on seniority or primogeniture, but these schemes came to nothing. Rejecting one such plot to assign early sovereignty, Akbar's courtiers, themselves 'descended from an ancient and illustrious Mughal family,' declared, 'This is contrary to the laws and customs of the Chaghatay Tartars and shall never be.'[94] Although it provoked devastating wars among brothers and produced an indirect dynastic line, the principle of tanistry remained firmly in place in India, forming a critical link to the Timurid steppe heritage, and defining individual rights to sovereignty and Mughal dynastic political legitimacy.

Restless Princes, Fratricide, and Timurid Imperial Partition

Succession by primogeniture was not generally the norm among the indigenous courts of South Asia, among whom inheritance and sovereignty were contested between sons and ruling fathers. A Buddhist narrative describes five murders of reigning kings by their sons and successors at the royal court of Magadha, while Hindu ruling traditions affirmed the devious nature of ambitious princes, advising that a king should control his sons, 'for princes, like crabs, eat their own parents.'[95] While parricide did not occur among the Mughal princes, open and sometimes flagrant acts of princely rebellion against paternal authority became a constant concern of Mughal kings from the reign of Akbar.

No mention of any assignment to a governorship occurs in Jahangir's memoirs until 1598, when his father departed for the Deccan and awarded his eldest son, the favorite and chosen successor, the province of Ajmer.[96] The prince was then already twenty-nine years old. He handled independence badly, committing serious acts of sedition, including the outrageous murder of his father's friend and biographer, Abu al-Fazl, before being brought to heel again by his father. Yet Jahangir's panegyrist insisted that Akbar was not entirely displeased by his insurrections, for 'through this act His Highness's [Jahangir's] bravery and manliness were noticed.'[97]

His two brothers, Danyal and Murad, had died young from 'overindulgence in wine' but Jahangir's succession came to be contested by his own son, Khusraw, who felt he had been Akbar's heir apparent.[98] In a notable commentary on the Mughal succession, Khusraw justified his filial insubordination by asserting, 'I shall certainly not become more criminal by taking arms against Jahangir than he himself was in revolting against Akbar. *If I offend, it will only be by following the example of my father.*'[99]

The emperor Jahangir composed bitter verses in response to the disloyalty of the royal princes:

Who could have known that this youth of tender years
    would in this way plot mischief against his elders?
With the first goblet he brought forth the dregs,
    bypassing my grandeur and his own shame.
He burned the throne of the sun
    in desiring the place of Jamshid.[100]

Ki danast kin kudak khurd sal
    shud ba bazurgan chunin bad sigal.
Ba avval qad' durdi arad
    guzarad shukuh-i man u sharm khuwish.
Ba suzand aurang-i khurshid ra,
    tamana kunad jay Jamshid ra.

At either end of his twenty-two year reign, Jahangir's restless and ambitious sons engaged in bloody rebellions, both of which were eventually defeated but at a high cost. Less than a year after Jahangir had ascended the throne, on the sixth of April 1606, Khusraw went into open rebellion. As Khusraw fled westward his undisciplined army swelled with the ranks of the disaffected and plundered the countryside. While passing through the Punjab, Khusraw begged for financial assistance from the Sikh patriarch, Guru Arjun Singh (1581–1606). The guru finally offered the desperate prince a charitable gift of 5000 rupees, which Jahangir would later interpret as support for the princely rebellion and punish by torturing and executing the guru, in what would prove to be a disastrously divisive moment in the history of Mughal-Sikh relations.

Jahangir rapidly quelled his son's rebellion. Although members of the imperial elite were generally forgiven, three hundred of the captured peasant-soldiers of his son's army were impaled alive, forming an avenue along which Khusraw was led on elephant-back in order to review the anguish of his followers. Only one year later Khusraw again became involved in a plot to overthrow his father's rule, but in this case a member of the cabal informed Jahangir of the plot. He was easily able to crush the conspiracy and execute the ringleaders. Following the pattern of remarkable intra-familial tolerance displayed by Babur, Humayun and Akbar, under threat of their rebellious brothers, even after two acts of open rebellion Jahangir could not bring himself to destroy his son. Khusraw was blinded and imprisoned, yet eventually, with the contrivance of his aunts, he was guardedly pardoned, doctors were called to attend to his blinded eyes, partial sight was restored, and he was yet again allowed to wait on his father. His depression and intransigence, though, prevented him from endearing himself to Jahangir, who eventually assigned him to the care of his equally ambitious younger brother, Khurram, the future Emperor Shah Jahan. Khusraw died under somewhat mysterious circumstances while in the custody of Khurram in 1622 in Burhanpur.

Khurram, Jahangir's third son, remained at court until the age of twenty-two, 'when the signs of bravery were resplendent from the auspicious face of His Majesty' and he was finally appointed to lead a military expedition to Ajmer.[101] In affirmation of the relatively late age at which the prince was assigned a role outside of the palace, when Khurram's *ateke*, Khan Azam, began behaving 'uncooperatively,' he was sent a letter from the emperor, remonstrating, 'At your advice I sent the imperial banners to Ajmer. Now that you have reasonably entreated me for the prince, and everything has been done as you advised and approved, what is wrong? ... I sent Baba Khurram, from whom I have never been separated (*Baba Khurram ra ki dar in muddat hargaz az khud juda nasakhte budam*), simply because I had confidence in your abilities.'[102]

Khurram's brilliance as a military leader in campaigns in the Deccan and Gujarat led his father to honor him with new titles, first *Shah Sultan Khurram* and, soon after, *Shah Jahan* (King of the World), and a special seat near his father's throne. He seems to have cultivated a fair degree of political influence and authority both at court and in the provinces, which he, like his father, eventually abused. At age thirty, his increasingly rebellious acts drove his father to re-name him '*bidawlat*' (unfortunate; wretched), adding in his manuscript, 'And every place in this *iqbalnama* [auspicious tale] "*bidawlat*" is mentioned, it will mean him.'[103] In irritation, Jahangir even returned to hunting, which he had in part foresworn five years earlier as an auspicious act of personal sacrifice for the benefit of Khurram's ailing son.[104] In his remarkably human memoir, Jahangir complains about his rebellious prince, 'About which of my afflictions should I write? In my grief and weakness, and with such warm weather, which is extremely debilitating to my constitution, is it really necessary for me to get on a horse and gallop in this condition after such a villainous (*na khalafi*) son?'[105]

And clearly the Mughal *ateke* had by now begun to identify with his prince more often than had been the case among Timur's immediate successors. Khurram was joined in his revolt by his *ateke*, the Khan Khanan, about whom Jahangir laments, 'If amirs like the Khan Khanan, who had been singled out for the exalted post of *ataliq* could dishonor himself at the age of seventy with such rebellious insolence and infidelity (*bagi u kafir*), what complaint could one have of others? It was as though insurgence and ingratitude were innate components of his nature.'[106]

Khurram's insurgency was unsuccessful, and he was forced to beg for pardon and send his eldest sons, Dara Shikoh and Aurangzeb, to live at his father's court as surety, but on the death of Jahangir he rushed to the capital and was able to overthrow his brothers and the son of Khusraw to become the new emperor, choosing as regnal name the title his father had bestowed upon him in happier times, Shah Jahan. In a dramatic act of innovation within the Mughal succession traditions, in what seems to have been recognition of the personal threat posed by the Timurid-Mughal principle of tanistry, Shah Jahan had the male members of his immediate family, a total of five princes, murdered within twenty-four days after his accession, 'for the exigencies of the affairs of state.'[107] He did not, however, threaten any of his own sons. For the first time in the history of the Timurid line, attempting to secure his reign against the threat of shared sovereignty, a newly enthroned Mughal ruler had even dependent and powerless male relatives, put to death, 'executing all those in whose veins flowed the royal blood.'[108]

Although Shah Jahan had been married and assigned his first rank at age fifteen, as well as given the income producing territory of Hissar Firoza, which had been the *jagir* of every previous Mughal emperor and a clear indication that he was the heir-apparent,[109] he had been kept at court until age twenty-one or two. While a few of his sons served as military commanders in their young adulthood, their first governorships were usually not assigned until much later. Aurangzeb, a military paragon, was sent to lead armies in the Deccan at age seventeen, but Dara Shikoh, the favorite, remained at court until he was nearly thirty. Murad Baksh was twenty-nine when he emerged from court to represent his father in Kabul, and Shah Shuja was seventeen when he was deputed as a military leader to the Deccan in 1633.

Shah Jahan, like Akbar and Jahangir, continually recalled his sons to court and rewarded their compulsory filial attentions with increased incomes and regular re-assignments. For example, his youngest son, Murad Baksh, was assigned to Kabul during his father's fourteenth regnal year, in March 1641. One year later he was recalled and sent to Kangra to lead a military expedition. After a brief but successful campaign, Murad Baksh was recalled to court and then sent to Qandahar to support Dara Shikoh's military expedition. He was recalled in July of the same year and married. He was then assigned the governorship of Multan but was then recalled a year and a half later when his father fell ill in his seventeenth regnal year. In June of 1644 he was returned to Multan for another year, after which he was again recalled and appointed to take part in the Mughal conquest of Balkh and Badakhshan. He was successful but resisted remaining in Balkh; his companions claimed to be 'dreading the hardship of a winter in that climate.'[110] Returning home without permission, he was stripped of his *mansab* (title) and *jagirs* (income-producing properties), but they were reinstated within a few months and he was then assigned the governorship of Kashmir. One year later he was recalled to court and re-assigned to the Deccan. A year after that, in his father's twenty-third regnal year, Murad Baksh was assigned to Kabul. Just over a year later, he was appointed to Malwa and a year and a half later, in March 1654, he was recalled and then sent on to Gujarat, where he was residing at the outbreak of the wars of the Shah Jahani succession. In all, Murad Baksh had been recalled and reassigned by his imperial father a total of eleven times in fourteen years.[111]

Brothers at War

The most famous of all Mughal succession wars was that which brought down a ruling emperor, Shah Jahan. When Shah Jahan fell ill in 1657, Shah Shuja was governor of Bengal, Murad Baksh was in Gujarat, Aurangzeb was leading military campaigns in the Deccan and Dara Shikoh was in Shahjahanabad, outside of Delhi, at his father's side. The sources indicate a clear preference for Dara Shikoh on the part of the emperor, for 'when his other sons departed to their respective governments, the Emperor from excessive love and partiality, would not allow Dara Shikoh to go away from him.'[112] Even when he was appointed provincial governor of Allahabad and the Punjab, Dara Shikoh remained at his father's side, sending his agents to rule his newly acquired territories in his stead.[113] His military record was not exemplary.[114] As heir apparent, Dara Shikoh was allowed to take on some of the duties of the reputedly ailing emperor, but his assumption of imperial power and attempts to prevent his brothers from communicating with their agents at court gave rise to rumors of the emperor's death. Later chroniclers accuse an 'unworthy and frivolous'[115] Dara Shikoh of encouraging a fraternal confrontation, claiming he conspired against his brothers, 'interfered in the affairs of State, and induced His Majesty to do many unwise things that tended to create disturbances.'[116]

Whether they rose up spontaneously at hearing rumors of their father's illness, or were compelled to rebel to protect interests threatened by their brother, the princes Shah Shuja and Murad Baksh, in their provincial capitals, each immediately declared himself emperor, appropriating the contents of his provincial treasury, issuing coins and having the *khutba* read in his name.[117] Having been kept at military service most of their adult lives, these Mughal princes were skilled military strategists, and the family tradition of succession war had certainly encouraged each to prepare for his own turn. Yet while artfully complaining of Dara Shikoh's high-handedness, Aurangzeb, serving as a general in the Deccan, evinced a lack of interest in his father's throne, claiming instead to be drawn to the life of a holy man. Writing to his brother, Murad Baksh, Aurangzeb claimed, 'I have not the slightest liking for or wish to take any part in the government of this deceitful and unstable world; my only desire is that I may make a pilgrimage to the temple of God.'[118] His actions belied claims to a desire for retirement, however, as he had already begun to prepare for war. 'To carry out his aims, Aurangzeb had set himself to win over to his side the great nobles of the State, some of whom he had made his own, and that he was endeavoring to effect his object by secret communications before his designs had become public. The money he had received in tribute from Kutbul Mulk [as leader of the victorious Mughal forces in the Deccan] he had spent without permission in the raising of forces, and it would not be long before he would cast off his obedience and commence a war.'[119] Claiming only to be interested in putting his brother Murad Baksh on the throne, Aurangzeb combined their armies and marched on Delhi.[120] Shah Shuja was routed early, and the carefully contrived strategic alliance between Aurangzeb and Murad Baksh was too powerful for the imperial armies. Defeating the forces of Dara Shikoh, Aurangzeb occupied Delhi and Agra, imprisoned his father, and forced him to abdicate in Aurangzeb's favor.

In addition to a general desire for personal sovereignty and the lifelong expectation of an eventual succession war, there is some suggestion that Shah Jahan's employment of a near Ottoman-style fratricide at the time of his own accession encouraged the four brothers in their murderous competition for the throne. An observer wrote, 'Not only was the crown to be gained by victory alone, but in the case of defeat life was certain to be forfeited. There was now no choice between a kingdom and death; as Chah-Jehan had ascended the throne by embrueing his hands in the blood of his own brothers, so the unsuccessful candidates on the present occasion were sure to be sacrificed to the jealousy of the conqueror.'[121]

Yet the fear of execution by whichever brother gained the throne might have been allayed by a remarkable gesture made by the weakened Shah Jahan. With Dara Shikoh still in the field, Shah Jahan made his sons an offer worthy of a Timurid ruler, proposing to partition the empire into classic Turco-Mongol appanages, shared among the four princes: Dara Shikoh would receive the Punjab, Murad Baksh would take Gujarat, Shah Shuja would have Bengal, and the remainder would be assigned to the clear victor, Aurangzeb, who would henceforth receive the title of *Shah Buland Iqbal* (King of Supreme Good Fortune) which had been formerly attached to their father's favorite, Dara Shikoh.[122] This attempt by Shah Jahan to revive ancient Central Asian appanage practices in order to defuse a succession conflict was unsuccessful. Perhaps doubting his father's sincerity, and justifiably confident that the entire empire lay within his grasp, Aurangzeb continued to pursue his rivals.

In an interesting rejection of his father's dramatic accessional murder of his brothers and nephews, Aurangzeb in his own turn, requested and received formal legal sanction for the execution of his last surviving rivals. It was more than a year after the war's commencement and six months after Aurangzeb's coronation that Dara Shikoh was captured and publicly humiliated. Tried in court as a heretic and danger to the state, on the basis of his attempts to identify and articulate a spiritual union between Hinduism and Islam, Dara Shikoh was executed.[123] Obtaining a legal ruling to support yet another fratricide, Aurangzeb handed his former ally, Murad Baksh, over to enemies, 'who had a charge against him for the murder of their father,' and who were therefore allowed to demand his assassination. Murad Baksh remained philosophical, saying 'If the Emperor [Aurangzeb] will accept my pledges and save my life, no harm will come to his throne; but if he is resolved to take my life ... he has the power and can do what he likes.'[124] Later chroniclers reflected on this 'simple mindedness' of Murad Baksh, explaining that his murder was required on the basis of the classic verse by Sa'di, oft quoted by their dynastic founder Babur, which declared that two kings cannot be contained in a single kingdom.[125] They ignored Babur's heartfelt injunctions for fraternal forgiveness.

Aurangzeb left unharmed, however, those of Dara Shikoh's sons, grandsons and daughters who had not participated in the succession war; Dara's favorite sister and active supporter throughout the succession war, Jahanara, he treated with respect and admiration for the remainder of her life. Not only to justify the murder of his brothers and nephew, but to legitimate his outrageous seizure of power from the living emperor, Shah Jahan, Aurangzeb enlisted the assistance of the religious legal community. When the Mughal's chief *qadi* (judge) refused to read the khutba in his name, Aurangzeb convinced the scholar, Shaykh Abd al-Wahhab (d. 1650), to insist on public acknowledgement of the legality of his claim to the throne.[126]

Shortly thereafter, Dara Shikoh's son, Suleiman Shikoh, was captured and imprisoned at the fort of Gwalior. A proven threat to his uncle, he was murdered without the sanction of legal proceedings like those which had preceded his father's execution. On the orders of his emperor-uncle, Suleiman Shikoh was buried next to his uncle, Murad Baksh.[127] Although skirmishes had continued until all of Aurangzeb's rivals had been found and executed, Aurangzeb resolved one of the dynasty's lengthiest and most destructive succession conflicts, concluding with the confinement of his father and the destruction of those brothers and nephews deemed dangerous, nearly all at least superficially legally sanctioned.

In the long years of his reign, Aurangzeb's relationship with his own sons seems to have been tortured and fearful, driven by the emperor's fear that he would suffer from his sons the fate he had meted out to his father. The mistrust which developed between the emperors and their rival sons led a bitter Aurangzeb to advise his successors to, 'Never trust your sons or treat them during your lifetime in intimate manner, because if the emperor Shah Jahan had not treated Dara Shikoh in this manner his affairs would not have come to such a sorry pass.'[128]

Over time, only one of his five sons escaped lengthy prison sentences meted out for real or imagined insurrection. His eldest son, Muhammad Sultan, had, during the war of succession, joined his uncle Shah Shuja in opposition to his father and, although he soon returned to the fold, for this betrayal he would be imprisoned by his newly enthroned father for the rest of his life.[129] Aurangzeb's second son, and eventual successor, Bahadur Shah, was found to be corresponding with the enemy and was imprisoned along with his sons for eight years until his release in 1695. His courage never returned, however, and his father 'taunted him with cowardice, though the prince was already a grandfather.'[130] Yet with all this, the only open revolt against Aurangzeb came from his fourth son, Akbar, who, while on military duty in Rajasthan, proclaimed himself emperor. He was quickly routed by the imperial forces and forced to flee to Iran. Aurangzeb never forgot the threat this rebellious son represented, and on finally hearing of Akbar's death years later, he expressed relief, exclaiming, 'The great troubler of the peace of India is gone.'[131]

On his deathbed Aurangzeb seems to have reflected on a long and bitter existence, writing to his sons, 'I have a dread for my salvation, and with what torments I may be punished. Though I have strong reliance on the mercies and bounties of God, yet regarding my actions, fear will not quit me;'[132] and, 'I have committed numerous crimes, and know not with what punishments I may be seized.'[133] Deeply fearful of the war of succession which he rightly suspected would follow his death, Aurangzeb, like his own father Shah Jahan, attempted to implement the Timurid solution, leaving a will which would partition the empire into appanages, divided amongst his three surviving sons. His divisions were generous: Kam Baksh would receive Bijapur and Haydarabad; Azam Shah (the later Emperor Bahadur Shah) would take Agra and the provinces of Deccan, Malwa, Ahmadabad, and Gujarat; while Muhammad Muazzam would receive Delhi, Kabul, and all other territories. Aurangzeb's attempt to return to the classic princely appanages of his Mongol-Timurid ancestors was as unsuccessful as his father's had been. Azam Shah urged his younger brothers to accept the terms, even offering to give them the additional territories of Gujarat and Ajmer, but the two brothers refused the offer. Both were killed in the succession war which followed.[134]

How Succession Wars Served the Dynasty: Benefits of Turco-Mongol Tradition

It is possible to identify in Islamic Central Asia the origins of notions of rivalry, loyalty and political entitlement which were embodied in Mughal imperial traditions and which defined Mughal acceptance of sovereignty and political viability. Other Turco-Mongolian empires, notably the Ottomans, Uzbeks, and Safavids, initially used similar succession practices (applying the principle of tanistry linked, as in the Mughal case, with the assignment of princely appanages), but they eventually created alternative systems which successfully contained succession rivalries within the palace, thereby avoiding expensive and destructive wars. Yet throughout the period of greatest Mughal prosperity and strength the absence of a fixed law of inheritance nearly guaranteed the outbreak of a war of succession on the death or deposition of each monarch, and although these wars are described in the chronicles as destructive, ranging across the land, laying waste and destroying property, the Mughals never successfully constructed an alternative, less traumatic, method of ordering succession. An examination of the roots of this tradition and its links to Mughal ideas of political legitimacy explains not only how the Mughals created their system of succession but also why they displayed such unwavering loyalty to a principle which has most often been viewed as inefficient and often wantonly destructive.

That the origins of their succession system can be directly traced to the practices of their Mongol-Timurid predecessors is a fact the Mughals themselves were quick to acknowledge, and the appanage system derived from Central Asian tradition surely played a role in inspiring and encouraging the bloody Mughal succession wars that occurred with almost every generation. Inexplicably, princely appanages have been consistently ignored in contemporary studies of Mughal succession conflicts, but the degree to which these positions, even modified to discourage childhood assignments, offered Mughal princes autonomous bases of power – military, economic, and political – must be explored as it relates to their ability to wage war and wield influence. The benefits to the dynasty were obvious, however, in that more often than not, a qualified candidate for king of an actively expansionist empire emerged from the fracas already in control of a successful ruling bureaucracy, military force, treasury, administrative system, and, perhaps most importantly, networks of influence and patronage that extended across the subcontinent, supporting and affirming his rule, drawing centralizing influences outward to the margins of empire. Even with sixteenth-century modifications of princely governorships and increased imperial control over the actions of the royal princes, Mughal wars of succession were allowed to rage unabated.

A further benefit accrued to the Mughals from their loyalty to Turco-Mongol tradition. While in Central Asia the tradition of tanistry had often 'resulted in the regular re-subjugation and reintegration of clans, affirming their social coherence among the otherwise centrifugal forces of steppe society,' hundreds of years later, in imperial India, as a recent study of princely politics has shown, tanistry continued to allow those in opposition to the center of power to remain within the orbit of the ruling family.[135] Through alliance with rival princes, leaders of viable factions were given a safe outlet for the expression of public opposition to their fathers and brothers. Several scholars have noted that princely factions were not defined by religion or race; instead, alliances could be, and often were, based on general dissatisfaction with the ruling center.[136] In his own rebellious youth, one of Jahangir's alliances had been with those who had formerly followed Akbar's rebellious brother, Mirza Hakim, in Kabul. Lala Beg Kabuli, Khwaja Dost

Muhammad and Zamana Beg all joined Jahangir's service and rose to power when he became emperor.[137] Having first allied with them as a mutinous prince, Jahangir brought a remarkable coalition of 'formerly marginal Afghans, Shaykhzadas, Mirzas, Kashmiris and Pahari and Bundela Rajputs' into the mainstream imperial establishment.[138]

As focal points of political opposition to their father and to each other, rival princes offered viable alternative loci of power to which the loyalty of alienated, disenfranchised, dissatisfied and recalcitrant elites could be attached. For example, Mughal courtiers and allied chieftains had justifiable qualms regarding the ability to rule of emperors Humayun and Jahangir – both were known drug addicts, among other concerns. During their reigns, rivals from *within* the royal family allowed the opposition to coalesce around alternative Mughal power centers; the threat of deposition was thereby expressed relatively harmlessly toward individuals rather than against the dynasty as a whole. Retaining Turco-Mongol traditions of universal legitimacy and princely power offered India's imperial dynasty a critical safety valve which effectively positioned the royal family above the individual, protecting and sustaining their power as a group. As in Timurid Mawarannahr until the arrival of the foreign power of the Uzbeks, individual rulers faced constant rivalries within the family but the skirmishes were internal scuffles that remained, however fierce and bloody, comfortably under the greater dynastic umbrella.

Divine Sanction

The Mughals were able to create a successful and centralized monarchy which faced remarkably little in the way of serious external threats. The subject population and the aristocracy seem to have accepted, with varying degrees of displeasure, this imperial lineage; for well over two hundred years the most serious threat to Mughal sovereignty lay in the regular bitter and bloody conflicts which sprang from within the royal family itself. Yet while the succession wars exposed the authority and legitimacy of each succeeding emperor to very public scrutiny at the time of his accession, there seems to have been no subsequent crises of legitimacy for the new monarch, for yet another survival of the

Central Asian past asserted that individual legitimacy was framed not only in dynastic claims but also in terms of divine sanction. Political legitimacy for Chingis Khan had included the conviction that 'God had designated him the sole legitimate ruler of the world,'[139] and biographers of Timur wrote, 'Whenever God Almighty exalts any person to the throne of sovereignty, he confers on him a special dignity and wisdom, by means of which he renders mankind obedient to him.'[140] By Akbar's time this heavenly sanction had evolved into an assertion of a 'divinely illuminated right of the Emperor to rule mortals with lesser qualities.'[141] While any and all Timurid royal sons had the right to claim political sovereignty, those successfully enthroned defended their victories with claims of heavenly support. Their very success served as evidence that their claim to power was legitimate.

Jahangir confirmed this in his commentary regarding the unsuccessful claims of his son Khusraw. 'They [the followers of Khusraw] were, of course, unaware of the fact that the rule of empire and royal command (*umur-i sultanat u jahanbani umari*) are not something which can be carried out by a couple of intellectually deficient (*naqis 'aqli*) individuals. Whom does the All-Giving Creator consider worthy (*shayista*) of this glorious and noble authority? And upon whose shoulders has he draped this robe of honor (*khil'at*)?'[142] The Mughal wars of succession, then, became an opportunity to illustrate the preference of the deity by establishing the identity of the next monarch. A chronicler explained the success of Aurangzeb in defeating his brother, the favorite and chosen successor, Dara Shikoh, as a heavenly intervention: 'The charge [of rule] was accordingly undertaken by the prince [Dara Shikoh], but Providence had determined otherwise. The country was destined to be ruled by a more just and better prince, and every circumstance which occurred in those days combined to assist him in obtaining the throne.'[143] In a letter to his father, Aurangzeb described a similar justification. 'It is clear to Your Majesty,' he wrote, 'that God Almighty bestows his trusts on one who discharges the duty of cherishing his subjects and protecting the people. It is manifest and clear to wise men that a wolf is not fit for a shepherd.'[144]

Indirect as the succession may have been, the legitimacy of the dynastic pattern would not be questioned. Not only did princely succession wars result in the reintegration of opposition groups, but they also offered Timurid-Mughal princes an opportunity to publicly establish their standing in the eyes of providence; the victorious successor to the Mughal throne proved God's sanction by the very fact of his victory. While the uncertainty of succession proved to be periodically divisive and destructive, it was closely bound to the Timurid tradition of universal sovereignty and supported by divine sanction, whereby individual and dynastic claims to rule 'rested on an ultimate legitimacy far surpassing the accidents of conquest, coup, or succession.'[145] As a critical link to their Timurid steppe heritage, the principle of tanistry remained central to Mughal understanding of dynastic legitimacy and was never substantially modified or reformed. Although it provoked devastating wars among brothers, and would eventually result in an indirect dynastic line, for the hundreds of years of Mughal rule in India, Turco-Mongol tradition defined individual rights to sovereignty and political legitimacy.

CHAPTER FIVE

CONCLUSION: IMAGINING KINGSHIP

The Uzbek confederation's conquest of Mawarannahr was absolute; having fled to India, the Timurid-Mughals would never return to their ancestral capitals of Samarqand and Herat. Those who survived the invasion and managed to make their way south were deeply aware of the cultural and political power of the Timurid legacy they had inherited, and in the bitterness of exile they remained devoted to developing and maintaining a set of shared Timurid symbols and ideals. Resounding imperial success apart, their forcible migration remained a defining event of the Timurid-Mughal community, inspiring regular efforts to assert their ancestral, cultural, ideological and territorial legacy.

Mughal loyalty to the Timurid legacy was demonstrated in almost all facets of imperial life. Scholars have explored Mughal military structures, for example, and affirm the dynasty's adherence, albeit with some modification, to Mongol military strategies and decimal-based troop organization.[1] Others have emphasized the entrenched loyalty of the Mughals to their ancestral allies among the Naqshbandi order of Sufis, whose expansion into the subcontinent had been facilitated by Mughal patronage during the imperial conquest, resulting in the establishment of 'an informal aristocratic Naqshbandi lobby at the Mughal court.'[2] Frustrated by his inability to influence the sixth Mughal emperor, Aurangzeb, a disgruntled Chishti shaykh wrote that, 'the Emperor of Hindustan is a descendant of Amir Timur and Amir

Conclusion: Imagining Kingship

Timur was spiritually attached to Shah-i Naqshband. These Turanians, all and every one of them, are connected with the Naqshbandi order and they do not attach value to any other *silsilah*.'[3] It was in many ways that the Mughals made deliberate efforts to 'remember' their legacy, privileging those components of their communal identity which would serve to unite, legitimize and sustain them: warfare and worship; charismatic ancestry and systems of political power; language, family relationships, inheritance and succession; aesthetic and literary understandings, among others.

Yet Timurid identity itself had been a profoundly hybrid cultural system, defined by regular deliberate references to those categories of culture recognized as Chingisid and Islamicate, themselves the accumulation of popular markers of kingship, spirituality and power. The boundaries of identity in Timurid Mawarannahr were drawn by porous and elastic membranes; its strength was driven by its highly adaptive character. It was an elaborate, complex and dynamic understanding of culture and legacy, developed at times deliberately and self-consciously over a hundred years of Timurid rule in Central Asia, that would be used to shape the Timurid royal court in India.

The protagonists of our discussion, the Timurid exiles – those imperial dynasts who invested time, energy and thought into the deliberate production of an imperial identity in India – were pehaps aware of the multi-valenced quality of their inheritance and of their continued fabrication. In forming a workable imperial narrative in India, the Timurid-Mughals did not draw absolute boundaries between the contingent cultural categories within which they were working. In the midst of conquest, their founder, Babur, even while describing both imperial identity and geography in sharp theatrical dichotomies – as Hindu versus Muslim; *ghazi* versus *kafir*; Indian versus Turk – employed and united men of 'different ethnicities and faiths (often against their coreligionists) and engender[ed] new patterns of circulation.'[4] In other words, while the establishment of Timurid kingship in India required the very public iteration of Timurid cultural and political loyalty, it was in a constant process of assimilation and adaptation that the Timurids culled and modified a wide variety of local and imported understandings of ethical and legitimate kingship. Having themselves sprung from a number of sources and influences, these attributes became welded to Mughal identity and rule.

It is in this context that the Mughal's adoption of the Hindu court tradition of the *darshan* can be best understood – its early acceptance and lasting power at the Mughal court perhaps due to its ability to simultaneously satisfy traditional understandings of kingship in both the Timurid dynastic and South Asian imperial ruling traditions. Darshan, with its origins in Hindu religious practices in viewing images of the gods, is 'the visual perception of the sacred,' in the form of an image or in the flesh.[5] Rather than simple passive viewing, darshan implies active and creative seeing: the worshippers take darshan (*darshan lena*), while the deity gives darshan (*darshan dena*).[6] Darshan is, in other words, mutually participatory – one sees the deity while being seen by the deity, in an act of reciprocity that 'lies at the heart of Hindu worship.'[7] At some point the auspicious act of darshan became an attribute of Hindu kingship – when used to describe a viewing of the king, by implication the act of offering darshan made explicit imperial claims of sacral kingship.

The gaze had enormous power at the royal court of Hindu kings. 'Let alone conversation, even the interchange of glances with the noble raises one to an exalted state ... Seeing was arguably the most developed sense in court circles and the act of looking and viewing was imbued with heavily coded meaning.'[8] A medieval sanskrit treatise, the Natyashastra, offered a list of one-hundred and forty-four types of 'glance' or 'look,' and twenty-five gestures of the eyeballs, eyelids, and eyebrows, 'clearly drawn from what must have been a complex ocular "language" at court.'[9] Medieval court manuals describe the character of a man, his internal disposition, as made clear by the movements of his eyes, and so laden with meaning did the movement of the eye become that the anxious courtier was advised to greet the king, quickly make his prostration, and then direct his eyes upon the ruler 'as if he were the newly risen moon,' the supplicant's frozen gaze thereby reducing the potential for any inauspicious blinks or facial twitches.[10] This can also be read as an affirmation of the sacred quality of Hindu kingship – the king's every act reflects divine references, and he is described as 'like the sun, because no one can dare look at him with hostile eyes, and like the moon because he gives satisfaction to all beings by appearing before them.'[11] So profound was the effect of the royal glance that what a courtier sought from the king was not, in fact, an audience but a viewing, *darshan*.

It would be a mistake to argue that Mughal allusions and references to sacred kingship originated solely in a desire to appeal to their non-Muslim subjects, among many of whom semi-divine kingship was an established norm. Long before their arrival in India, the Timurids had expressed personal and dynastic connections to the divine and sacred. Timur and/or his immediate successors had toyed with the imagery of divine kingship in taking the title *Sahib Qiran*, among other manipulations of locally legitimizing signs and symbols.[12] As for Babur, 'even though he was a Muslim king ruling over a largely Muslim population, the aspect of religion that he had to interact with had little to do with law and doctrine. Instead, much of his time was spent in engaging with embodied symbols and performed myths.'[13] Humayun famously drew inspiration from astrology and the occult and at times deliberately designed his royal court as a backdrop for elaborate performances of imperial sacrality, such as the slow removal of a veil from before his face, accompanied by his courtiers' cries that, 'Light has shined forth.'[14]

It was surely no ideological leap for Akbar to have actively sought identification with the divine, and it was to that end that Akbar's panegyrist and chronicler Abu al-Fazl originally conflated the need for Timurid kings to be publicly accessible with the Hindu tradition of darshan, 'with all its connotations – secular and sacred.'[15] Abu al-Fazl describes Akbar as offering two forms of darshan, the first being a less publicly accessible appearance by the king in a palace audience hall, which limited the spectators to members of the nobility.[16] A visitor to the royal court emphasized the theatrical quality of the deliberately staged presentation: 'I found him in a Court, set above like a King in a Play, and all his Nobles and my selfe below on a stage covered with carpets,' and 'the Kinge sits in a little Gallery overhead ... the great men lifted on a stage as actors; the vulgar below, gazing on – that an easy description will informe of the place and fashion.'[17]

For the second, however, the king would appear to the general public at a palace window, known as the *jharoka-i darshan*. Akbar, who played with the imagery of the sun king, displayed himself daily, just after sunrise. A sect of emperor-worshippers, known as the *darshani-yya*, gathered at the daily imperial audience to prostrate themselves before the king and receive his blessing, they offered prayers for the emperor's health and safety, and many would fast until they had gazed upon the emperor's face.[18]

'Upon His Majesty's appearance, the assembled masses in the plain beneath the window perform their obeisance and all their temporal and spiritual desires are gratified ... The object of the institution of this mode of audience, which originated with the late Emperor Akbar, was to enable His Majesty's subjects to witness the simultaneous appearance of the sky-adorning sun and the world-conquering Emperor, and thereby receive without any obstacle or hindrance the blessing of both luminaries.' Abu al-Fazl may be describing an actual interaction between subject and ruler in this moment, adding, 'By their presence in this space ... the harassed and oppressed of the population may freely represent their wants and desires.'[19] Shah Jahan's chronicler, Lahauri, also seems to suggest the Mughal darshan as an opportunity to directly petition the emperor. 'Upon His Majesty's appearance, the assembled masses in the plain beneath the window perform their obeisance and all their temporal and spiritual desires are gratified.'[20] At the very least, petitions could be presented to the emperor's lackeys at the darshan: 'Written petitions gathered beneath the jharoka by the administrators of justice were then brought to the public audience hall (*Dawlat Khana-i Khass*) at the second court, where the emperor regularly held audiences after the darshan ceremony.'[21] The darshan became so integral a component of Mughal rule that not only did the emperor offer regular staged viewings at the window of the imperial palace, but even the imperial household tent of the relentlessly peripatetic Mughal kings, the *du ashiyana manzil*, was designed with a second story balcony and viewing window.[22] Although access to the ruler in fact varied wildly in different settings and periods, a regnal appearance at the *jharoka-i darshan*, balcony of viewing, at the very least implied the possibility of imperial intervention and the dispensation of justice.

Imperial Dispensation of Justice

As Muslims kings, a primary imperative of Timurid kingship lay in their close attention to perceived Islamic norms of legitimate rule. Across the fourteenth and fifteenth century Islamic world, the 'classical' understanding of the responsibilities of kingship emphasized above all else *'adalet*, justice, and the 'theme of the ruler as shepherd of his people.'[23] This popular understanding of the fundamental responsibilities of medieval and early modern Muslim rulers was believed to be an inheritance from the great pre-Islamic kings of Sassanid Persia, most specifically that of the legendary Iranian ruler Khusrau I Anushirvan (531–579 CE), who is famed for having hung a bell outside his palace so that any of his subjects who might require royal intervention could easily gain the attention of the king. The reasons and rewards of good kingship were described as a 'Circle of Justice': 'There is no king without an army, no army without wealth, no wealth without material prosperity, and no material prosperity without justice.'[24] *'Adalet* was of course interpreted in a variety of ways, yet in its most general form described the ruler rewarding those who do good and punishing those who do evil. The 'medieval Islamic theory of kingship' found support across the popular consciousness and became the most universally recognized trope of Islamic rule, public deference to which supported all of the region's ruling dynasties.

The Timurids were, of course, no exception, yet just how the Timurids chose to interpret the imperial responsibility of justice was perhaps most heavily influenced by a thirteenth-century Persian treatise, the *Akhlaq-i Nasiri*, composed by Khwaja Nasir al-Din Tusi.[25] Originally intended as advice literature for the Ismaili rulers of thirteenth-century Iran, in the wake of the Mongol invasion of west Asia its author merely re-wrote the introduction and presented his manuscript to the region's new conquerors – evidence and confirmation of the work's universal qualities, as was its immediate popularity within the medieval Mongol, Persian and Turkish political milieus. In later centuries Timur's descendant, the famed Sultan Husayn Bayqara of Herat, patronized scholarship based on the Nasirean ethos, and at least two imitations of the advice treatise were produced at his court.[26] In an illustration of the ubiquitous quality of Tusi's work, on the heels of the Uzbek rout of the Timurids, the author of one of these simplified, local interpretations of Tusi's political philosophy, Ikhtiyar al-Din al-Husayni, re-entitled his work *Akhlaq-i Humayun* and formally presented it to Babur, then in Kabul, to serve as an ethical and political guide to the last independent Timurid prince and his descendants.[27] Although offered a variety of local interpretations, the Mughals in India chose to return their allegiances to the earliest version and Tusi's original study became the central text representing Mughal morality and ruling ethics.

Tusi affirmed the concept of justice as the single most important attribute of kingship, yet his interpretation represented true justice as an act of balance among diverse and sometimes conflicting special interest groups within a single state. 'The affairs of living thus must be administered through cooperation (*shirkat u mu'awant*) which in turn depends on justice (*'adl*). If *'adl* disappears each will then follow his own desire ... But *Shari'a* cannot work without it being administered by a just king, whose principal duty is to bring the people in control with affection and favors.'[28] The necessity of tolerance, mutuality of interests, even the existence of a social contract between ruler and subject, are implicit in Tusi's argument. 'The principles underlying states derive from the agreement of the opinions of a community who, in respect of cooperation and mutual assistance, are like the members belonging to an individual; if such an agreement be commendable, we have a true state; otherwise it is false.'[29]

It is easy to understand Timurid-Mughal loyalty to Nasirean ethics, which was after all originally presented by the author to the non-Muslim Mongol rulers of newly conquered Iran as a manual for kingship – if it were to be appropriate for Mongol rule, Tusi's ethical construct could not advocate narrow, legalist adherence to Islamic law. The government of the realm, writes Tusi, must be virtuous, 'its purpose being the perfection of men, and its consequence the attainment of felicity.' In a statement remarkable in the context of medieval monarchy, Tusi asserts that legitimate government, 'holds fast to justice (*'adalat*), treating its subjects (*ri'ayat*) as friends ... [rather than] servants and slaves (*khawal u 'abid*).'[30]

Conclusion: Imagining Kingship

Tusi's message of justice found fertile ground in a society informed by Islamic mysticism and the Persian poetic culture which was ubiquitous in Ilkhanid, and later Timurid, Transoxiana. In the spirit of the 'questioning and self-reflection within Islam' that emerged in the wake of the Mongol conquest of Muslim west Asia and the steadily increasing involvement and engagement of the Sufi orders in regional politics, which operated as 'an assertion of the right of the individual to experiment with Islamic religious truth,' a remarkably influential literature of spirituality and ethics emerged, arguably the three most influential authors being Jalal al-Din Rumi, Hafez of Shiraz and Sa'di.[31] Their poetry shares a focus on issues of ethics and morality, articulates a vision of tolerance and social justice, rejects narrowly imagined religious heterodoxies, and offers a passionate spirituality grounded in Islam. Without denying the power of royalty, all three affirm Tusi's insistence on the existence of a social contract in which the ruler is required to impose justice and protect the subjects. In Sa'di's ethical construct, justice is key to legitimate rulership and it is the task of the ruler to serve his subjects.

> When an unjust ruler commits an injustice
> The world survives but he dies with his injustice ...
> The ruler does not deserve to sleep well
> When under him the strong exploit the weak.[32]

> Try to look after the poor and needy
> Do not think of your own well-being
> No-one will live in peace and comfort
> If you seek only your own betterment ...
> The sultan is a tree, his subjects are the roots
> The tree stands on the strength of its roots.[33]

Sa'di's direct advice to rulers, as much as that of Tusi, resonates in the history of Timurid-Mughal princely ethics; the influence of Sa'di's parables is evident in the behaviors and religious/ethical understandings of the Mughal kings of India, strongly evoking Jahangir's respectful visit to the Hindu ascetic, Jadrup.

> 'A reclusive dervish was living in an isolated spot,' Sa'di wrote. 'A Shah passed him by but, given the lack of need associated with

the realm of contentment, the dervish did not acknowledge him. Given the majesty of kingship, the sultan was hurt and said, 'These ascetics are like animals and lack civility and humanity.' The vizier approached the dervish and said, 'Chivalrous sir, the lord of the land passed you by. Why did you not display humbleness and show respect to him?' He replied, 'Tell the Sultan to expect service from one who expects a favor from him. And further than that, he should know that *shahs exist for protecting the subjects, not the subjects for serving the shah* .... The sheep do not exist for the shepherd, it is the shepherd that must serve the sheep.'[34]

For all their liberality and willingness to forgive libertine excesses, the *ghazals* of Hafiz, like the other texts held most dear at the Timurid-Mughal courts, reflect a general preoccupation with the ethics of kingship. Hafiz offered a running commentary on courtly behavior, emphasizing the transience of power and riches, the need for justice and social harmony. Reinforcing the Timurid-Mughal's highly developed sense of the centrality of regnal justice, Hafiz wrote, 'The king will gain more from one hour of justice, than from one hundred years of worship and prayer.'[35] Modern scholarship has made the connection to a broader popular engagement with these questions, writing of the ruler, as portrayed by Hafiz, 'If the king is, ideally, the Perfect Man of his age, he is also, in a particular sense, Everyman, embodying the highest ideals of humanity. Combining temporal and spiritual rule, he *incarnates the dual idea of justice and love expressed by Nasir al-Din Tusi* and bears the responsibility for upholding and maintaining the social order of which love is the guiding force.'[36] And while Hafiz was willing to step well outside of the boundaries of Islamic law, engaging in and excusing behaviors condemned in narrower legalist understandings, he, like the mutually reinforcing Rumi and Sa'di, carefully presented a fundamentally Muslim identity, positioning his ethical imprecations in an Islamic context, writing 'I have seen no verses sweeter than yours, Hafiz, {I swear} by that Quran you hold in your breast.'[37]

Rather than speculate on the degree to which this body of literature may have influenced the construction of religio-political thought in medieval Central Asia, we can at least assert that it found comfortable

CONCLUSION: IMAGINING KINGSHIP

accommodation in the pre-existing conditions of Timurid society. These texts represent the culmination of a ruling ideology that became a critical common reference point for Timur's successors, defining and articulating a vision of human relations, ethics, justice and kingship. The presence of this literary canon, embodying a set of moral and political understandings, may explain the highly resistant Timurid character of Mughal political culture and ethics. Articulating what was an already firmly held ethical paradigm, the literature came to serve a central importance in supporting the claims of the Mughals in India, where they supplied the dynasty with an articulate and scholarly argument which could be strategically expounded to make possible and to justify rulership of South Asia within the context of a recognized and legitimate Sunni political discourse, and without threatening their formal religious loyalties.

The paternalist benevolence of this tolerant humanism[38] suited well the reigning ethos of the Mughal kings who ruled over a diverse and polyglot empire in which Islam was a minority religion. The emperor Akbar's chief minister, Abu al-Fazl, declared the *Akhlaq-i Nasiri* among the five most important works in the library of the emperor Akbar, had it read aloud to the emperor nearly every day, and claimed it had enormous influence on Akbar's governing philosophy. Not only did it become a staple in the curriculum of Mughal madrasas but the imperial comittment to Tusi's vision of rule was made explicit to local Mughal administrators across the empire, when they were instructed to be particularly attentive to Tusi's message of acceptance.[39]

The imperial library of the Mughals reflects intellectual shifts in the interests of the various emperors yet illustrates the degree to which the Mughal dynasty remained loyal to the personal and political values of their ancestors in Central Asia. With a library of twenty-four thousand volumes available to him, the intellectual foundations of even the most spiritually curious of kings, Akbar, were reflected in the texts he chose to have read aloud to him daily: Tusi's *Akhlaq-i Nasiri*, Sa'di's *Gulistan*, Rumi's *Masnawi* (which Akbar is said to have memorized), Firdowsi's *Shahnama* and various works of local and family history.[40] While the list of most favored books affirms the dynasty's religious loyalty, not surprisingly, it additionally supports the perception that most Mughal kings retained a personal and informal approach to religion and were not terribly interested in Quranic exegesis or law. On the death of Akbar's court poet, Abu al-Fazl's brother Fayzi, his library of four thousand manuscripts was placed in the larger imperial Mughal library and classified by merit, in categories of superior, middling and inferior. Mughal literary tastes and values can be perhaps understood by the organization of these additions to the imperial library: those judged superior were works of poetry, medicine, astrology and music. Middling books included philosophy, tasawwuf (Sufism) and astronomy. The least valued were works of tafsir (exegisis), hadith (tradition), fiqh and sacred law.[41] The emperor Aurangzeb has been portrayed as an exception to the Mughal pattern of religious toleration, yet he too left his handwriting in the margins of the Mughal library's *Diwan-i Hafiz* and *Shahnama* manuscripts, the latter of which had been signed by all of the Mughal emperors from Babur to Aurangzeb.[42]

The influence of this literature came to be acknowledged and absorbed by not only the Persian and Turkic Central Asian individuals associated with the dynasty, nor even exclusively the Muslim members of the aristocracy, but by the entire Mughal court. As late as the reign of Shah Jahan, the Hindu court poet Chandra Bahan Brahman asserted that a particular selection of texts: Nasir al-Din Tusi's *Akhlaq-i Nasiri*, a respected later interpretation of it, the *Akhlaq-i Jalali*, by Jalal al-Din Davvani and the *Gulistan* and *Bustan* of Sa'di, defined the Mughal cultural code. It was through an awareness and understanding of this literature, he wrote in a letter of advice to his son, that young men could 'earn their capital, and be blessed with the fortunes of knowledge and good moral conduct.'[43] The markers of kingship described in these works were universally acknowledged among the northern Indian elites: Turani and Persian noblemen, local Muslims and even non-Muslims, easily and comfortably recognized the regular, deliberate references to the Mughal dynasts as 'just kings,' benevolent and tolerant, dispensing justice and charity. Descriptions by their courtiers of the Mughal kings as 'Anushirvans of their time,' can be read as obvious tropes, the most basic of legitimizing panegyrics.

The emperor Jahangir, perhaps more deliberately than his immediate forebears, demonstrated a fascination with the Persianate model of Islamic sovereignty and its demands for royal justice and charity. Much of his memoir is devoted to asserting his compliance with medieval Islamic understandings of legitimate kingship. At least in theory, Jahangir accepted the responsibility of a Nasirean social contract, and described his own interpretation of the classic 'Circle of Justice': 'Whenever a just and equitable monarch's (*sulatin ma'dalat a'yin masruf*) mind and intention are turned to the people's welfare and the peasant's tranquility (*rafahiyat-i re'aya*), then prosperity, blessings, good crops and produce are immeasurable.'[44] Sensitive to calls for royal acts of justice, Jahangir's response to news of tyrannical behavior by the eunuchs of an important amir was to write immediately to chastise the offenders, claiming in his missive that his own 'sense of justice did not tolerate oppression and that in the scales of justice, greatness and smallness were not sanctioned.'[45]

Jahangir regularly and publicly confirmed his regnal emphasis on Islamic ideas of justice within the ideology of kingship as 'refuge to the oppressed and a protector of the fallen.'[46] His absorption with Perso-Islamic precedents for imperial responsibility was illustrated by his very first act as sovereign, ordering a golden 'Chain of Justice' (*silsilah-i 'adl* or *bustan zanjir-i 'adl*) strung with sixty bells and hung between the banks of the Yamuna river and the peak of the citadel at Agra, enabling petitioners to bypass those clerks at the imperial law courts (*mutasadiyan-i muhimat dar al-'adalat*) who were not attentive to the needs of the empire's subjects.[47] Those of the king's subjects who felt they had been wronged could in this way gain personal and direct access to the king, wellspring of imperial justice, in time of need. Miniature paintings of the period indicate that the 'chain of justice' remained in place in the period of Shah Jahan, who, like his father, was portrayed with it as backdrop. The first British ambassador to the Mughal court, Sir Thomas Roe, described Jahangir's subjects as slaves but commented that Jahangir too was 'in a kynd of reciprocal bondage,' describing the requirement of the king to make himself available at particular times of the day to dispense justice.[48]

During the reign of Jahangir, the compulsion to perform public displays of Perso-Islamic imperial justice could be satisfied by daily appearances at the viewing balcony; in acting out an explicitly Hindu religio-political ritual, an increasingly theatrical and performative darshan emerged at the Mughal court. Sir Thomas Roe describes a compulsory daily viewing, with personal justice meted out weekly. 'He comes every morning to a window called the *Jarruco* looking into a playne before his gate, and shows himself to the Common People ... he is tyed to observe these howres and Customes so precisely that if he were unseene one day and noe sufficient reason rendered the people would mutinie; two dayes noe reason can excuse, but that he must consent to open his doores and be seene by some to satisfye others. On Tuesday at the *Jarruco* he sitts in Judgment, never refusing the poorest mans Complaynt, where he hears with patience both parts.'[49]

The Hindu origins of the viewing tradition were universally known but not publicly acknowledged by members of the Mughal royal court, yet the act of darshan and the emperor's active and public dispensation of justice had become openly conflated as an ideal of legitimate kingship. The emperor's absence from the jharoka for more than a day or two was seen as a reason for public unrest, even mutiny.[50] Jahangir's memoirs describe the jharoka, like the regular offering of alms to the poor, as a duty of kingship, sometimes painful but always necessary. Powerfully affirming the access he offered to the general public, Jahangir explains his the public audience, 'as demanded by justice,' while on a journey to Ahmadabad. Complaining of pain, illness, and the severity of the heat, the emperor yet dispensed imperial law 'by the side of the river, where there is no kind of impediment like gates, walls, watchmen and guards.'[51]

Shah Jahan, noted for the increasingly rigid and formal setting of his court, would sit at the jharoka-i darshan every morning just at sunrise in order that 'the assembled masses in the plain beneath the window perform their obeisance and all their temporal and spiritual desires are satisfied.'[52] In its increasingly elaborate and unsubstantial manifestations, the jharoka yet satisfied Mughal promises of direct access, imperial intercession and justice, although it seems that few plaintiffs came before Shah Jahan.[53] While this public audience was staged as an affirmation of the accessibility of imperial justice, Shah Jahan's court historian mused that, due to the emperor's 'great solicitude,' Mughal imperial justice was already so complete and universal that few supplicants could be found who required the personal intervention of the king![54]

Of course maintaining a theoretical interest in the wellbeing of their subjects, no matter how well intentioned, did not always translate into successful imperial actions. A facetious comment made by Jahangir to a village blacksmith, at court to appeal for the emperor's intervention in a matter of the heart, ended with the blacksmith throwing himself from the palace window to prove to the emperor the depths of his passion for a local widow. Although Jahangir called for court physicians to tend to the man, the blacksmith died of his injuries. While his careless words had caused the death of the lovelorn blacksmith yet Jahangir did, somewhat apologetically, include the story in his memoirs, illustrating to his readers the degree to which this monarch, though a descendant of the world's greatest empire builders and appointed by God, was enacting the rites and rituals of legitimate Islamic kingship, personally and publicly dispensing justice amongst even the most lowly of his subjects.[55] And it was through the regular performance of Hindu acts of kingship that the Timurid kings of India came to express the responsibilities of Perso-Islamic rule.

The Timurid Kings of India

When the reluctant Central Asian prince Babur first conquered northern India he complained bitterly about the Indian climate and culture, the lack of melons and of medreses, but when, over one hundred years later, Shah Jahan sent armies north to re-conquer Transoxiana, his son, Murad Baksh, fled the city of Balkh, returning to India in disgrace. In a very telling commentary on the adaptation of the Timurid-Mughals to their subcontinental empire, when the outraged emperor demanded to know for what reason his son had deserted the Mughal army the prince replied that he could not bear the cold; he and his nobles 'were dreading the hardship of passing a winter in that clime.'[56] Although the re-conquest of Samarqand remained an evocative dream and the Mughal emperors continued to cling to their charismatic lineage, it is clear that by the end of the seventeenth century the Mughals had adapted to South Asia, and Timurid steppe culture had become a component, albeit foundational, of the greater Mughal-Indian synthesis.

Yet it is also clear that the political and social culture which which had been carefully constructed over generations to define and defend Timurid identity and legitimacy in Central Asia, had been neither lost nor abandoned in the Timurid flight, but would instead, to varying degrees, continue to be meticulously maintained at the Mughal royal court in India. Even as Babur and his following of refugees celebrated their remarkable new success in India, their fervent identification with the Timurid cultural complex – grounded in a bedrock of longing, bitterness and loss – led them and their descendants to remain loyal to those familiar, potent symbols of power and royalty which had so well defined and oriented Timurid imperial identity and legitimacy in Central Asia.

A recent study of Babur's memoirs describes his writings as an effort to demonstrate his legitimate right to rule due to his nature as 'the perfect man, or perfect ruler.'[57] In late Timurid Transoxiana the perfect ruler was a 'Persianized, Islamicized Turco-Mongol aristocrat ... an *adib*, a cultured, civilized man and therefore, partly for that reason, qualified to rule.'[58] It is clear that through the device of his own royal memoirs, Babur's descendant Jahangir articulated an ideology of kingship and right to rule that remained loyal to the model of his ancestors. His presentation of himself as a legitimate ruler had become embellished by powerful local attributes and acts of kingship such as the darshan, yet the ideology, the ethics, the aesthetics and values of the Mughal king were little modified in the generations since Babur's reluctant conquest of northern India.

The resulting cultural expression was neither unique nor original, but the result cannot be seriously contested. Despite the real fluidity of cultural boundaries in Mughal India, the identity of the ruling dynasty continued to be presented as self-evident, successfully supplying the Mughals with a shared bond which tied the community together culturally around a universally recognizable and legitimate kingship. The past served the dynasty as a source of inspiration, with which to revitalize, renew, even re-invent the Mughal understanding of their own political, spiritual and social selves. Even more fundamentally, it was through identifying as Timurids in exile that the Mughals and their followers understood their own place in the world and asserted a public face of legitimate rule. Their loyalty to the Timurid past would forever affect their ability as a dynasty to adopt and accept local customs or derive new understandings of culture, family relationships, politics, religion and law under the influence of their South Asan conquest territories.

NOTES

Introduction

1. Peter Jackson, *The Delhi Sultanate*, NY: Cambridge University Press, 1999, 3.
2. These few include Maria Eva Subtelny, who has worked on the Mughal retention of Timurid gardens, Richard Foltz, who published a study of Mughal links to Central Asia, and Stephen F. Dale, who has identified the Mughals as the principal heirs of the Timurids, among others.
3. John Richards, *The New Cambridge History of India: The Mughal Empire*, New Delhi: Cambridge University Press, 1993, repr. 1995, 2.
4. Ibid.
5. Ibid., 3.
6. Letter from Abu al-Fadl Allami, a grandson of Sultan Husayn Bayqara of Herat, to Abd al-Rahim Khan-i Khanan, in Riazul Islam, *A Calendar of Documents on Indo-Persian Relations (1500–1700)*, Tehran, 1979/ 1982, 15.
7. Gulbadan Begim, *Humayunnama* (Persian text) *or The History of Humayun* (English text), Annette S. Beveridge, ed. and trans., Delhi: Idarah-i Adabiyat-i Delli, 1972. Quotes from Persian text, with translations by this author, unless noted. *Humayunnama*, 13–14.
8. Maria Eva Subtelny, "The Timurid Legacy: A Reaffirmation and a Reassessment," *Cahiers D'Asie Centrale*, 3–4 (1997), 14.
9. Muzaffar Alam and Sanjay Subrahmanyam, *The Mughal State, 1526–1750*, New Delhi: Oxford University Press, 1998, p. 5.
10. Stephen Frederick Dale, "The Legacy of the Timurids," *Journal of the Royal Asiatic Society*, Series 3, 8, 7 (1998), 43.

11. In so writing, I have been influenced by the writings of Finbarr Flood, *Objects of Translation: Material Culture and Medieval "Hindu-Muslim" Encounter*, Princeton University Press, 2009, 3.
12. Timon Screech, *The Shogun's Painted Culture: Fear and Creativity in the Japanese States, 1760–1829,* London: Reaktion Books, 2000, 12.

Prologue   Timurid Political Charisma and the Ideology of Rule

1. No region was as thoroughly destroyed in the Mongol onslaught as Transoxiana, and Khurasan was "comprehensively wrecked by Chingis Khan's youngest son, Tolui." See David O. Morgan, *The Mongols*, Cambridge, MA: Blackwell Publishers, 1986, reprint 1994, 41.
2. For a description of Chingis Khan's distribution of tribes, see Paul Kahn, *A Secret History of the Mongols: an Adaptation of the Yuan Cha'o Pi Shih*, Francis Woodman Cleaves, trans., Boston: Cheng & Tsui Company, 1984, 1998, 114–145. See also Morgan, *Mongols*, 89–90.
3. Douglas E. Streusand, *The Formation of the Mughal Empire*, Delhi: Oxford University Press, 1989, 29.
4. Morgan, *Mongols*, 41.
5. Thomas W. Lentz and Glenn D. Lowry, *Timur and the Princely Vision: Persian Art and Culture in the Fifteenth Century*, Los Angeles and Washington, D.C.: Los Angeles County Museum of Art and the Arthur Sackler Gallery, Smithsonian Institution, 1989, 24.
6. The *ulus* was a territorial unit, described variously as a tribe, community, "nation." See Stephen F. Dale, *The Garden of the Eight Paradises: Babur and the Culture of Empire in Central Asia, Afghanistan and India (1483–1530)*, Leiden: Brill, 2004, 111.
7. Beatrice Forbes Manz, *The Rise and Rule of Tamerlane*, NY: Cambridge University Press, 1999, 4.
8. Beatrice Forbes Manz, "Mongol History rewritten and re-lived," *REMMM* 89-90 (2002), 136.
9. Timur is better known in the West as Tamerlane, which is itself a convolution of the Persian name which was given to him after an early accident crippled an arm and leg: *Timur-i Leng*, or Timur the Lame.
10. The Chaghatay ulus, so-called because it was the inheritance of Chingis Khan's second son Chaghatay, was originally made up of those Central Asian regions later known as Transoxiana in the west and Mughulistan in the east. The split into two parts occurred gradually during the fourteenth century. A fuller description of this territory is included below, in the discussion of the region at the time of Timur's death.

11. The peoples of twelfth century Mongolia had become so intermarried with Turkic tribes that to distinguish one from another is impossible on any basis beyond that of the language spoken by a particular group. See Morgan, *Mongols*, 56. Some consider the Barlas to have been a Turkicized (Turkish speaking) Mongol clan, rather than of pure Turkish origin. Timur himself claimed to share an ancestor with Chingis Khan, although never claimed direct descent. Fifteenth century Timurid histories state that the Barlas tribe had been assigned as a military adjunct to the Chaghatay retinue prior to the death of Chingis Khan in 1227. See Lentz and Lowry, *Timur and the Princely Vision*, 27. His descendants, however, emphasizing Timurid genealogy over Chingisid, were careful to refer to themselves as Turks.
12. Beatrice Forbes Manz, "Tamerlane's Career and Its Uses," *Journal of World History*, 13.1 (2002), 3.
13. It has been suggested recently that this title was not chosen by Timur but assigned to him by his immediate successors. See Ahmad Azfar Moin, "Islam and the Millenium: Sacred Kingship and Popular Imagination in early Modern India and Iran," unpublished PhD dissertation, University of Michigan, 2010.
14. Manz, "Tamerlane's Career," 1.
15. Manz, "Mongol History," 138.
16. *Tuzukat-i Timuri*, ed. Major Davey, Oxford, 1783, 32, as quoted in Hamid Algar, "Political Aspects of Naqshbandi History," *Naqshbandis: Cheminements et situation actuelle d'un ordre mystique musulman*, Actes de la Table Ronde de Sèvres, ed. Marc Gaborieau, et al., eds., Editions Isis: Istanbul, 1985, 1990,124.
17. His captive biographer Ibn Arabshah, accused Timur of preferring Chingisid law over that of Islam, and claimed "he must be accounted an infidel." See Ahmed Ibn Arabshah, *Tamerlane or Timur, the Great Amir*, J.D. Sanders, trans., Lahore: Progressive Books, 1976, 299.
18. Manz, "Mongol History," 142.
19. Ibn Arabshah, *Tamerlane*, 321.
20. Ibid., 298, for a discussion of Timur's choice of companions. In illustration of the Timurid cultural fusion, Timur's marriage to Tukal Khanim, daughter of Khizr Khwaja Oghlan, was celebrated in Muslim and Mongol traditions. As the bride approached, the men of Timur's retinue set out to greet her. "They went for fifteen days and performed the rituals of *nithar* [the ceremony of coins and jewels sprinkled over the heads of bride and groom] and the presentation of horses ... All along the way elaborate *toys* [feasts] were held at every *yurt* and on Wednesday the first of Rabi' 800 [November 22, 1397] the *Nushuba* of the age [Nushuba was the queen of ancient Barda in Azerbaijan; the name also means "the water of life"] was ushered with all

ceremony into the world-receiving court of the Alexander of his time ... The *qadis* [judges] and *ulama* [religious scholars] were summoned." Sharafuddin Ali Yazdi, "Zafarnama," *A Century of Princes*, Wheeler M. Thackston, trans. and ed., Cambridge, MA: The Aga Khan Program for Islamic Architecture (1989), p. 87. Of course, the reference to an "Alexander of his age" would have been a common trope for rulers in the Islamic world, but here we see it coupled with pre-Islamic Turco-Mongol traditions as well as locally meaningful evocations of legitimate kingship and power--an illustration of the author's more general assertion that identity and legitimacy are understood to be contingent and multiple.

21. No evidence of a kitabkhana in Timur's Samarqand exists, although his interest in the capture of artists of the book (calligraphers, literary scholars, miniaturists and book binders) suggests that manuscript production was occurring in his capital city. His successors, beginning immediately with Shahrukh, are known to have established kitabkhanas in the major cities of Mawarannahr and Khurasan.
22. Ibn Arabshah, *Tamerlane*, 299.
23. Ibid., 222–3.
24. Zahir al-Din Muhammad Babur, *Baburnama (Vekayi), Critical Edition Based on Four Chaghatay Texts*, Eiji Mano, ed., Japanese and Chaghatay, 4 vols., Kyoto: Syokado,1995, p. 69. Citations from Mano edition with translations by this author unless noted.
25. Ibn Arabshah, *Tamerlane*, 223.
26. Ruy Gonzales de Clavijo, *Embassy to Tamerlane, 1403–1406*, Guy le Strange, trans., NY and London: Harper Brothers, 1928, 280.
27. Ibn Arabshah, *Tamerlane*, 216.
28. Clavijo, *Embassy*, 238 and Ibn Arabshah, *Tamerlane*, 216. See also Lentz and Lowry, *Princely Vision*, 34.
29. At the time of Timur's death, the heartland of his conquest territories had been the sparsely populated region known as *Mawarannahr* (Transoxiana), the land area between the two great rivers of Central Asia, the Amu Darya and the Syr Darya (known in the Western world by their Greek names, the Oxus and the Jaxartes). In the fourteenth century, the northern portions of this territory comprised primarily an arid steppe populated sparsely by nomadic pastoralists, surrounding the oasis cities of Khiva and Tashkent. In the south, high mountains were split by small, fertile river valleys in which semi-nomadic peoples traveled fixed seasonal migration routes, settled populations farmed, and the cities of Samarqand and Bukhara were sustained and linked by ancient trade routes. The Iranian territories were markedly urban, settled, Islamicate and culturally sophisticated, including

the rich oasis city of Herat, the capital city of Khurasan, the northeastern portion of the Iranian plateau and the only part that remained closely tied to Mawarannahr after Timur's death.
30. Manz, "Tamerlane's Career," 6.
31. Lentz and Lowry, *Princely Vision*, 74.
32. This genealogy is also included within the Timurid biographies, such as Mir Dawlatshah Samarqandi's *Tadhkirat al-shu'ara* (a partial translation of which has been included in the bibliography), which contains biographical sketches of Timurid rulers as well as of contemporary poets. It was completed in 1487.
33. Dale, *Garden*, 135.
34. Lentz and Lowry, *Princely Vision*, 95.
35. Ibid., 168 and 162.
36. Ibid., 113.

Chapter 1   Babur and the Timurid Exile

1. Edward Said, "Reflection on Exile," *Granta* 13 (1984), 159.
2. The reasons for and expressions of general admiration for Timurid court culture by rivals kingdoms are covered more thoroughly in chapter two of this study.
3. In his rich and thoughtful study of Babur and the Timurid movement into India, *The Garden of the Eight Paradises*, Stephen Dale identifies the development of nostalgia among Babur's refugee following. I have found it very useful to explore in greater detail the elements of that nostalgia, driven not only by territtorial loss but perhaps due to an even greater degree by the nature of the Uzbek conquest of Mawaarannahr, accompanied as it was by humiliation and trauma.
4. Screech, *Painted Culture*, 11.
5. At the time of Babur's birth Mawarannahr was ruled by five autonomous Timurid princes, including Babur's father and three paternal uncles, all descendants of Timur's third son Miranshah. The nominal governor of the region was Sultan Ahmad Mirza (1451–1494), who was the eldest of Miranshah's sons but in fact controlled only the two great cities of Samarqand and Bukhara. His brother, Sultan Mahmud Mirza (1453–1495) ruled until a year before his death the region of the upper Oxus river valley, including the centers of Hisar, Termez, Qunduz and Badakhshan. The third brother, Ulugh Beg Kabuli (d. 1502), was ruler of Kabul, while Babur's father, Umar Shaykh Mirza (1456–1494), fourth brother, ruled the valley of Ferghana, a rich agricultural region in eastern Mawarannahr. The fifth ruling Timurid prince was Sultan Husayn Bayqara (1469–1506), a descendant

of Timur's eldest son Umar Shaykh, who controlled the enormous appanage of Iranian Khurasan, centered on Shahrukh's capital city of Herat, and Khwarazm, stretching from below the Aral Sea to Qandahar in Central Afghanistan. To the east, between Mawarannahr and Western China, was the region known as Mughulistan, Mongol territories ruled by Babur's maternal grandfather Yunus Khan (d. 1487), who was descended from Chingis Khan through his second son Chaghatay. Yunus Khan's eldest son, Sultan Mahmud Khan (d. 1509), ruled the city and hinterland of Tashkent, while his brother Sultan Ahmad Khan (d. 1504) controlled Aqsu and the region of Alti Shahr (Six Cities) in northern and eastern Mughulistan along the southern skirt of the Tien Shan Mountains. Both sons were married to women of the Dughlat Mongol clan, who historically had been the amirs of Kashgar under Chaghatay.

6. Uzbek is perhaps an inappropriate term to use for this group, although it is the common usage among modern scholars. Properly speaking, these are Jochids, descendants of Chingis Khan through his eldest son, Jochi, with the group we are most interested in being the descendants of Jochi's son Shiban, hence the appellation "Shibanid." The descendants of another of Jochi's sons, Toqay Timur, became known in the Persian sources as the Ashtarkhanids, because of their origins in Astrakhan. Within a year of Shibani Khan's death the Shibanid Uzbeks lost control of Mawarannahr to rival clans. They competed with the Ashtarkhanids for control of Central Asia through the late sixteenth century in a relationship that resulted in a bipartite Uzbek state from 1612 to the early eighteenth century, when it disintegrated under the pressure of decentralizing amirs.

7. Babur, *Baburnama*, Mano, ed., 152.
8. Ibid., 290.
9. Ibid., 321-2.
10. Ibid., 322.
11. Ghiyas al-Din Muhammad Khwandamir, "Habib al-Siyar," *Century of Princes*, 232-3.
12. Claudia Card, "Rape as a Weapon of War," *Hypatia*, Vol. 11, No. 4, Women and Violence (Autumn, 1996), 5-18. The particulars of these events were carefully recorded in the chronicles of the period, most notably, the Baburnama and Tarikh-i Rashidi. In a very useful appendix to her translation of the Humayunnama, relying on these earlier works as her sources, Annette Beveridge detailed, without comment, the names and fates of many of these women. It is surprising, then, that while there have been several important studies of the late Timurid world, and of Babur, in the past decade, to this date no examination of the Timurid expulsion has addressed

this aspect of the the Uzbek conquest of Timurid Mawarannahr. That nearly all of Babur's immediate female relatives (among many others) were subject to rape, conquest marriage and/or enslavement in the decades of the Uzbek advance, must have greatly increased the degree of humiliation and trauma felt by the Timurids as they fled as refugees—a not inconsequential component of their cultural and political recovery in their new South Asian territories. While our sources are not explicit in describing the impact of these traumas on the survival and re-establishment of the Timurids in India, I have found it very useful to establish a context for these events in modern studies of refugee and exile. This scholarship argues that the degree of humiliation felt by surviving refugee communities is directly tied to the depth of their nostalgia and efforts to memorialize that which has been irrevocably lost.

13. Babur, *Baburnama*, Mano, ed., p. 141.
14. Mirza Haydar Dughlat, *Tarikh-i Rashidi: A History of the Khans of Moghulistan*, W.M. Thackston, ed. and trans. Persian and English 2 vols. Cambridge, Massachusetts: Harvard University Department of Near Eastern Languages and Civilizations, 1996, 133; Gulbadan, *Humayunnama*, 3 (Persian text). Of course, Uzbek marriages to the women of the Chaghatay branch of Chingisid Mongols would also have been a conscious enhancement of their Jochid lineage, particularly in the Timurid-Chaghatayid lands of Mawarannahr and Mughulistan. Hence Khanzada's value as half-Timurid, half-Chaghatay, like her full brother Babur.
15. Babur, *Baburnama*, Mano, ed., 142. She is listed as a guest at the wedding feast of Babur's son, Mirza Hindal, held in Agra in 1537 and, according to Beveridge, seems to have been given a village near Kabul by Babur as reward for her loyalty. It was during this episode in Pishgar, by the way, that Babur records having met a 111-year-old woman who remembered the occasion of Timur's invasion of Hindustan. She herself had a relative who had served in that army. It is interesting to speculate how this conversation may have influenced Babur's thinking when he much later chose to expand from Kabul into Hindustan. See Babur, *Baburnama*, Mano, ed.,143.
16. Dughlat, *Tarikh*, 132.
17. Ibid., 133; Gulbadan, *Humayunnama*, Appendix, 264, 265 and 284.
18. Gulbadan, *Humayunnama*, Appendix, 290.
19. Dughlat, *Tarikh*, 95; Gulbadan, *Humayunnama*, Appendix, 272.
20. Gulbadan, *Humayunnama*, Appendix, 223- 24.
21. Dughlat, *Tarikh*, 63–4; Gulbadan, *Humayunnama*, Appendix, 274.
22. Gulbadan, *Humayunnama*, Appendix, 289.

NOTES

23. Dughlat, *Tarikh*, 116; Gulbadan, *Humayunnama*, Appendix, 236.
24. Gulbadan, *Humayunnama*, Appendix, 294.
25. Babur, *Baburnama*, Mano, ed., 14; Gulbadan, *Humayunnama*, Appendix, 275.
26. Babur, *Baburnama*, Mano, ed., 323.
27. Gulbadan, *Humayunnama*, 31 and Appendix, 252.
28. Khwandamir, *Habib al-Siyar*, 232. See also Gulbadan, *Humayunnama*, Appendix, 263. She too is listed among the guests at Humayun's accessional feast in Agra, where she was described as living with a female cousin, wearing men's clothing, playing polo and manufacturing thumb-rings and arrows. See *Humayunnama*, p. 33. See also Balabanlilar, "Begims of the Mystic Feast," *The Journal of Asian Studies* Vol. 69, No. 1 (February) 2010, 123–147.
29. Gulbadan, *Humayunnama*, Appendix, 234.
30. Babur, *Baburnama*, Mano, ed., 322–3.
31. Ibid., p. 323. See also Gulbadan, *Humayunnama*, Appendix, 252.
32. Dughlat, *Tarikh*, 105.
33. Gulbadan, *Humayunnama*, Appendix, 271.
34. Shah Begum had good reasons to leave Kabul, for there she had attempted to foment rebellion against Babur in favor of her own grandson, and of course it was to find the grandson an appropriate kingdom that she eventually left.
35. Gulbadan, *Humayunnama*, Appendix, 265.
36. Babur, *Baburnama*, Mano, ed., 199.
37. Ibid., 334.
38. Dale, *Garden*, 292.
39. Ibid.
40. Gulbadan, *Humayunnama*, 13–14.
41. Ibid.
42. Ibid.; It is highly significant that the Timurid refugee community in Agra included many of the very same women we have previously counted among the direct victims of the Uzbek onslaught. Their influence on the emergent Timurid royal court in India should not be underestimated. Within five or six years, seven of Babur's paternal aunts, the daughters of Sultan Abu Sa'id Mirza (1424–1469), had made their way south, including Gauhar Shad Begim, Fakhr Jahan Begim along with her daughter, Kichak Begim, Badi al-Jamal Begim, Aq Begim Miranshahi and Bakht Sultan Begim, who came to India at Babur's request shortly after his conquest accompanied by her daughter, Afaq Begim, who arrived in Agra in 1528. Khadija Sultan Begim's circumstances are unclear; as a wife of Sultan Husayn Mirza, she had been enslaved by Shibani Khan on the conquest of Herat, but the sources place her in India in 1526. Also in India by 1531 was Agha Sultan Aghacha, a widow of Umar Shaykh Mirza and mother of Babur's half-sister Yadgar Sultan Begim. The daughters of

Babur's Chaghatay maternal uncles, Zaynab Sultan Khanim and Muhibb Sultan Khanim, made their way to Timurid India. Babur's sister, Khanzada Begim, who had been left as ransom in Samarqand and forcibly married to Shibani Khan, was divorced by the Uzbek leader after several years--having originally forced her into marriage he seems to have grown afraid that her resentment might prove fatal to him. He gave her in marriage to a follower, Sayyid Hada. In 1511 Khanzada Begim, by then aged thirty-three, was graciously returned to Babur, then in Agra, by the Safavid Shah Ismail, victor at the battle of Merv in which both Sayyid Hada and Shibani Khan were killed. Some of the Timurid refugee women who made it to Babur's Kabul did not survive the second leg of the journey, to India. Afaq Begim, a wife of Sultan Husayn Mirza, died in Babur's Kabul in 1527 or 1528. Sultanum Begim Bayqara, eldest daughter of Sultan Husayn Mirza Bayqara, fled Herat for Khwarazm in 1507, eventually making her way to Kabul by 1519, where Babur showed her great respect and gave her the gift of a garden, the *Bagh-i Khilwat* (Garden of Retirement). She died at the Indus River while traveling to Babur's court in Agra in 1527. Another of Sultan Husayn Bayqara's daughters, Ayisha Sultan Begim Bayqara, had been married successively to two Uzbek nobles, by each of whom she had sons who eventually joined Babur's service in India. She was in India by 1531, dying in Humayun's military rout at the battle of Chausa in 1539. Mihrangaz Begim, whose fate has already been mentioned, having been forced into marriage with an Uzbek warrior, Ubaydullah, at the conquest of Herat, somehow managed to extricate herself and make her way to India by 1531, where she attended Humayun's feast with a female cousin, Shad Begim, also a refugee from Timurid Herat. A few half sisters of Babur were noted in India by 1535, including Mihr Banu Begim and Yadgar Sultan Begim, who had been a captive of the Uzbeks as a child. Even Babur's first wife, a daughter of Sultan Ahmad Mirza Miranshahi, was reported at the neo-Timurid court in India by 1535, although she had divorced Babur thirty-two years earlier, in 1503! These details are cited in, variously, the major sources of the period: Babur, *Baburnama* and Dughlat, *Tarikh*, as well as the somewhat later, Gulbadan, *Humayunnama*.

43. Babur, *Baburnama*, Mano, ed., 148. It is perhaps worthy of note that the Turkish word for a state of exile, *ghariplik*, rather than simply implying a loss of home or displacement, much more powerfully emphasizes the idea of *strangeness*. It is the sense of foreignness, of not belonging or fitting in, that is expressed here.
44. Ibid., 437.
45. Ibid., 466–7.
46. Susheila Nasta, *Home Truths: Fictions of the South Asian Diaspora in Britain*, NY: Palgrave, 2002, 7.

47. Pier M. Larson, "Reconsidering Trauma, Identity and the African Diaspora: Enslavement and Historical Memory in Nineteenth Century Highland Madagascar," *William and Mary Quarterly*, 3rd Series, LVI, 2 (April 1999), 335. Italics mine.
48. Babur, *Baburnama*, Mano, ed., 473.
49. Ibid., 475; Thackston, trans., 635.
50. For a more detailed discussion of this event, see chapter two, this book.
51. Babur, *Baburnama*, Mano, ed., 575.
52. Ibid., 577. Though no longer drinking alcohol, Babur was not entirely abstemious. He continued to indulge regularly in *majun*, the mild narcotic concoction, and described taking opium, both to cure illness and because "the moon influenced him." He complained bitterly of the hangover he suffered next day.
53. Ibid., 573; Thackston, trans., 761.
54. Stephen F. Dale, "A Safavid Poet in the Heart of Darkness," *Iranian Studies*, 36/ 2 (June 2003) p. 209.
55. Sunil Sharma, *Persian Poetry at the Indian Frontier*, Delhi: Permanent Black, 2000, 38–39.
56. Nasir Khusraw (d. ca. 1072), in Sharma, 51- 3.
57. Quoted and translated by Dale, "A Safavid Poet," 210–11.
58. Babur, *Baburnama*, Mano, ed., 454.
59. Ibid., 458.
60. Ibid., Mano ed., 468; Thackston, trans., 625.
61. Ibid.
62. Ibid., Mano, ed., p. 469.
63. Ibid., p. 468.
64. Ibid., p. 475; Thackston, trans., 635.
65. Ibid., Mano ed., 527–8.; Thackston, trans., 701.
66. Ibid., Mano, ed., 607; Thackston, trans., 803.
67. This perhaps further illustrates Mughal ambivalence, for it was Shah Jahan who had inscribed on his throne room wall in the imperial Mughal capital of Shahjahanabad, the famous verse by Amir Khusraw, "If there is a paradise on the face of the earth, this is it!"

Chapter 2   Dynastic Memory and the Genealogical Cult

1. Arthur F. Buehler, *Sufi Heirs of the Prophet: The Indian Naqshbandiyya and the Rise of the Mediating Sufi Saint,* Columbia: University of South Carolina Press, 1998, 107.
2. Mir Dawlatshah Samarqandi, "Tadhkirat al-Shu'ara" *Century of Princes,* 15.

3. Ghiyas al-Din Muhammad Khwandamir, "Habib al-Siyar," *Century of Princes*, 101.
4. Sholeh Quinn, *Historical Writing During the Reign of Shah Abbas I, Ideology, Imitation and Legitimacy in Safavid Chronicles*. Salt Lake City: University of Utah Press, 2000, 89.
5. Cornell Fleischer, *Bureaucrat and Intellectual in the Ottoman Empire: The Historian Mustafa Ali (1541–1600)*, Princeton, NJ: Princeton University Press, 1986, 284–5.
6. Ibid., 278.
7. Peter Avery, "Nadir Shah and the Afsharid Legacy," *The Cambridge History of Iran*. VII, " Nadir Shah to the Islamic Republic," Peter Avery, Gavin Hambly and Charles Melville, eds. Cambridge: Cambridge University Press (1991) 10. See also Thomas Allsen, *The Royal Hunt in Eurasian History*, Philadelphia, PA:University of Pennsylvania Press, 2006.
8. Richard Eaton, *A Social History of the Deccan, 1300–1761, Eight Indian Lives*, Cambridge University Press, 2005, 51.
9. Ibid., 61.
10. See Abdul al-Razzaq Samarqandi, "Mission to Calicut and Vijayanagar," *Century of Princes*, 308. See also Phillip Wagoner, "Sultan among Hindu Kings: Dress, Titles, and the Islamicization of Hindu Culture at Vijayanagara," "The Journal of Asian Studies", Vol. 55, No. 4 (Nov., 1996), 851–880.
11. Ali Anooshahr, *The Ghazi Sultans and the Frontiers of Islam*, London and NY: Routledge, 2009.
12. J. M. Rogers, *Mughal Painting*. London: British Museum Press 1993, 28.
13. Babur, *Baburnama*, Mano, ed., 507.
14. For example, see Ibn Arabshah, *Tamerlane*, 298–9.
15. *Beg* and *noker* can be (loosely) translated as 'lord and liege man.'
16. Babur, *Baburnama*, Thackston, trans., 691.
17. Dale, *Garden*, 351.
18. Babur, *Baburnama*, Mano, ed., 521; Dale, *Garden*, 351.
19. In his description of this one battle Babur quotes verses of the Quran a remarkable total of nine times.
20. Least of all can we draw sharp dichotomies in Babur's "transition from Mongol to Islamic rule," (Anooshirvan, *Ghazi Sultans*, p.51). It should be very clear by this point that Babur's pre-Hindustan model(s) of kingship cannot and should not be classified as simply "Mongol," but understood to include a dynamic array of Mongol, Turkic, Persianate and Islamic "embodied symbols and performed myths." (See Moin, "Islam and the Millenium," 156)
21. Babur, *Baburnama*, Mano, ed., 352.

NOTES

22. Richard C. Foltz, *Mughal India and Central Asia,* Karachi: Oxford University Press, 1998, 134.
23. Gulbadan, *Humayunnama,* 88–9.
24. Abu al-Fazl, *Akbarnama,* Delhi: Low Price Publications, 1st ed., 1902- 39, reprints 1989, 1993, 1998, 2002, III, 616.
25. Riazul Islam, *Calendar of Documents,* p. 207; Mutribi al- Asamm of Samarqand, *Conversations With Emperor Jahangir,* Richard C. Foltz, trans. and ed., Costa Mesa, CA: Mazda Publishers, 1998, 8.
26. Nur al-Din Muhammad Jahangir, *Jahangirnama (Tuzuk-i Jahangiri),* Tehran: Buny adi Farhangi Iran, 1359 (1980), p. 16. Cited henceforth as *Tuzuk*; translations by this author unless noted.
27. Ibid., 16 and 53.
28. Abdul Hamid Lahori [Lahauri], "Badshahnama," *The History of India As Told by Its Own Historians,* Elliot and Dowson, eds., Vol VII, NY: AMS Press, Inc. (1966), VII, p.70. In the case of minor or less readily available sources, I have made use of available collections, including the famously incomplete translations of Elliot and Dowson. Fortunately, they have been critiqued and annotated and I have relied heavily on these studies to guide my use of the texts. See Shahpurshah Hormasji Hodivala, *Studies in Indo-Muslim History: A Critical Commentary on Elliot and Dowson's History of India as Told by its Own Historians,* Lahore: Islamic Book Service, 1st ed. 1939, Pakistan reprint 1979. At no time have I allowed a potentially unreliable translation to inspire, suggest or support alone a new line of argument.
29. Mughal efforts to re-conquer Mawarannahr ended with Shah Jahan, whose successor, Aurangzeb, broke with dynastic tradition to the extent of focusing all of his military efforts in the Deccan. While this surely speaks to the increasingly assimilated nature of the Mughal dynasty, Aurangzeb did, in other ways, regularly re-affirm his lingering loyalty to the Timurid legacy by, for example, educating his children in Turkish, and employing traditional Turco-Mongol titles for his elites. Of course in the years after Aurangzeb's death, the dynasty suffered steady impoverishment and political instability – surely enough to prevent any renewed effort to invade north, regardless of the still powerful claims of revanchist nostalgia.
30. Jahangir, *Tuzuk,* 16 and 53.
31. Ibid.
32. Ebba Koch, "My Garden is Hindustan: The Mughal Padshah's Realization of a Political Metaphor," *Middle East Garden Traditions: Unity and Diversity,* Michel Conan, ed., Washington, DC: Dumbarton Oaks, 2007, 162.
33. "Murtib" al-Asamm Samarqandi, *Conversations,* 22–3.
34. Ibid., 24.

35. Ibid., 87.
36. Ibid., 352 and 357.
37. Dale, *Garden*, 297.
38. Ibid, 297 and 299.
39. Wheeler Thackston suggests that the term "Mughal" was "a misnomer picked up in the sixteenth century by Europeans, mainly the Portuguese, from a local usage, probably derogatory." As an example of the difficulties involved in determining an ethnic identity in sixteenth century Central Asia, Thackston also asserts that even Babur's mother (the daughter of Ulus Khan, d. 1487), who is generally considered to have descended directly from Chaghatay, son of Chingis Khan, was not truly Mongol but that her people were "highly Mongolianized Turks." See *Jahangirnama,* Thackston, editor's preface, p. xxiii.
40. It has been noted that Babur's emphasis on Timurid genealogy may have been in part due to the pure Chingisid descent of his arch-rivals, the Uzbeks, through Chingis Khan's son Jochi and through marriage with women from the lineage of Chingis Khan's son Chaghatay. See Maria Eva Subtelny, "Arts and Politics in Early Sixteenth-Century Central Asia," *Central Asiatic Journal* 27, 1–2 (1983), 131–2.
41. See Moin, "Islam and the Millenium."
42. Dawlatshah Samarqandi, "Tadhkirat " *Century of Princes,* 15.
43. "Murtib" al-Asamm Samarqandi, *Conversations*, Foltz, trans. and ed., 30. As explained in Thackston, *Jahangirnama*: "The letters in the words *Sahib qiran-i sani* (second Sahib Qiran) yield 1013. To this is added the first letter of *iqbal* (fortune's head) which has a numerical value of one, for the Hegira date of 1014 (1605)," 28.
44. Muhammad Hashim Khafi Khan, "Muntakhab'ul-Lubab Muhammad Shahi,"*The History of India,* VII, 228.
45. Sakinat ul-Awliya, quoted in *Majma' ul- Bahrain (The Mingling of Two Oceans)* by Prince Muhammad Dara Shikoh, M. Mahfuz-ul-Haq, trans. and ed., Calcutta: The Asiatic Society, 1929, reprint 1982, 8.
46. An important study of this genealogical chart has been done by John E. Woods, *The Timurid Dynasty*, Bloomington: Indiana University Research Institute for Inner Asian Studies, Papers on Inner Asia, No. 14, 1990.
47. Eventually the Mughal manuscript made its way to London, where it currently resides in the British Library (MS. OR 467). A more complete copy of the original Timurid manuscript, which never entered Mughal India, was carried to Istanbul and then to France, where it is housed in the national archives. It has no illustrations.
48. British Library, MS. OR182.

49. Annabel Teh Gallop, "The Genealogical Seal of the Mughal Emperors of India," *Journal of the Royal Asiatic Society*, 3/9/1 (April 1999) 77.
50. Ibid., 80.
51. Ibid., 81. See also Abu al-Fazl, *Akbarnama*, III, 1033.
52. Gallop, "Genealogical Seal," 84.
53. Ibid., 77.
54. For a full discussion see John Richards, "The Formulation of Imperial Authority Authority Under Akbar and Jahangir," *The Mughal State, 1526–1750*, Muzaffar Alam and Sanjay Subrahmanyam, eds., New Delhi: Oxford University Press (1998), 268–9.
55. Abd al-Qadir ibn Muluk Shah Badauni, *Muntakhabu al-Tawarikh*, Sir Wolseley Haig, trans., Brahmadeva Prasad Ambashthya, ed., Patna, India: Academica Asiatica, 1973, II, 350.
56. Jahangir, *Tuzuk*, 152. Jahangir also dabbled in identifying himself as a near deity or Sufi *pir* (leader) while relinquishing his father's more extreme religious interpretations. In the middle of his reign he had his ears pierced and strung with pearl earrings as a gesture of affection and loyalty to "the great [Chishti] *khwaja*," and this act seems to have been replicated by his closest courtiers as a mark of personal discipleship.
57. Mirza Nathan (Ala al-Din Isfahani), *Baharistan-i Ghaybi*, M. I. Borah, trans. and ed., Gauhati, Assam: Narayani Handiqui Historical Institute, 2 vols., 1936.
58. Ibid., I, 17.
59. Ibid.
60. Ibid., 74.
61. Ibid.
62. Babur, *Baburnama*, Mano, ed., 559. Complaining of Humayun's reported solitude, Babur wrote to him, "Solitude is a flaw in kingship ... If you are fettered, resign yourself (*agar payband-i rida pish gir*)."
63. John E. Woods, "The Rise of Timurid Historiography," *Journal of Near Eastern Studies*, 46/2 (April 1987), 82.
64. Yazdi, "Zafarnama," *Century of Princes*, 65. A "sharp proliferation" of histories in the fourteenth century included chronicles in Persian produced or begun during Timur's lifetime, including *Jush-i khurush* (*The Raging and Roaring*) by Shaykh Mahmud Zangi Ajami Kirmani and its *Zayl* (*Continuation*) by his son Qutb al-Din; *Futuhat-i Miranshahi* (*The Conquests of Miranshah*) of Sa'id Allah Kirmani; *Ruznama-i futuhat-i Hindustan* (*Journal of Indian Conquests*) of Qazi Nasir al-Din Umar; and the *Zafarnama* (*Book of Conquests*) of Nizam al-Din Ali Shami, written in 1404. Early Timurid-era chronicles composed in Chaghatay Turkish included the *Tarikh-i khani* (*Khanid History*) and

Zafarnama (*Book of Conquests*) of Safi al-Din Khuttalani Samarqandi. Of these works none is extant, although fifteenth-century copies of the *Zafarnama* of Nizam al-Din Ali Shami do exist. This is considered to have been the most important of the Timurid histories, commissioned personally by Timur and intended to be a work "free from rhetorical artifice" and "preciosity." It was finished in 1404 and served as the basis of other surviving histories of Timur, including the *Zafarnama* of Sharaf al-Din Ali Yazdi, completed in 1425 for Ibrahim Sultan ibn Shahrukh, then governor of Shiraz. The popularity and influence of these works was enormous; Yazdi's *Zafarnama* was copied and illustrated no fewer than thirty times in the years between 1425 and 1507. For a compete discussion, see Woods, "Timurid Historiography."

65. Dale, *Garden*, 41. Anooshahr has raised a debate regarding the Baburnama in its original Turki and the driving force behind its later translations into Persian (see Anooshahr, *Ghazi Sultans*). My comments follow below, endnote 90.

66. Khwandamir, "Habib al-Siyar," *Century of Princes*, 118.

67. Gulbadan Begim, *Humayunnama*, 2.

68. The most recent translation is that of Wheeler Thackston, including all three in a single volume. See *Three Memoirs of Homayun*, Wheeler M. Thackston, trans. and ed., Costa Mesa, CA: Mazda Publishers, 2009.

69. Gülru Necipoğlu, "Word and Image: The Serial Portraits of Ottoman Sultans in Comparative Perspective," *The Sultan's Portrait*, Istanbul: Işbank, 2000, 51.

70. Abu al-Fazl, *Akbarnama*, I, 17. In the same section, among other epithets, Abu al-Fazl describes Akbar as "heir apparent of the sun," "quintessence of the co-mingling of nights and days" and "the cheek mole of sovereignty and fortune!"

71. Ibid., Akbar's Greek horoscope, 67–84, Indian horoscope, 85–95, and discussion of the differences between them, 119–128. Akbar's Shirazi horoscope, 96–116, and Ilkhanid horoscope, 117–128

72. Ibid., 167. Japheth, as "Father of the Turk," is also described as the original possessor of a rain stone (tr: *yedatash*, per: *sang-i yada*). Belief in a stone which could summon rain and control weather has been ubiquitous in Central Asia and Mongolia, in some regions to the present day. Babur mentions the use of rain stones among the Timurids in the *Baburnama*.

73. Sharifuddin Ali Yazdi wrote this in the *Zafarnama* and it was repeated in the *Habib al-Siyar* by Khwandamir. Abu al-Fazl's censure is described in *Akbarnama*, 205.

74. Four members of the immediate dynasty wrote their own personal histories: Babur; his Mongol cousin, Haydar Dughlat; his daughter, Gulbadan Begim; his great-grandson, the emperor Jahangir.

75. Jahangir, *Tuzuk*, 270.
76. Ibid. Also see p. 276: the second and third copies were made shortly after the first and were distributed at the king's request to his father-in-law and close advisor, Itimad al-Dawla, and to his brother-in-law, Asaf Khan.
77. Ibid., 285–6.
78. Ibid., 30.
79. The childhood and final years of Jahangir's life were chronicled as an appendix to his personal memoirs by Muhammad Hadi, probably a member of Muhammad Shah's royal court, who had become ""enamored by the science of history and the craft of biography." He claims to have relied on "several reliable manuscripts." See *Jahangirnama*, Thackston, editor's preface, p. xii, and (translation) p. 3.
80. Inayat Khan, *Shah Jahan Nama*, A.R. Fuller, trans. W.E Begley and Z.A. Desai, eds., Delhi, NY, and London: Oxford University Press, 1990, 2.
81. As described in an essay by Ebba Koch, this refers to the Shah Burj pavilion, Shah Jahan's most private gathering place, reserved for meetings with the highest dignitaries and princes of the royal blood. See Ebba Koch, "The Heirarchical Principles of Shah Jahani Painting," *Mughal Art and Imperial Ideology*, Ebba Koch, ed., New Delhi: Oxford University Press, 2001, 132.
82. Ibid., 132. [quoting from Kaswini, "Padshahnama"]. Given the intensity of the emperor's involvement in the writing process, it is easy to see why the official histories of the reign of Shah Jahan consistently lack the charm and spontaneity of those written for and by his predecessors.
83. Muhammad Amin Kaswini, "Padshahnama," *History of India*, VII, 1–3, 1. "Alamgir," Seizer of the Universe, was the regnal name chosen by Aurangzeb (perhaps in direct response to the choices of his grandfather Jahangir, Seizer of the World, and his father Shah Jahan, King of the World).
84. Muhammad Kazim, "Alamgirnama," *History of India*, VII, 175. In one of the more delightful condemnations of Mughal court prose, the editor of the *Alamgirnama*, describes the style as "strained, verbose and tedious; fulsome in its flattery, abusive in its censure." See Ibid., 177. Perhaps this was the factor that influenced Aurangzeb's disinclination to allow further court histories!
85. Ibid., p. 174.
86. Letter by Aurangzeb to his son, Shah Azam Shah, in Iradat Khan, "Tarikh-i Iradat Khan,"in *History of India*, Elliot & Dowson, VII, 562.
87. Muhammad Shafi Tehrani, "Tarikh-i Chaghatai," *History of India*, VIII, 21–22. Italics mine.
88. For example, see *Baburnama*, Mano, ed., p. 351, when Babur uses the *Zafarnama* to identify geographic landmarks in former Timurid conquest territories.

89. Rogers, *Mughal Painting*, 32.
90. The fragments are in the British Library, MS Add. No. 26, p. 202; MS OR 1, p. 999. See Abu al-Fazl, *Akbarnama*, 248–9, note 5. Anooshahr, *Ghazi Sultans*, argues that Zayn's Persian translation was part of a concerted, even institutionalized, effort by Babur to engage local idioms of power, rejecting the limitations of a Turkish-Timurid set of politically legitimizing symbols. Muzaffar Alam seems to decisively refute this, however, arguing that Persian was not, in fact, dominant in the region at the time of Babur's conquests. Babur himself asserts that most of the Afghans in the area could not speak Persian. An explanation for the Mughal emphasis on Persian, writes Alam, "may then be sought in a convergence of factors within the Mughal regime than within the Indo-Persian heritage of preceding Muslim regimes." See Muzaffar Alam, *The Languages of Political Islam, India 1200–1800*, Chicago: University of Chicago Press, 2004.
91. Babur, *Baburnama*, Abdul-Rahman Khan-i Khanan, trans., British Library, MS OR 3714.
92. Abu al-Fazl, *A'in-i Akbari*, 3 vols., H. Blochmann, trans., Delhi: Low Price Publications, I, 115. For a thorough discussion of Akbar's translation movement and increasing use of Persian, see Alam, *Languages*, chapter 4.
93. Inayat Khan, *Shah Jahan Nama*, 573.
94. Jahangir, *Tuzuk*, 64.
95. Richard Foltz, *Mughal India and Central Asia*, NY: Oxford University Press, 1998, 37.
96. Bakhtawar Khan, "Mirat-i Alam," *History of India*, VII, p. 162. See also Saqi Musta'id Khan, *Ma'asir-i Alamgiri (History of the Emperor Aurangzeb-Alamgir)*, Jadunath Sarkar, trans., Calcutta: Royal Asiatic Society of Bengal, 1947, and New Delhi: Munshiram Manoharlal Publishers Pvt. Lmt., 1986, 195–6, who describes Aurangzeb's sons Muhammad Kam Baksh and Muhammad Sultan as proficient in Turkish.
97. Jahangir, *Tuzuk*, 270.
98. Jahangir, *Jahangirnama* (in Ottoman translation), British Library, OR 6441.
99. Mu'tamid Khan, *Iqbalnama-i Jahangiri*, British Library, Add 26218. The decline of the imperial workshops is evident. Illustrations for the nineteenth-century version are extremely basic and neither Timurid nor Mughal in style. The figures are posed in the Timurid tradition, but all of the faces have Indian features rather than Turkish or Mongol, and Mughal use of perspective and shading are entirely lacking.
100. Timur himself is believed to have been illiterate, as is his distant descendant, the Mughal emperor, Akbar.

101. Ibn Arabshah, *Tamerlane*, 310.
102. Thomas W. Lentz, "Dynastic Imagery in Early Timurid Wall Painting," *Muqarnas*, Vol. 10 (1993), 253. See also Ibn Arabshah, *Tamerlane*, 216.
103. Ibid.
104. Jafar Tabrizi, "Arzadasht," *Century of Princes*, 326.
105. Lentz, "Dynastic Imagery," 254–5.
106. Ibid.
107. Shah Tahmasp is reputed to have decorated the Chihil Palace at Qazvin with, among other scenes, portrayals of Joseph appearing before Zulaykha. Traces of these small-scale paintings could be detected in the 1960's. See Rogers, *Mughal Miniatures*, 34.
108. Gülru Necipoğlu, "Word and Image," *The Sultan's Portrait*, Selim Kangal, ed., Istanbul: Işbank, 2000, 54–5. Necipoğlu's interest is in Ottoman portraiture; her points are, however, equally relevant to the production of Timurid/Mughal royal portraits.
109. Lentz and Lowry, *Princely Vision*, 115.
110. Ibid., 114.
111. Ibid., 171.
112. Necipoğlu, "Word and Image," 24.
113. Ibid., 25.
114. Ibid.
115. Lentz, "Dynastic Imagery," 263.
116. Ironically, he died in a fall from the steps of his library in Delhi. As for his love of books, according to his biographer, Jauhar Aftabchi, even while in desperate flight from his disloyal brother Kamran, Humayun thought to ask after the safety of his library. Jauhar Aftabchi, *Tazkirat-i Waqi'at*, British Library MS Add. 16711, fol. 99b.
117. Shah Tahmasp seems to have had a crisis of conscience regarding the production of portraiture at his highly religious conservative court and was clearly willing to let his court painters depart for India.
118. Joseph M. Dye III, "Imperial Mughal Painting," *The Magnificent Mughals*, Zeenat Ziad, ed., Oxford University Press, 2002, 147.
119. Ibid., 39.
120. Abu al-Fazl, *A'in-i Akbari*, 115.
121. Rogers, *Mughal Painting*, 77. The *Tutinama* is a collection of Hindu morality tales, written in Persian in the period of the early Delhi Sultanate. The *Hamzanama* is an adventure story extolling the highly idealized exploits of the Prophet Muhammad's uncle.
122. Manuscripts at the Safavid court prior to the reign of Shah Tahmasp averaged only 40 illustrations; see Dye, "Imperial Mughal Painting," 152.

123. Badauni, *Tawarikh*, II, 329.
124. Abu al-Fazl, *Akbarnama*, 115.
125. The painting by Govardan is now housed in the Victoria and Albert Museum, London; reproduced by Annemarie Schimmel, *The Empire of the Great Mughals*, London: Reakton Books, LTD, 2004 16.
126. Sheila Canby, ed., *Humayun's Garden Party: Princes of the House of Timur*, Bombay: Marg Publications, 1994.
127. These are the three sons of Jahangir, and the state of their portrayal within the painting is a good indication of the years of its modification. Khusraw was in full rebellion in the first year of Jahangir's reign and may have had the progress of his portrait halted for that reason. Shah Jahan (Khurram), while seeming very young, is already clearly the chosen successor and still in good favor--unlike his brothers, he is posed within the pavilion alongside the current and former emperors.
128. On display at the Archeological Museum, The Red Fort (Shahjahanabad), Delhi, as of January 2006.
129. Ibid.. While the Chishti order is identified as a South Asian sufi movement, it was well known to the Timurid-Mughals well before their establishment as kings of northern India. When Babur arrived as conqueror of Delhi, among his earliest acts was the respectful circumambulation of the tomb of the Chishti sheiykh, Nizam al-Din Auliya (d. 1325). Each of his royal descendants performed pilgrimage to the tomb and even the austere Aurangzeb, having died in the Deccan, was buried in the courtyard of the tomb of Auliya's disciple, the Chishti Sheikh Burham al Din Gharib (d. 1331), in Ahmednagar.
130. Abu al-Fazl, *Akbarnama*, 113.
131. Jahangir, *Tuzuk*, 266–7; Thackston, trans., 268.
132. Ebba Koch, "Shah Jahani Painting," 131.
133. Ibid., 130.
134. Ibid., 131.
135. Jahangir, *Tuzuk*,173.
136. Ibid.; Thackston, trans., 182.
137. Jahangir, *Tuzuk*, 83. The white jade Ulugh Beg cup is now on display at Museu Calouste Gulbenkian, Lisbon.
138. Ibid., 302–3.
139. Ibid., 323.
140. Ibid.
141. Ibid., 88.
142. Ibid., 369.
143. The Safavids successfully retook Qandahar in 1622.
144. Lahori, "Badshahnama," 46.

145. Ibid. See also Inayat Khan, *Shah Jahan Nama*.
146. Satish Chandra, *Parties and Politics at the Mughal Court, 1707–1740*, New Delhi: Oxford University Press, 2002–3, 257.
147. John Keay, *India, A History*, NY, NY: Grove Press, 2000, p. 438–9. Bahadur Shah II Zafar was eighty years old when the rebellion began.
148. Ibid.
149. William Dalrymple, *The Last Mughal: The Fall of a Dynasty: Delhi, 1857*, NY: Alfred A. Knopf, 2006, 278.
150. Ibid., 342.
151. Description of a visit to Delhi in 1842, which remained unpublished until the 1857 rebellion, "Voyages dans les Etats du Grand Mogol," (author unknown) *L'Illustration*, 12 September 1857, in Valerie Berinstain, *India and the Mughal Dynasty*, NY: Harry N. Abrams, 1997, 146.
152. *Proceedings on the Trial of Muhammad Bahadur Shah, Titular King of Delhi, before a Military Commission, upon a charge of Rebellion, Treason and Murder*, Calcutta: John Gray, Calcutta Gazette Office, 1858.
153. Catherine B. Asher, "Architecture," *The Magnificent Mughals*, Zeenut Ziad, ed., Oxford, UK: Oxford University Press (2002), 225.

Chapter 3   The Peripatetic Court and the Timurid-Mughal Landscape

1. Ruby Lal, *Domesticity and Power in the Early Mughal World*, Cambridge: Cambridge University Press, 2005.
2. Monika Gronke, "The Persian Court Between Palace and Tent: From Timur to 'Abbas I," *Timurid Art and Culture*, ed. by Lisa Golombek and Maria Subtelney, Leiden: E.J. Brill, 1992, 18–22. Mughal court travels can be viewed in sharp contrast to their Turkish and Afghan predecessors in north India, whose movements were for the most part limited to military campaigning, pilgrimage and the hunt, and for whom permanent capitals, as the base of a sedentary imperial administration, were the norm.
3. Babur, *Baburnama*, Mano, ed., 16.
4. Francois Bernier, *Travel in the Mogul Empire, AD 1656–1668*, Archibald Constable, trans. and ed., London: Cambridge University Press, 1934; New Delhi: Munshiram Manoharlal Publishers Pvt, Ltd., Oriental Reprint, 1983, 358.
5. Ibid., 365.
6. Ibid.
7. Ibid., 380–81; also, Montserrate, *The Commentary of Father Montserrate, SJ, On His Journey to the Court of Akbar*, trans. J.S. Hoyland, ed., S.N. Bannerjee, Oxford, 1922, 79.

8. Bernier, *Travel*, 365.
9. Montserrate, *Commentary*, 108.
10. Bernier, *Travel*, 380–1.
11. Ibid.
12. Ibid., 365
13. Peter Mundy, as quoted in *Jahangirnama*, Thackston, p. xix.
14. Apart from a period in the seventeenth century during which the sultans moved to Edirne in an effort to escape the political factionalism of Istanbul, from the time of Mehmet Fatih's conquest of the city in 1453 Istanbul remained the economic, political and spiritual center of Ottoman identity until the complete collapse of empire in the early twentieth century.
15. Of course when Aurangzeb seized control of Delhi in 1658, he essentially took control of the empire. However, this was not because he took the capital of the empire but because he simultaneously seized his father, the emperor Shah Jahan, who afterwards remained a prisoner of his son, housed in Agra for eight years, until his death in 1666. See chapter four of this study for an full discussion of the event in the context of Turco-Mongol succession traditions.
16. Akbar's departure from Fatehpur Sikri for Lahore seems to have been initially inspired by military threats to northern Mughal territories, but the emperor and his court remained away permanently, even when the need for a powerful imperial presence was no longer necessary in the north. Lahore did not become the new capital and from this time no single city served as a central capital under the Mughals until Shah Jahan built his new city, Shahjahanabad, in the suburbs of Delhi. There has been the strong suggestion, as yet unconfirmed, that Sikri may have had water shortages and could not sustain the demanding presence of the royal court and all of its attendants.
17. M. E. Subtelny, "Mirak-i Sayyid Ghiyas and the Timurid Tradition of Landscape Architecture," *Studia Iranica* 24 (1995), 20.
18. Among these historical kings of note was the first Muslim Ilkhanid king, Ghazan Khan (r.1295–1304), who probably influenced by the same aesthetic-political considerations, built the *Bagh-i Adalet* (Garden of Justice) near Tabriz---a square, walled enclosure with a golden platform and a golden pavilion, towers, baths, streams fed by tanks and cisterns, in order "to provide a pleasant and agreeable meadow for the sojourn of the emperor." See Penelope Hobhouse, *Gardens of Persia*, Kales Press Inc, 2003–4, 82.
19. Sharaf al-Din Ali Yazdi, "Zafarnama," *Century of Princes*, 91.
20. Clavijo, *Embassy*, pp. 215–17; Yazdi, "Zafarnama," *Century of Princes*, pp. 85–87; and Arabshah, *Tamerlane*, 309–310.

21. Clavijo, *Embassy*, 243.
22. Ibid., 216.
23. Ibid., 243.
24. Ibn Arabshah, *Tamerlane*, 216.
25. The Ottoman Sultan Bayezid I was defeated by Timur at the Battle of Ankara in 1402. See chapter two, above, for the comments by the political commentator Mustafa Ali in an Ottoman interpretation of the contest between the two great kings.
26. Thomas W. Lentz, "Memory and Ideology in the Timurid Garden," in *Mughal Gardens: Sources, Places, Representations and Prospects*, James L. Westcoat, Jr. and Joachim Wolschke-Bulmahn, eds., Washington, D.C.: Dumbarton Oaks, 1996, 39.
27. Babur, *Baburnama*, Mano, ed., 468.
28. Ibid., 482.
29. Gulbadan Begum, *Humayunnama*, 12.
30. Babur, *Baburnama*, Mano, ed., 482.
31. Ibid., 483.
32. Ahmad Yadgar, *Tarikh-i Shahi*, as quoted in Ebba Koch, "The Mughal Waterfront garden," *Gardens in the Time of the Great Muslim Empires*, ed. Attilio Petruccioli, Leiden: Brill, 1997, 140.
33. Ibid.
34. Babur, *Baburnama*, Mano, ed., 483.
35. Anthony Welch "Gardens That Babur Did Not Like: Landscape, Water and Architecture for the Sultans of Delhi," *Mughal Gardens*, J.L. Westcoat and J. Wolschke-Bulman, eds., Dumbarton Oaks, 1993, 66.
36. Dale, *Garden*, 186.
37. Jahangir, *Tuzuk*, 62–63.
38. Ibid.
39. Ibid.
40. Asher, "Architecture," 209.
41. Abdul Rehman, "Garden Types in Mughal Lahore," *Gardens in the Time of the Great Muslim Empires*, Attilio Petruccioli, ed., Leiden: Brill, 1997, 166.
42. Ibid.,164.
43. Inayat Khan, *Shah Jahan Nama*, 298.
44. Quoted in, R.E.M. Wheeler, *Five Thousand Years of Pakistan*, London: Royal India and Pakistan Society, 1950, 87. The most famous Mughal gardens of Lahore, the *Shalimar Bagh* of Shah Jahan and the *Bagh-i Jahangiri*, constructed for the emperor Jahangir, are the only Mughal gardens still intact of the city's original fifty.
45. Scholars have pointed out what they consider specifically Persian influences in the architecture of Humayun's tomb, but we must remember that

Humayun's widow, Hamida Banu Begim, was from Khurasan, the former heartland of Timurid rule and Timurid culture and, as such, cannot be described as bringing foreign influences to the Mughal aesthetic. See Gavin Hambly, *Cities of Mughal India*, NY: G.P. Putnam's Sons, 1968, 41, where he asserts that the tomb "exemplifies the alien Persian element" and that "Iran ... [was] the main inspiration for this great mausoleum." I argue that these so-called Persian characteristics are in fact a part of what should be described as a greater Perso-Islamic, Ilkhanid-Timurid cultural vocabulary.

46. Ebba Koch, "Delhi of the Mughals," *Mughal Art and Imperial Ideology: Collected Essays,* Ebba Koch, ed., New Delhi: Oxford University Press, 2002, 174.
47. D. Fairchild Ruggles, "Humayun's Tomb and Garden: Typologies and Visual Order," *Gardens in the Time of the Great Muslim Empires*, Attilio Petruccioli, ed., Leiden: Brill, 1997, 174.
48. Akbar also constructed a large mosque at the Chishti shrine complex in Ajmer in Rajasthan, to which the emperor, and later his sons, regularly made pilgrimages, at times barefoot.
49. Jahangir, *Tuzuk,* 210.
50. My discussion of the social and political role of the hunt in the Mongol, Timurid and Mughal royal courts, has been heavily influenced by the encyclopedic and fascinating monograph, *The Royal Hunt in Eurasian History*, by Thomas Allsen (Philadelphia: University of Pennsylvania Press, 2006) and by personal conversation with him, Eugene, Oregon, summer 2008. I would like to express my thanks for his superb scholarship and his gracious hospitality.
51. Allsen, *Royal Hunt,* 183.
52. Ibid., 181.
53. Kami Shirazi, *Waqa-i-uz-Zaman (Fath Nama-i-Nur Jahan Begam),* W.H. Siddiqi, ed and trans., Rampur, Uttar Pradesh: Rampur Raza Library 2003, 156.
54. Allsen, *Royal Hunt,* 194.
55. Sir Thomas Roe, *Embassy to the Court of the Great Mogul, 1615-1619.* W. Foster, ed., London: Hakluyt Society, 1899, 438; also Allsen, *Royal Hunt,*194.
56. Niccolao Manucci, *Memoirs of the Mogul Court*, Michael Edwardes, ed., London: Folio Society, publication date unknown, 112. According to Manucci, the prince, Sultan Muhammad, was jailed and eventually killed by Aurangzeb because he was known as "a brave soldier," and therefore seen as a threat by the king. Previous to this, however, Sultan Muhammad had supported his father's insurgency, "obediently" assisted in arresting Shah Jahan, and had successfully led his father's armies in the Deccan.

57. Several Mughal miniature paintings illustrate the vast numbers of men employed and game captured in the Mughal circle hunt. That it continued to be referred to as the "qamargha," is attested by many of the court chronicles. For exmple, the emperor Jahangir describes a lenghty hunting trip in his first regnal year, when three months and six days of hunting resulted in five-hundred and eighty-one animals taken through the use of guns, traps, trained hunting leopards and the qamargha. See Jahangir, *Tuzuk*, p. 49. See also Mu'tamid Khan, *Iqbalnama*, British Library, Add 26218, f. 128.
58. Roe, *Embassy*, 377.
59. Bernier, *Travels*, 374–5.
60. Clavijo, *Embassy*, 215–6.
61. William Howard Adams, *Gardens Through History: Nature Perfected*, NY: Abbeville Press, 1991, 24.
62. Jahangir, *Tuzuk*, 53.
63. Ibid., 54.
64. Allsen, *Royal Hunt*, 130.
65. Ibid.,196.
66. Clavijo, *Embassy*, 231.
67. For a thorough discussion of early modern Iranian drug and alcohol usage, see Rudolph P. Matthee, *The Pursuit of Pleasure: Drugs and Stimulants in Iranian History, 1500- 1900*, Princeton, NJ: Princeton University Press, 2005.
68. Khwandamir, "Habib al-Siyar," *Century of Princes*, 118.
69. Dughlat, *Tarikh*,179.
70. Babur, *Baburnama*, Mano, ed., 360.
71. Ibid., 392.
72. Gulbadan Begim, *Humayunnama*, 38.
73. Asad Beg, "Wikaya," 155. No one, of course, has suggested that Akbar was an addict like his father.
74. Comments by the editor, *History of India*, Elliot and Dowson, VI, 260.
75. Jahangir, *Tuzuk*, 360.
76. Written by Taleb Amuli, a Persian immigrant, appointed poet laureate in 1618 and entitled by the emperor Jahangir, *Malik al-Shu'ara*, the King of Poets. Quoted by Jahangir, *Tuzuk*, 324; Thackston trans., 320.
77. Babur, *Baburnama*, Mano, ed., 497.
78. Prasun Chatterjee, "The Lives of Alcohol in Pre-Colonial India," *The Medieval History Journal*, 8/1 (2005) pp. 189–225. (My gratitude to Thomas Allsen for the reference.)
79. Ibid., 560. See also Dale, *Garden*, 148.
80. Matthee, *Pursuit of Pleasure*, 67.

81. Jahangir, *Tuzuk*, 212.
82. Ibid., 224.
83. Ibid., 286.
84. Koch, "My Garden is Hindustan," 162.
85. Ibid., 29.
86. Ibid.; Hafez, *Divan*, 6, line 10, in *Jahangirnama*, Thackston, trans. and ed., 46.
87. Chatterjee, "Lives of Alcohol," 199.
88. Ibid., 200. Quote from Foster, *English Factories in India*, 149.
89. Jahangir,*Tuzuk*, 207; Thackston, trans., 214.
90. Roe, *Embassy*, 375.
91. Ibid., 368.
92. Ibid.
93. Henri Hosten, "Three letters of Fr. Joseph de Castro, S.J., and the Last Year of Jahangir," *Mughal India According to European Travel Accounts; texts and studies*, 1998, I, 247.
94. Elizabeth ten Grotenhaus, *Japanese Mandalas: Representations of Sacred Geography*, University of Hawai'i Press, 1998.
95. Kautilya, *The Arthashastra*, L.N. Rangarajan, ed. and trans., New Delhi and NY: Penguin Books, 1992. See also, *Kautilya's Arthashastra*, R. Shamasastry, trans., Mysore Printing and Publishing House, 1967.
96. Bharati Mukherjee, *Kautilya's Concept of Diplomacy, A New Interpretation*, Calcutta: Minerva Associates, 1976, 24-26.
97. J. Gonda, *Ancient Indian Kingship From the Religious Point of View*, Leiden: E. J. Brill, 1969, 104.
98. William S. Sax, "The Ramnagar Ramlila: Text, Performance, Pilgrimage," *History of Religions*, 30/2, Nov. 1990, 143. My warm thanks to Professor Jeffrey Kripal of Rice University for introducing me to the work of William S. Sax.
99. Respectively, D. Devahuti, *Harsha, A Political Study*, Oxford: Clarendon, 1970, 230, and Ronald Inden, "Ritual, Authority and Cyclic Time in Hindu Kingship," in *Kingship and Authority in South Asia*, ed. J.F. Richards, Madison: University of Wisconsin, 1978, 28.
100. Benoy Kumar Sarkar, "The Hindu Theory of International Relations," American Political Science Review, 1919.
101. Daud Ali, *Courtly Culture and Political Life in Early Medieval India*, Cambridge University Press, 2004, 35.
102. Literary references to the digvijaya are numerous, the earliest described in the *Mahabharata*, during which four of the five Pandava brothers perform a ritualized digvijaya simultaneously. See Sax, "Ramnagar Ramlila," 143.
103. Ronald Inden, "Cultural and Symbolic Constitutions in Ancient India," Institute for Advanced Study, Princeton, 1978, in Sax, "Ramnagar Ramlila,"143.

104. Shivaji's *digvijaya* was only one part of a large and complex effort to assert and defend his claims to *kshatriya* caste, including lengthy purification rites, a coronation carefully contrived in reference to ancient Hindu texts, a thread ceremony for himself and his son, and remarriage, now under kshatriya custom, to each of his wives. Stewart Gordon, *The Marathas, 1600–1818*, Cambridge University Press, 1993, 87–90. Shivaji ritually visited both religious shrines and a series of the royal courts of subjugated Muslim and Hindu kings of the Karnatak, including that of his brother Ekoji. See G. S. Sardesai, "Shivaji," in *The Mughal Empire*, Bombay: Bharatiya Vidya Bhavan, 1974, R.C. Majumdar, ed., 271–2; see also B. K. Apte, ed., *Chhatrapati Shivaji*: Coronation Tercentenary Commemoration Volume, Bombay: University of Bombay, 1874–5 and John Keay, *India*, 354. It has been suggested that the Vedic tradition of the *digvijaya* continues to resonate in South Asian society, remaining a common point of reference in modern performances of political theatre-- an example being Advani's *rath yatra*, or "chariot procession," from Somnatha to Ayodhya in 1990. See William S. Sax, "Conquering the Quarters: Religion and Politics in Hinduism," *International Journal of Hindu Studies*, 4/1, April 2000, 39.

105. The twelfth-century Rajput king Prithviraj, having succeeded in uniting some of the Rajput princes and cordoning off the Muslim Panjab, seems to have been performing a ritual digvijaya when he was attacked by the eventually victorious Muhammad Ghori, who established what became known as the Delhi sultanate.

106. Mu'tamid Khan, *Iqbalnama,* British Library, Add 26218, f. 138

107. Muhammad Hadi, Appendix to the *Jahangirnama*, Thackston, trans., 456.

108. Milo Cleveland Beach and Ebba Koch, *King of the World: The Padshahnama,* NY: Azimuth Editions Limited and Smithsonian Institution, 1997, 11.

109. Hamid ud-Din Bahadur, *Anecdotes of Aurangzeb {Ahkam-i Alamgir}*, Jadunath Sarkar, trans., London: Sangam Books Limited, 1988 (1st and 2nd ed. 1925; 3rd 1949), 74.

110. Ibid., 37.

111. Ibid., 41.

Chapter 4 Legitimacy, Restless Princes and the Imperial Succession

1. Beatrice Forbes Manz, "Women in Timurid Dynastic Politics," *Women in Iran from the Rise of Islam to 1800*, Guity Nashat and Lois Beck, eds. Champagne-Urbana: University of Illinois Press (2003), 121. Of course, one must not ignore the influence of the many non-Muslim, non-Turco-Mongol Mughal

wives. Their marriages into the ruling family were often performed for the same sort of political alliance as had Timurid-Mongol matches, affirming yet again that the lineage of his mother would be respected and could offer a critically important network for a Mughal prince, in the ties of loyalty they often created with her father and brothers. Perhaps even more importantly, the influence these women must have had in the cultural and political assimilation of the Mughal dynasty must have been very great, although that rich subject matter is fated for another book.

2. Leslie Pierce, *The Imperial Harem: Women and Sovereignty in the Ottoman Imperial Harem*, Oxford University Press, 1993, 16 and 23.
3. This did not of course prevent the development of powerful political factions around the princes and their mothers, but merely removed maternal relations as possible players in the regular succession wars and power struggles which rocked the Ottoman palace.
4. Pierce, *Imperial Harem*, 23.
5. Ibid.
6. Manz, "Dynastic Politics," 12.
7. Clavijo, *Embassy*, 310.
8. Manz, "Dynastic Politics," 12.
9. Ibid., 122.
10. Ibid.
11. Babur, *Baburnama*, Mano, ed., 253.
12. Ibid., p. 96.
13. Manz, "Dynastic Politics," 11.
14. Ibid.
15. Ibid.
16. Ibid.
17. Gulbadan Begim, *Humayunnama*, Appendix, 203.
18. Ibid., 235–6. Habiba Sultan Khanish Dughlat led a life of adventure deserving of comment: taken captive by the Uzbeks as a child, she was raised in the household of Shibani Khan and eventually married to his nephew, Ubaydullah, whom she left c. 1511 when the Uzbeks retreated to Turkestan. She remained in Samarqand, joined her Dughlat uncle, married her cousin, was widowed in 1533 and was present in India for the Timurid celebration of 1531 and the wedding of Babur's son Hindal in 1537.
19. Ibid., 244–5.
20. Ibid., 9.
21. Jahangir, *Tuzuk*, 20.
22. Manz, "Dynastic Politics," 11.
23. Streusand, *Formation*, 29.

24. Joseph Fletcher, "Turco-Mongolian Monarchic Traditions in the Ottoman Empire," *Eucharistion*, Harvard Ukrainian Studies, III-IV, 1979–80, 239. Fletcher uses the Celtic term "tanistry" to describe the Turco-Mongol system of inheritance and legitimacy. This system of succession, which allows the most able male member of the royal clan to inherit the throne, has been identified in such diverse regions as the British Isles, Central Asia, sub-Saharan Africa and Southeast Asia.
25. Ibid.
26. Maria Eva Subtelny, "Babur's Rival Relations: A Study of Kinship and Conflict in 15th and 16th Century Central Asia," *Der Islam*, 66 (1989), 106.
27. Munis Faruqui, "Princes and Power in the Mughal Empire, 1569- 1657," unpublished PhD dissertation, Duke University, 2002, 34.
28. Subtelny, "Rival Relations," 107.
29. Ibid., 104.
30. Gulbadan Begim, *Humayunnama*, 2.
31. Babur, *Baburnama*, Mano, ed., 558–9; Thackston, trans., 741–3.
32. Ram Prasad Tripathi, "The Turko- Mongol Theory of Kingship," *The Mughal State, 1526- 1750*, Alam and Subrahmanyam, eds., New Delhi: Oxford University Press, 1998.
33. Babur, *Baburnama*, Mano, ed., 187 and 285.
34. Ibid., p. 264; Thackston, trans., 353.
35. The eldest, Jochi, pre-deceased his father so it was his descendants who were given the western portion of the empire; the second son, Chaghatay, received steppe Transoxiana; and Ogodei was given the territory east of Lake Balkhash. The youngest son, Tolui, received the Mongolian heartland of the empire, as well as Chingis Khan's personal guard and the larger portion of his army; this was the usual share of the youngest heir and did not imply enhanced status.
36. Manz, *Rise and Rule*, 4.
37. Ibid., 15. Also Streusand, *Formation of the Mughal Empire*, 29.
38. Manz, *Rise and Rule*, 77.
39. Ibid.. Manz warns her readers that the ten thousand soldiers each implied by the word *tumen* is an unlikely number and that perhaps not all *tumens* mentioned in the sources, nor soldiers in each *tumen*, in fact existed. *Tumen* perhaps should be taken to mean "a large military force."
40. Ibn Arabshah, *Tamerlane*, 241–2.
41. Pierce, *The Imperial Harem*, 43.
42. Manz, *Rise and Rule*, 84–5.
43. Ibid., 86.
44. Babur, *Baburnama*, Reşit Rahmeti Arat, trans. and ed., [*Vekayi Babur'un Hatıratı*], Ankara: Türk Tarih Kurumu Basımevi, 1946, II, 579. As a

Central Asian tradition, the office of *ateke* was common among many groups of Turkish and Mongol descent, such as the Aqquyunlus, Qaraquyyunlus, Seljuk Turks, Ottomans and Safavids, among others.
45. As in Beveridge translation of Gulabadan Begim's *Humayunnama*.
46. As in Thackston translation of Jahangir's *Jahangirnama*.
47. Babur *Baburnama*, Arat, trans., 579–80.
48. Manz, *Rise and Rule*, see ch.7.
49. Ibid., 87.
50. In the northwest quadrant, Amiranshah's sons controlled the *ulus* of Hulegu Khan; Khalil Sultan governed Baylaqan, Arran, Armenia and Georgia; Abu Bakr took Iraq, Kurdistan, Mardin, Diyarbakir, and the Oyirat tribe; while Umar governed Azerbaijan. Umar Shaykh had died in 1394, so his son Pir Muhammad governed the southeast quadrant, in Fars, while in the southwestern sector, Iskandar governed Hamadan, Nihawand, Burujird and Lur-i Kuchik, and Rustam governed Isfahan. In the northeast quadrant, Shahrukh governed Khurasan and his sons ruled to its north: Ibrahim Sultan ruled on the borders of Moghulistan, in Andijan and Kashghar, while Ulugh Beg ruled along the border of Turkestan, in Tashkent, Sayram and Ashbara.
51. Ibn Arabshah, *Tamerlane*, 242. Khalil Sultan was the son of Miranshah (1367–1408), Timur's third son.
52. Lentz and Lowry, *Princely Vision*, 68 and 155.
53. Gulbadan Begim, *Humayunnama*, p. 10. Babur's four sons were all born in Kabul: Humayun (1508–1556), Askari (d. 1558), Hindal (1518–1551) and Kamran (d. 1557), in addition to several daughters.
54. Ibid., 11.
55. Babur, *Baburnama*, Arat, trans., 580.
56. Gulbadan Begim, *Humayunnama*, 11.
57. Ibid., 22.
58. Babur, *Baburnama*, Mano, ed., 558- 61; Thackston, trans., 741- 43.
59. Abu al-Fazl, *Akbarnama*, I, 586. Italics mine.
60. Ibid., 587.
61. Ibid., 588.
62. Ibid., 596.
63. Ibid.
64. Gulbadan Begim, *Humayunnama*, 50.
65. Ibid., 61.
66. Ibid., 65.
67. Ibid., 61–2.
68. The exception is, of course, the accession of Shah Jahan, who acknowledged the continued relevance of the principle of tanistry through the immediate

order to murder of all of his male relatives, even those who were too young to seem an immediate threat to the throne. His own successor, Aurangzeb, also carefully rid himself of rivals, but those not killed outright in actual succession battles were "legally" executed as demanded by a public court order the emperor had requested and, of course, received. See below, this chapter.

69. Abu al-Fazl, *A'in-i Akbari*, III, 428–9. Akbar's forgiveness did not extend to Mirza Hakim's sons. When their father died of alcohol poisoning in 1585, Akbar refused a position of substantial power to any of the three.
70. Abu al-Fazl, *Akbarnama*, III, 105.
71. Ibid.; For an alternative view of Akbar's talents as a father, see Fr. Monserrate, who wrote that "The king's nature is such that, though he loved his children very dearly, he used to give them orders rather roughly whenever he wanted anything done; and he sometimes punished them with harsh blows as well as harsh words." See Monserrate, *Commentary*, 53.
72. They were, of course, assigned income-producing properties, *jagirs*, but as children were not expected to govern these territories themselves, but merely to profit from them.
73. Abu al-Fazl, *Akbarnama*, III, 288.
74. cited in Faruqui, "Princes and Power," 43- 4. See Shaykh Farid Bhukhari, *Zakhirat al-Khawanin*, Ziya al-Din Desai, trans., Delhi, 1993, I, 58,
75. Sa'id Khan Chaghatay descended from a line of Timurid military men in Transoxiana. His grandfather, Ibrahim Beg Chabuq, had come to India in the service of Humayun, and his father had served Akbar. Shah Nawaz Khan, Nawab Shams ud- Daula, and Abdul Hayy, *Maathir (Ma'asir)-ul-Umara: biographies of the Muhammadan and Hindu Officers of the Timurid Sovereigns of India from 1500 to about 1780 A.D.*, 2 vols., H. Beveridge, trans., Baini Prashad, ed. Calcutta: The Asiatic Society, 1952. Delhi: Low Price Publications, 1999, II, 679–82.
76. Abu al-Fazl, *Akbarnama*, III, p. 308.
77. Ibid., pp. 463–4.
78. Inayat Khan, *Shah Jahan Nama*, 537.
79. Sayyid Tabib Hasan Ramzi, *Ruka'at-i Alamgiri*, Jamshid H. Bilmoria, ed., Delhi: Idarah-i Adabiyat-i Delli, 1972, 40- 41.
80. H.K. Naqvi, *History of Mughal Government and Administration*, Delhi: Kanishka Publishing House, 1990, p. 65. Also, "The Timurid-Mughal tradition demanded an end to the appointment of *ataliqs* once princes attained adult status," in Faruqui, "Princes and Power," 46.
81. Abu al-Fazl, *A'in-i Akbari*, III, 1081.
82. Mu'tamid Khan, *Iqbalnama*, British Library, Add 26218, f. 87.

83. Manucci, *Memoirs*, pp. 37–8.
84. Iradat Khan, "Tarikh-i Iradat Khan," *History of India*, VII, 555.
85. Of noble descent, son of Mirza Rustam of Qandahar, Shah Nawaz Khan was made *ateke* to Shah Jahan's son, prince Murad Baksh, at the time of his assignment to the Deccan. On his death in the succession wars, because of his royal lineage, Shah Nawaz Khan Safavi was buried in the Chishti shrine in Delhi on orders of Emperor Aurangzeb. See Shah Nawaz Khan, *Ma'athir ul-Umara*, II, 767- 71.
86. Faruqui, "Princes and Power,"12.
87. Jahangir, *Tuzuk*, 14. Jahangir took over the patronage of Mirza Sultan, the son of Mirza Shahrukh, a Timurid descendant through the line of Mirza Sultan Abu Sa'id and governor of Badakhshan.
88. In modern Persian, *naukar* has come to mean "servant," indicating a trend in definition towards increasing personal loyalty.
89. Jahangir, *Tuzuk*, 294 and 403. The size of the retinues developed by the adult princes could be enormous. It has been estimated that by the 1580's Salim's personal household reached 30,000 people, 6,000 horsemen and 24,000 retainers, in addition to the personnel required to service these multitudes. See Faruqui, "Princes and Power," 51.
90. Muhammad Hashim Khafi Khan, "Muntakhab'ul-Lubab (Tarikh-i Khafi Khan)," *History of India*, VII, 229.
91. Colin Imber, *The Ottoman Empire, 1300–1650*, NY: Palgrave Macmillan, 2002, 97.
92. Ibid., 99.
93. See Pierce, *The Imperial Harem* and Imber, *Ottoman Empire*, for a discussion of the Ottoman succession. See Roger Savory, *Iran Under the Safavids*, Cambridge: Cambridge University Press, 1980 and H.R. Roemer, "The Safavids," *Cambridge History of Iran*, Vol. 6: The Timurid and Safavid Periods, Peter Jackson and Lawrence Lockhart, eds., Cambridge University Press, 1986, for information regarding the Safavid succession.
94. Asad Beg (Kaswini), "Wikaya-i Asad Beg," *History of India*, VI, 170.
95. R.P. Kangle (ed. and trans.), *The Kautilya Arthashastra*, Bombay, 1960–1965, III, 17.
96. Muhammad Hadi, *Preface to Jahangirnama*, Wheeler M. Thackston, trans., 8.
97. Ibid.,11.
98. Ibid.,18.
99. Ram Prasad Khosla, *Mughal Kingship and Nobility*, New Delhi: Idarah-i Adabiyat-i Delli, 1976, 100.
100. Jahangir, *Tuzuk*, 38; Thackston, trans., 55. Jamshid is among the pre-Islamic kings of Iran listed in Ferdowsi's *Shahnama*. Jamshid's reputation

for justice made him an imperial icon within the Persian speaking world. The imagery of his cup has generally been interpreted as "an emblem of mystical gnosis and divine love," but as it was employed by the favorite poet of the Jahangiri Mughal court, the medieval Persian composer of ghazals, Hafiz, the "cup of Jamshid" has a courtly context, both generally and more specifically to signify the transience of kingly power and glory" (See Julie Scott Meisami, *Medieval Persian Court Poetry*, Princeton, NJ: Princeton University Press, 1987, 288.). Surely it is this interpretation which inspired Jahangir's evocation of pre-Islamic Persianate kingship. In a certainly deliberate play on words, the name *Khurshid* is here translated as sun, but it was also the name of the mistress of Jamshid, see F. Steingass, *Persian-English Dictionary*, New Delhi: Munshiram Manoharlal Publishers, Pvt., 2000, 484.

101. Muhammad Hadi, *Preface*, Thackston, trans., 6.
102. Jahangir, *Tuzuk*, 147; Thackston, trans., 155. *Baba* was commonly used by the Mughals in India as an affectionate nickname, meaning baby or child, although its Persian meaning is grandfather or father. Note the tellingly childish and diminutive nickname used by the emperor in referring to his twenty-two-year-old son in a letter to a third party.
103. Ibid., 403.
104. Ibid., 395.
105. Ibid., 403. (*nā khalafi*: wicked, dastardly, ignoble)
106. Ibid., 404.
107. Inayat Khan, *Shah Jahan Nama*, 14. "On royal command," the new emperor's brother, Shahryar, and nephews Bulaqi (Dawar Bakhsh), son of the emperor's deceased brother Khusraw, another brother, Gurshasp, along with Danyal's sons Tahmuras and Hushang, were put to death on February 2, 1628, four days after the *khutba* was read in Shah Jahan's name in Lahore.
108. Khosla, *Mughal Kingship*, 102.
109. Inayat Khan, *Shah Jahan Nama*, 119.
110. Ibid., 356. What would Babur, whose men complained of the heat in India, have thought!
111. Ibid.
112. Kambu, "Amal-i Salih," 128.
113. Dara Shikuh (Shikoh), *Majma' ul-Bahrain (The Mingling of Two Oceans)*. M. Mahfuz-ul-Haq, trans. Calcutta: The Asiatic Society, 1929, reprint 1982, 3.
114. Ibid.
115. Muhammad Kazim, "Alamgirnama," *History of India*, VII, 178.
116. Kambu, "Amal-i Salih," *History of India*, VII, 129.

117. Inayat Khan, *Shah Jahan Nama*, 545.
118. Khafi Khan, "Muntakhab'ul Lubab," *History of India*, VII, 217.
119. Kambu, "Amal-i Salih," *History of India*, VII, 129.
120. Khafi Khan, "Munakhab'ul Lubab," *History of India*, VII, 217–18.
121. Francois Bernier, *Travels*, 25.
122. Inayat Khan, *Shah Jahan Nama*, 554.
123. For a discussion of the "heresy of Dara Shikoh," see Muhammad Kazim, "Alamgirnama," *History of India*, VII, 179, and Khafi Khan, "Muntakhab'ul Lubab," *History of India*, VII, 214.
124. Salih Kambu, "Amal-i Salih," *History of India*, VII, 132
125. Khafi Khan, "Muntakhab'ul Lubab," *History of India*, VII, 228.
126. Alan M. Guenther, "Hanafi *Fiqh* in Mughal India: The *Fatawa-i Alamgiri*," *India's Islamic Traditions, 711- 1750*, Richard M. Eaton, ed., New Delhi: Oxford University Press, 2003, 211.
127. Salih Kambu, "Amal-i Salih," *History of India*, VII, 131.
128. Hamid al-Din Khan Bahadur, *Ahkam-i Alamgiri*, Sir Jadunath Sarkar, trans. as *Anecdotes of Aurangzeb*, Calcutta: M.C. Sarkar and Sons, 1927.
129. Sir Jadunath Sarkar, *History of Aurangzib*, London: Orient Longman Limited, 1973, III, 4.
130. Ibid., 30.
131. Ibid., 34.
132. Letter from Aurangzeb to his grandson Shah Azam Shah, in Iradat Khan, "Tarikh-i Iradat Khan," *History of India*, VII, 563.
133. Letter from Aurangzeb to his son, Kam Bakhsh, in ibid., 65.
134. Khosla, *Mughal Kingship*, 111–113.
135. Faruqhi, "Princes and Power."
136. For example, Faruqui, "Princes and Power," and Chandra, *Parties and Politics*.
137. Faruqui,"Princes and Power," 52.
138. Ibid., 128.
139. Streusand, *Formation of the Mughal Empire*, 29.
140. Khosla, *Mughal Kingship*, 9.
141. Richards, "Formulation of Imperial Authority," 260.
142. Jahangir, *Tuzuk*, 30.
143. Mufazzal Khan, "Tarikh-i Mufazzal," *History of India*, VII, 43.
144. Khafi Khan, "Muntakhab'ul Lubab," *History of India*, VII, 253.
145. Richards, "Formulation of Imperial Authority," p. 260. One of the chief concerns of the nineteenth-century Mughal dynasty was the attempt by the British to impose a rule of primogeniture on the royal family. See Dalrymple, *Last Mughal*.

Chapter 5   Conclusion: Imagining Kingship

1. See Jos J.L. Gommens, *Mughal Warfare: Indian Frontiers and High Roads to Empire, 1500–1700,* NY:Routledge, 2002; and the same, with Dirk H. A. Kolff, *Warfare and Weaponry in South Asia, 1000–1800, AD,* Delhi: Oxford University Press, 2001.
2. Dale, "Legacy of the Timurids," 47. See (listed in alphabetical order), Hamid Algar, "The Naqshbandi Order: A Preliminary Survey of Its History and Significance," *Studia Islamica* 44/136 (1976), pp. 123–152; Arthur F. Buehler, *Sufi Heirs of the Prophet: The Indian Naqshbandiyya and the Rise of The Mediating Sufi Saint,* Columbia: University of South Carolina Press, 1998; Stephen F. Dale and Alam Payind, "The Ahrari Waqf in Kabul in the Year 1546 and the Mughal Naqshbandiyyah," *The Journal of Asian Studies* 119, 2 (1999), pp. 210–33; Johanan Friedman, "Nizami, Naqshbandi Influence on Mughal Rulers and Politics," *Islamic Culture* XXXIX (1965), pp. 40–43; K.A. Nizami, "Naqshbandi Influence on Mughal Rulers and Politics," *Islamic Culture* 39 (1965), pp. 41–52, among others.
3. *Maktubat-i Kalimi, Letters of Shah Kalimullah of Delhi,* quoted in Khaliq Ahmad Nizami, *State and Culture in Medieval India,* New Delhi: Adam Publishers, 1985, p. 160.
4. Finbarr Flood, *Objects of Translation,* 4.
5. Diana L. Eck, *Darsan: Seeing the Divine Image in India,* Columbia University Press, 2nd ed., 1996, 3.
6. Ibid., 6.
7. Ibid., 7.
8. Daud Ali, *Courtly Culture in Medieval India,* Cambridge: Cambridge University Press, 2004, 133; quote from the *Harsa-carita of Bana.*
9. Ibid.
10. Ibid.; quote from the *Manosollasa of King Somesvara*
11. Ram Charita Prasad Singh, *Kingbsip in Northern India (c. 600–1200 AD),* Delhi: Motilal Banarsidass, 1968, 31.
12. Moin, "Sacred Kingship."
13. Ibid., 156.
14. al-Badaoni, *Muntakhab,* 573.
15. Catherine Asher, "Sub-Imperial Palaces: Power and Authority in Mughal India, *Ars Orientalis,* Vol. 23, Pre-Modern Islamic Palaces (1993), 282. Ultimately, the source of darshan in Hindu religious tradition motivated the Mughal emperor Aurangzeb to end the practice.
16. Asher, "Sub-imperial Palaces," 283.
17. Roe, *Embassy,* 112 and 108, respectively.

18. Asher, "Sub-Imperial Palaces," 30.
19. Abu al-Fazl, *A'in-i Akbari*, I, 165.
20. Abd al-Hamid Lahori, "Daily Activities of the Emperor Shah Jahan from cAbd al-Hamid Lahori's Padshah Nama," appendix in A.R. Fuller, trans. W.E. Begley and Z.A. Desai, eds., Delhi, NY, and London: Oxford University Press, 1990, 567.
21. Gülru Necipoğlu, "Framing the Gaze in Ottoman, Safavid, and Mughal Palaces," *Ars Orientalis*, 23, Pre-Modern Islamic Palaces (1993), 579.
22. Abu al-Fazl describes Akbar's massive two- story imperial tent/mobile royal dwelling as containing a jharoka, a small upper-story window and balcony, from which the ruler could be viewed but also observe performances, "inspect the rations for the elephants and camels," watch animal fights, etc.. See *A'in-i Akbari*, I, 55.
23. A.K.S. Lambton, "Justice in the Medieval Persian Theory of Kingship," *Studia Islamica*, No 17 (1962), 94. The earlier mirrors for princes' literature may have put more emphasis on wisdom, but by the medieval period, in the writings of the majority, justice had become the central tenet of legitimate kingship.
24. In Lambton, "Justice," 100. Attributed by al-Tha'alibi to the Sassanid emperor, Arashir.
25. Nasir al-Din Tusi, *Akhlaq-i Nasiri*, 5th ed., Tehran: Shirkat-i Salami-ye Intishirat-i Khorazm, 1373 (1994). See Alam, *Languages of Political Islam, India 1200–1800*, University of Chicago Press, 2004; and Alam, "Akhlaqi Norms and Mughal Governance," *The Making of Indo-Persian Culture*, Muzaffar Alam, et al., eds., New Delhi: Manohar, 2000.
26. Muzaffar Alam, "State Building Under the Mughals,"126.
27. The assumption by modern scholars is that this work was his earlier study, the *Dastur al-Vizarat*, given a new title to better suit the author's new patron, Babur. Ibid., 14.
28. Alam, "Akhlaqi Norms," 78.
29. Ibid., 229.
30. Ibid., 227.
31. Muzaffar Alam, *Languages of Political Islam*, 6.
32. Sa'di Shirazi, *Thousand Years of Persian Rubaiya*, Reza Saberi, trans. Bethesda, Maryland: IBEX Publishers, 2000, 130.
33. Ibid.
34. Ibid., 132–33.
35. Haleh Pourafzal and Roger Montgomery, *The Spiritual Wisdom of Hafiz*, Rochester, Vermont: The Spiritual Traditions, 1998, 201.
36. Meisami, *Court Poetry*, 297. Italics mine.

37. Ibid., 297.
38. Tusi claims that while justice is the most important virtue in a king, it is closely followed by benevolent kindness (*ihsan*). Tusi, *Nasirean Ethics*, 233.
39. Alam, "Akhlaqi Norms," 84–85.
40. Ibid., 34.
41. Abdul Aziz, Sh., *The Imperial Library of the Mughals*, Delhi: Idarah-i Adabiyat-i Delli, 1974, 57. It is unclear just who determined the ranking of these works.
42. Ibid., p. 31.
43. Alam, "State Building," 116
44. Jahangir, *Tuzuk*, 285.
45. Ibid., p. 9. Thackston, trans., 28.
46. Linda T. Darling, "'Do Justice, Do Justice, For That is Paradise!': Middle Eastern Advice for Indian Muslim Rulers,"*Comparative Studies of South Asia, Africa, and the Middle East*, XXII, 1&2 (2002),10.
47. Jahangir, *Tuzuk*, 5.
48. Roe, *Embassy*, 108.
49. Ibid., 106 and 108.
50. Ibid, 108.
51. Jahangir, *Tuzuk*, p. 242. Thackston, trans., 264.
52. Ibid.
53. Ibid.
54. Rai Bhara Mal. "Lubbu-t Tawarikh-i Hind," *History of India*, VII, 172.
55. Ibid., 366–67.
56. Inayat Khan, *Shah Jahan Nama*, 356.
57. Dale, *Eight Paradises*, 466.
58. Ibid.

BIBLIOGRAPHY

Primary Sources:

Ahmad, Bakhshi Khwajah Nizam al-Din, *Tabaqat-i Akbari (a history of India from the early musalman invasions to the 38th year of the reign of Akbar)*, Brajendranath De (trans.), Baini Prashad (ed.), Delhi: Low Price Publications 1939, reprint 1990.

Alamgir (Aurangzeb), *Dastur al 'Amal-i Agahi* (Collected letters), British Library MS Add 18881.

_____ *Ruka'at-i-Alamgiri.* (Collected letters), Jamshid H. Bilmoria (ed.), Delhi: Idarah-i Adabiyat-i Delli, 1972.

Allami, Abu al-Fazl, *'Ain ('Ayn)-i Akbari*, Vol. 1, H. Blochmann, (trans.) 2nd ed., Lieut. Colonel D.C. Phillott, (ed.), New Delhi: Munshiran Manoharlal Pub. Pvt. Ltd., 3rd ed., 1977. Vols. 2 and 3, Colonel H.S. Jarrett, (trans. and ed.), 2nd ed., Sir Jadunath Sarkar, (ed.), 3rd ed., 1977.

_____ *Akbarnama*, H. Beveridge (trans.), 3 Vols., Delhi: Manmohan Satish Kumar, Rare Books, 1st Indian edition, 1972.

Anonymous (I), "Synoptic Account of the House of Timur," *A Century of Princes: Sources on Timurid History and Art*, Wheeler Thackston (trans.), Cambridge, MA.: The Aga Khan Program for Islamic Architecture (1989), pp. 237–246.

Asad Beg (Kaswini), "Wikaya-i Asad Beg," *History of India, As Told by Its Own Historians*, Sir H.M. Elliot & John Dowson (eds.), NY: AMS Press, Inc. (1966), VI, pp. 150–174.

Babur, Zahir al-Din Muhammad, *Vaqi'at-i Baburi*, Original translation from Chaghatay Turkish into Persian by 'Abdul Rahim Khan-i Khanan for Emperor Akbar, c. 1590, (includes 68 entire pages of miniatures and 48 smaller drawings in body of text), British Library MS OR 3714.

_____ *Baburnama (Vekayi), Critical Edition Based on Four Chaghatay Texts*, Eiji Mano (ed.), Japanese and Chaghatay, 4 vols., Kyoto: Syokado, 1995.

Bibliography

_____ *Baburnama*, Wheeler M. Thackston (trans.), text in Chaghatay, Persian and English, 3 vols., Cambridge, MA: Harvard University Department of Near Eastern Languages and Civilizations, 1993.

_____ *The Baburnama in English*, Annette Susannah Beveridge (trans.), London: Luzac and Company, Ltd., 1969.

_____ *Vekayi Babur'un Hatıratı*, Reşit Rahmeti Arat (trans.), Turkish text, 3 vols., Ankara: Türk Tarih Kurumu Basımevi, 1946.

al-Badauni (Badaoni), Abdul Qadir Ibn Muluk Shah, *Muntakhabut al-Tawarikh*, W.H. Lowe (trans.), 3 vols., Patna, India: Academica Asiatica, 1973.

_____ *Muntakhabu-t-tawarikh*, 2 vols., G. S. A. Ranking, trans., Calcutta, 1898.

Bahadur, Hamid al-Din Khan, *Ahkam-i Alamgiri*, British Library, BM 14807.a.10.

_____ *Anecdotes of Aurangzeb [Ahkam-i Alamgiri]*, Jadunath Sarkar (trans.), Calcutta: M.C. Sarkar and Sons, 1927.

Bakhtawar Khan, "Mirat-i Alam [Mirat-i Jahun Nama]," *History of India, As Told by Its Own Historians*, Sir H.M. Elliot & John Dowson (eds.), NY: AMS Press, Inc. (1966) VII, pp. 145–65.

Bayat, Bayazid, *Tazkirah-i Humayun ve Akbar*, M. Hidayet Hosayn (ed.), Calcutta: Bibliotheca Indica, 1941.

_____ "Tarikh-i Humayun," *Three Memoirs of Homayun*, Wheeler M. Thackston (trans./English and Persian texts), Costa Mesa, CA: Mazda Publishers, 2009, II.

Bayqara, Mirza Sultan Husayn, "Apologia," *A Century of Princes: Sources on Timurid History and Art*, Wheeler Thackston (trans.), Cambridge, MA: The Aga Khan Program for Islamic Architecture (1989), 373–78.

Bernier, Francois. *Travels in the Mogul Empire, AD 1656- 1668*, Archibald Constable, (trans.), London: Cambridge University Press, 1934; New Delhi: Munshiram Manoharlal Publishers Pvt. Ltd., Oriental Reprint, 1983; Delhi: Low Price Publications, 2005.

Bhukari, Shaykh Farid, *Zakhirat al-Khawanin*, Ziya al-Din Desai (trans.), Delhi, 1993.

Clavijo, Ruy Gonzales de, *Embassy to Tamerlane, 1403–1406*, Guy Le Strange (trans.) NY and London: Harper Brothers, 1928.

Coverte, Robert, *A True and Almost Incredible Report of an Englishman*, London, 1612; Amsterdam and NY: Da Capo Press, reprint 1971.

Dara Shikuh (Shikoh), *Majma' ul- Bahrain (The Mingling of Two Oceans)*, M. Mahfuz-ul-Haq (trans.), Calcutta: The Asiatic Society, 1929, reprint 1982.

_____ *Sirr-i Akbar (Upanishads)*, Tara Chand and J. Na'ini (eds.), Tehran, 1957–60.

Dawlatshah, "Tadhkirat al- shu'ara," *A Century of Princes: Sources on Timurid History and Art*, Wheeler M. Thackston (trans.), Cambridge, MA: The Aga Khan Program for Islamic Architecture, 1989, pp. 11–62.

Dughlat, Mirza Haydar, *Tarikh-i Rashidi: A History of the Khans of Moghulistan*, W.M. Thackston (trans./Persian and English texts), 2 vols., Cambridge, MA: Harvard University Department of Near Eastern Languages and Civilizations, 1996.

East India Company, *Letters received by the East India Company from Its Servants in the East*, 2 vols., London, 1896; reprint Amsterdam: N. Israel, 1968.

Elliot, Sir H.M. and John Dowson (eds.), *The History of India, As Told by its Own Historians: the posthumous papers of Sir H.M. Elliot*, 8 vols., London: Trubner and Co. 1872, NY: AMS Press, Inc., 1966.

Ferishta, Muhammad Kasim, *Gulshan-i Ibrahimi (History of the Rise of Mahomedan Power in India)*, John Briggs (trans.), Calcutta: Editions Indian 1829; reprints 1908, 1966.

Foster, Sir William, *The English Factories in India, 1618–1621* (a calendar of documents in the India Office and British Museum), Oxford: Clarendon Press, 1906.

Gulbadan Begim, *Humayunnama (The History of Humayun)*, Annette S. Beveridge, (trans. and ed./ English and Persian texts), Delhi: Idarah-i Adabiyat-i Delli, 1972.

_____ "Humayunnama," *Three Memoirs of Homayun*, Wheeler M. Thackston (trans./English and Persian texts), Costa Mesa, CA: Mazda Publishers, 2009.

Hadi, Muhammad, "Preface to the Jahangirnama," *The Jahangirnama, Memoirs of Jahangir, Emperor of India*, Wheeler M. Thackston, (trans.), NY: Oxford University Press, in association with the Freer Gallery of Art and the Arthur Sackler Gallery, Smithsonian Institution, Washington, D.C., 1999.

Hafiz (Hafez), *Drunk on the Wine of the Beloved: 100 Poems of Hafiz*, Thomas Rain Crowe (trans.), Boston and London: Shambhala, 2001.

Hosten, Henri, "Three letters of Fr. Joseph de Castro, S.J., and the Last Year of Jahangir," *Mughal India According to European Travel Accounts; texts and studies*, vol.1, 1998, pp. 243–268.

Ibn Arabshah, Ahmed ibn Muhammad, *Tamerlane, or Timur the Great Amir*, J.H. Sanders (trans.), Lahore: Progressive Books, 1936, reprint 1976.

Ibn Arabi, *Tarjuman al-Ashwaq*, R.A. Nicholson (trans.), London, 1911.

Islam, Riazul, *A Calendar of Documents on Indo-Persian Relations (1500–1700)*, Tehran, 1979.

Husaini, Khwaja Kamgar, *Maathir (Ma'asir)-i Jahangiri*, India Office MS OR 171.

_____ *Ma'asir-i Jahangiri (A Contemporary Account of Jahangir)*, Azra Alavi (ed.), (Persian text with English introduction), NY: Asia Publishing House, Inc., 1978.

Inayat Khan, *Shah Jahan Nama*, A.R. Fuller (trans.), W.E Begley and Z.A. Desai (eds.), Delhi, NY, and London: Oxford University Press, 1990.

Iradat Khan, "Tarikh-i Iradat Khan," *History of India, As Told by Its Own Historians*, Sir H.M. Elliot & John Dowson (eds.) NY: AMS Press, Inc. (1966),VII, pp. 534–564.

Jahangir, Nur al-Din Muhammad, *Jahangirnama*, British Library MS OR 1644. (See also Ottoman Turkish trans., British Library MS OR 6441).

_____ *Jahangirnama (Tuzuk-i Jahangiri)*, Tehran: Buny adi Farhangi Iran, 1359 (1980).

_____ *The Jahangirnama, Memoirs of Jahangir, Emperor of India*. Wheeler M. Thackston (trans.), NY: Oxford University Press, in association with the Freer Gallery of Art and the Arthur Sackler Gallery, Smithsonian Institution, Washington, D.C., 1999.

_____ *Jahangir, memoirs of the Emperor Jahangueir written by himself*, Major David Price (trans.), London: Oriental Translation Committee, 1829.

Jauhar Aftabchi, Tazkirat-i Waqi'at *(*Tadkhirat-i Waqi'at, Tarikh-e-Humayun, Humayun Shah, Jawahir-e-shahi*)*, *British Library MS Add 16711.*

_____ "Tadhkiratu'l-waqiat," *Three Memoirs of Homayun*, Wheeler Thackston (tans.), Costa Mesa, CA: Mazda Publishers, 2009, Vol.1, English text, pp. 69–175/ Persian text, pp. 1–214.

al-Juwayni (Juvaini), Ala-ad-Din Ata Malik, *Tarikh-i Juhan Gusha*, M.M. Qazvini (ed.), 3 vols., Leiden and London, 1912, 1916, 1937.

_____ *The History of the World Conqueror*, John Andrew Boyle (trans.), 2 vols., Cambridge: Cambridge University Press, 1958.

Kambu (Kambo), Muhammad Salih, "Amal-i Salih," *History of India, As Told by Its Own Historians*, Sir H.M. Elliot & John Dowson (eds.), NY: AMS Press, Inc. (1966), VII, pp. 123–132.

Kautilya, *The Arthashastra*, L.N. Rangarajan (trans.), New Delhi and NY: Penguin Books, 1992.

_____ *Kautilya's Arthashastra*, R. Shamasastry (trans.), Mysore Printing and Publishing House, 1967.

_____ *The Kautilya Arthashastra*, R.P. Kangle (trans.), Bombay, 1960–1965.

Kazwini, Muhammad Amin, "Padshahnama," *History of India, As Told by Its Own Historians*, Sir H.M. Elliot & John Dowson (eds.), NY: AMS Press, Inc. (1966), VII, pp. 1–3.

Kazim, Muhammad, "Alamgirnama," *History of India, As Told by Its Own Historians*, Sir H.M. Elliot & John Dowson (eds.), NY: AMS Press, Inc. (1966), VII, pp. 174–180.

Khafi Khan, Muhammad Hashim, *History of Alamgir*. S. Moinul Haq (trans.), Calcutta: Bibliotheca Indica, 1860–74; Reproduction, Karachi: Pakistan Historical Society, 1975.

_____ "Muntakhabu-l Lubab Muhammad Shahi," *History of India, As Told by Its Own Historians*, Sir H.M. Elliot & John Dowson (eds.), NY: AMS Press, Inc. (1966), VII, pp. 207–533.

Khan, Nawab Shams ud- Daula Shah Nawaz and Abdul Hayy, *Maathir (Ma'asir)-ul-Umara: biographies of the Muhammadan and Hindu Officers of the Timurid Sovereigns of India from 1500 to about 1780 A.D.*, 2 vols., H. Beveridge (trans.), Baini Prashad (ed.), Calcutta: The Asiatic Society, 1952; Delhi: Low Price Publications, 1999.

Khwandamir, Ghiyas al-Din Muhammad, "Habib al- Siyar," *A Century of Princes: Sources on Timurid History and Art,* Wheeler M. Thackston (trans.), Cambridge, MA: The Aga Khan Program for Islamic Architecture, 1989, pp. 101–235.

_____ *Qanun-i Humayuni (Humayunnama of Khwandamir),* M. Hidayat Hosain (ed.), Calcutta: Royal Asiatic Society of Bengal, 1940.

Lahori [Lahauri], Abdul- Hamid and Muhammad Waris, *Padshahnama,* Kabir al-Din Ahmad and Abdal Raman (eds.), Calcutta: Royal Asiatic Society of Bengal 1867; A. R. Fuller (trans.) 1851, reprint. 1990.

_____ "Badshahnama," *History of India, As Told by Its Own Historians,* Sir H.M. Elliot & John Dowson (eds.), NY: AMS Press, Inc. (1966), VII, pp. 3–72.

_____ "Daily Activities of the Emperor Shah Jahan from Abd al-Hamid Lahori's Padshah Nama," appendix in Inayat Khan, *Shah Jahan Nama,* A.R. Fuller (trans.), W.E Begley and Z.A. Desai (eds.), Delhi, NY, and London: Oxford University Press, 1990, pp. 567–73.

Manucci, Niccolao, *Memoirs of the Mogul Court,* Michael Edwardes (trans.), London: Folio Society, 1957.

al-Marghinani, 'Ali ibn Abi Bakr, *The Hedaya or Guide: A Commentary on the Mussulman Laws,* Charles Hamilton (trans.) 2nd ed. 1870, reprint Lahore: Premier Book House, 1963.

Mir Khan (Subadar of Kabul), or Sayyid Mir, *Zafarnama-i Padishah Alamgiri,* British Library MS Add 26234.

Montserrate, Fr., *The Commentary of Father Monserrate, SJ, On His Journey to the Court of Akbar,* J.S. Hoyland (trans.), S.N. Bannerjee (ed.), Oxford, 1922.

Moosvi, Shireen, *Episodes in the Life of Akbar; Contemporary Records and Reminiscences,* New Delhi: National Book Trust, 1994.

Mufazzal Khan, "Tarikh-i Mufazzal," *History of India, As Told by Its Own Historians,* Sir H.M. Elliot & John Dowson (eds.), NY: AMS Press, Inc. (1966), VII, pp. 141–145.

Muhammad (Mirza), *T'arikh-i Jahan Gusha,* London, 1912/ J.A. Boyle (trans.), Manchester, UK, 1958.

Mu'tamid Khan, Muhammad Sharif, *Iqbalnama-i Jahangiri,* British Library Add 26218/ see also, OR 14342.

Najm-i Sani, Muhammad Baqir, *Art of Governance: An Indo-Islamic Mirror for Princes (Ma'uizah-i Jahangiri),* Sajida S. Alvi (trans.), State University of NY Press, 1989.

Nathan, Mirza ('Alau'd- Din Isfahani), *Baharistan-i Ghaybi,* M. I. Borah (trans.), 2 vols. Gauhati, Assam: Narayani Handiqui Historical Institute, 1936.

Nawa'i, Mir Ali Sher [Shir], "Preface to his First Turkish Divan: Gharayib al-Sighar," *A Century of Princes: Sources on Timurid History and Art,* Wheeler Thackston (trans.), Cambridge, MA: The Aga Khan Program for Islamic Architecture (1989), pp. 363–372.

Pelsaert, Francis, *A Dutch Chronicle of Mughal India,* Brij Narain and Sri Ram Sharma (trans. and eds.), Lahore: Sang-e-Meel Publications, 1978.

BIBLIOGRAPHY

Qabil Khan, Musavvadat Munshi al Mamalik Shaykh Abu al- Fath Sadiq Mutlabi Anbalvi, *Adab-i Alamgiri*, British Library OR 177.

——— *Adab-i Alamgiri*, Abdul Ghafur Chaudhari (ed.), Lahore: Idarah-i Tahqiqat-i Pakistan and People's Publishing House, 1941.

Rai Bhara Mal, "Lubbu-t Tawarikh-i Hind," *History of India, As Told by Its Own Historians*, Sir H.M. Elliot & John Dowson (eds.), NY: AMS Press, Inc. (1966), VII, pp. 168–173.

Ramzi, Sayyid Tabib Hasan, *Ruqa'at-i Alamgiri*, British Library Per D, 1861.

——— *Ruqa'at-i Alamgiri*, Jamshid H. Bilmoria (ed.), Delhi: Idarah-i Adabiyat-i Delli, 1972; previously published as: *Ruka'at-i Alamgir*, Diyoband: Mas'ud Publishing Haus, 1968.

Rashid al-Din, *The Successors of Genghis Khan*, John Andrew Boyle (trans.), New York: Columbia University Press, 1971.

Razi, Aqil Khan, *Waqiyat-i Alamgiri*, British Library MS Per. D. 84.

——— *Waqiyat-i Alamgiri*, Khan Bahadur Mawlvi Haji Zafar Hasan (ed.), Delhi: Mercantile Printing Press, 1946.

Roe, Sir Thomas, *Embassy to the Court of the Great Mogul, 1615–1619*, W. Foster (ed.), London: Hakluyt Society, 1899.

Sa'di Shirazi, *A Thousand Years of Persian Rubaiyat*, Reza Saberi (ed.), Bethesda, Maryland: IBEX Publishers, 2000.

Samarqandi, Abdul al-Razzaq, "Mission to Calicut and Vijayanagar," *A Century of Princes: Sources on Timurid History and Art*, Wheeler Thackston (trans.), Cambridge, MA: The Aga Khan Program for Islamic Architecture (1989), pp. 299–321.

Samarqandi, Mir Dawlatshah, "Tadhkirat al-shu'ara" *A Century of Prince: Sources on Timurid History and Art*, Wheeler Thackston (trans.), Cambridge, MA: The Aga Khan Program for Islamic Architecture (1989), 11–62.

Samarqandi, Mutribi al-Asamm, *Khatirat-i-Mutribi*, Abdul Ghani Mirzoyef (ed.), Karachi: University of Karachi, 1977.

——— ["Murtib" al-Assam], *Conversations With Emperor Jahangir*, Richard C. Foltz, (trans.), Costa Mesa, CA: Mazda Publishers, 1998.

Saqi Must'ad Khan, *Ma'asir-i Alamgiri*, British Library MS B.I. 269.

——— *History of the Emperor Aurangzeb-Alamgir*, Jadunath Sarkar (trans.), Calcutta: Royal Asiatic Society of Bengal, 1947, and New Delhi: Munshiram Manoharlal Publishers Pvt. Lmt., 1986.

Shafi, Muhammad (Tehrani), "Tarikh-i Chaghatai," *History of India, As Told by Its Own Historians*, Sir H.M. Elliot & John Dowson (eds.), NY: AMS Press, Inc. (1966), VIII, pp. 21–22.

Shah Nawaz Khan, Nawab Samsam ud- Daula, and Abdul Hayy, *Maathir (Ma'asir)-ul-Umara: biographies of the Muhammadan and Hindu Officers of the Timurid Sovereigns of India from 1500 to about 1780 A.D.*, 2 vols., H. Beveridge (trans.), Baini Prashad (ed.), Calcutta: The Asiatic Society, 1952; Delhi: Low Price Publications, 1999.

Shirazi, Kami, *Waqa-i-uz-Zaman (Fath Nama-i-Nur Jahan Begam)*, W.H. Siddiqi (trans.), Rampur, Uttar Pradesh: Rampur Raza Library 2003.

Tabrizi, Jafar, "Arzadasht," *A Century of Princes: Sources on Timurid History and Art,* Wheeler M. Thackston (trans.), Cambridge, MA: The Aga Khan Program for Islamic Architecture, 1989, pp. 323–327.

Tavernier, Jean- Baptiste, *Travels in India,* V. Ball (trans., from French edition of 1676) 2nd ed., William Crooke (ed.), London: Oxford University Press 1925; Delhi: Low Price Publications, 2000.

Thackston, Wheeler M. (trans. and ed.), *A Century of Princes: Sources on Timurid History and Art,* Cambridge, Massachusetts: The Aga Khan Program for Islamic Architecture, published in conjunction with the exhibition "Timur and the Princely Vision," 1989.

Tirmizi, S.A.I., *Edicts from the Mughal Harem,* Delhi: Idarah-i Adabiyat-i Delli, 1979.

Tusi, Nasir al-Din, *Akhlaq-i Nasiri,* Tehran: Shirket-i Salami-ye Intishirat-e Khorazm, 5th ed., 1373 (1994).

_____ *Akhlaqi Nasiri (The Nasirean Ethics),* G.M. Wickens (trans.), London: George Allen and Unwin, Ltd., 1964.

Yazdi, Sharafuddin Ali, "Zafarnama," *A Century of Princes: Sources on Timurid History and Art,* Wheeler M. Thackston (trans.), Cambridge, MA: The Aga Khan Program for Islamic Architecture (1989), pp. 63–100.

Miscellaneous:

Proceedings on the Trial of Muhammad Bahadur Shah, Titular King of Delhi, before a Military Commission, upon a charge of Rebellion, Treason and Murder, Calcutta: John Gray, Calcutta Gazette Office, 1858/ printed 1895/ reprint Karachi : Royal Book Company (1972).

Silsilahnamas (genealogical scrolls):

_____ Ottoman genealogy from Adam to Abdul Mecid, British Library, OR 7309.

_____ Biographical notices and portraits of Ottoman sultans to Abdul Mecid, British Library, OR 9505.

_____ *Mir'at al-ashbah-i salatin-i asman jah,* Timurid chronological tables, British Library, OR 182.

_____ *Mu'izz al- Ansab,* Timurids through Badi' al-Zaman [illustrated], British Library, OR 467.

Secondary Sources:

Adams, William Howard, *Gardens Through History: Nature Perfected,* NY: Abbeville Press, 1991.

Alam, Muzaffar, "Guiding the Ruler and Prince," *Islam in South Asia in Practice*, Barbara Metcalf (ed.), Princeton, NJ: Princeton University Press, 2009.

―――― *The Languages of Political Islam, India 1200–1800*, Chicago: University of Chicago Press, 2004.

―――― "Akhlaqi Norms and Mughal Governance," *The Making of Indo-Persian Culture*, Muzaffar Alam, Francoise 'Nalini' Delvoye and Marc Gaborieau (eds.), New Delhi: Manohar (2000), pp. 67–95.

――――, Francoise 'Nalini' Delvoye and Marc Gaborieau (eds.), *The Making of Indo-Persian Culture*, New Delhi: Manohar, 2000.

―――― and Sanjay Subrahmanyam, *The Mughal State, 1526- 1750*, New Delhi: Oxford University Press, 1998.

―――― "The Pursuit of Persian: Language in Mughal Politics," *Modern Asian Studies* 32, 2 (1998), pp. 31–49.

―――― "State Building Under the Mughals," *L'Heritage Timouride, Iran- Asie Central-Inde, XVe- XVIIIe Siecles, Les Cahiers d'Asie Centrale*, Maria Szuppe (ed.), Tachkent- Aix-en-Provence (1997), pp. 105–128.

Algar, Hamid, "The Naqshbandis and Safavids: A Contribution to the Religious History of Iran and Her Neighbors," *Safavid Iran and Her Neighbors*, Michel Mazzaoui (ed.), Salt Lake City, Utah: The University of Utah Press (2003), pp. 7–48.

―――― "Political Aspects of Naqshbandi History," *Naqshbandis: Cheminements et situation actuelle d'un ordre mystique musulman*. Actes de la Table Ronde de Sèvres, Marc Gaborieau, et al. (eds.), Editions Isis: Istanbul (1985, 1990), pp. 123–152.

―――― "The Naqshbandi Order: A Preliminary Survey of Its History and Significance," *Studia Islamica* 44/136 (1976), pp. 123–152.

Ali, Daud, *Courtly Culture and Political Life in Early Medieval India*, Cambridge: Cambridge University Press, 2004.

Ali, M. Athar, "Towards an Interpretation of the Mughal Empire," *Journal of the Royal Asiatic Society*, No. 1 (1978), pp. 38–49

―――― "The Passing of Empire: The Mughal Case," *Modern Asian Studies* 9, 3 (1975), pp. 385–96.

Allen, Terry, *Timurid Herat*, Weisbaden: Ludwig Reichart, 1983.

Allsen, Thomas T., *The Royal Hunt in Eurasian History*, Philadelphia, PA: University of Pennsylvania Press, 2006.

―――― *Culture and Conquest in Mongol Eurasia*, Cambridge: Cambridge University Press, 2001.

―――― *Commodity and Exchange in the Mongol Empire*, Cambridge: Cambridge University Press, 1997.

Alvi, Sajida S., "Religion and State During the Reign of Mughal Emperor Jahangir (1605–27): Nonjuristical Perspectives." *Studia Islamica*, 69 (1989), 95–119.

Andrews, Walter G., Najaat Black and Mehmet Kalpaki, eds. and trs., *Ottoman Lyric Poetry*, Austin, Texas: University of Texas Press, 1997.

Anooshahr, Ali, *The Ghazi Sultans and the Frontiers of Islam*, London and NY: Routledge, 2009.

Apte, B.K. (ed.), *Chhatrapati Shivaji: Coronation Tercentenary Commemoration Volume*, Bombay: University of Bombay, 1874–5.

Arberry, A.J., *Fifty Poems of Hafiz*, Richmond, Surrey: Curzon Press Ltd., 1947;corrected 1953, reprints 1962, 1970.

Asher, Catherine B., "Architecture," *The Magnificent Mughals*, Zeenut Ziad, ed., Oxford, UK: Oxford University Press (2002), pp. 183–228.

——— "Sub-Imperial Palaces: Power and Authority in Mughal India," *Ars Orientalis*, Vol. 23, Pre-Modern Islamic Palaces (1993), pp. 281–302.

Avery, Peter, "Nadir Shah and the Afsharid Legacy," *The Cambridge History of Iran*, VII, " Nadir Shah to the Islamic Republic," Peter Avery, Gavin Hambly and Charles Melville eds.), Cambridge: Cambridge University Press (1991), pp. 3–62.

——— Gavin Hambly and Charles Melville, eds., *The Cambridge History of Iran*, VII [Nadir Shah to the Islamic Republic], Cambridge: Cambridge University Press, 1991.

Aziz, Abdul Sh., *The Imperial Library of the Mughals*, Delhi: Idarah-i Adabiyat-i Delli, 1974.

Aziz, Ahmad, *Studies in Islamic Culture in the Indian Environment*, New Delhi: Oxford University Press, 1964; reprint 2002.

Babayan, Kathryn, "The 'Aqa'id al-Nisa:' A Glimpse of Safavid Women in Local Isfahani Culture," *Women in the Medieval Islamic World*, Gaven Hambly (ed.), NY: St. Martin's Press (1998), pp. 349–382.

Balabanlilar, Lisa, "Begims of the Mystic Feast," *The Journal of Asian Studies*, Vol. 69, No. 1 (February) 2010, pp. 123–147.

——— "The Emperor Jahangir and the Pursuit of Pleasure," *Journal of the Royal Asiatic Society*, Series 3, 19, 2 (2009), pp. 1–14.

——— "Lords of the Auspicious Conjunction: Turco-Mongol Imperial Identity on the Subcontinent," *The Journal of World History* 18, 1 (2007) pp. 1–39.

——— "Lords of the Auspicious Conjunction: Turco- Mongol Imperial Identity on the Subcontinent," unpublished PhD dissertation, The Ohio State University, 2007.

Barnett, Richard B., "Embattled Begims: Women as Power Brokers in Early Modern India," *Women in the Medieval Islamic World*, Gaven Hambly (ed.), NY: St. Martin's Press (1998), pp. 521–36.

Beach, Milo C. and Ebba Koch, *King of the World: The Padshahnama*, NY: Azimuth Editions Limited and Smithsonian Institution, 1997.

Beach, Milo C., "Jahangir's Jahangir- Nama," *Powers of Art*, Barbara Stoler Miller (ed.), Delhi: Oxford University Press (1992), pp. 224–234.

Berinstain, Valerie (ed.), "Voyages dans les Etats du Grand Mogol," *L'Illustration*, 12 September 1857, *India and the Mughal Dynasty*, NY: Harry N. Abrams, 1997.

Blake, Stephen, "Contributors to the Urban Landscape: Women Builders in Safavid Isfahan and Mughal Shahjahanabad," *Women in the Medieval*

Islamic World, Gavin R.G. Hambly (ed.), NY: St. Martin's Press (1998), pp. 407–428.
_____ *Shahjahanabad: The Sovereign City in Mughal India, 1639–1739*, Cambridge University Press, 1991, 2002.
_____ "The Patrimonial- Bureaucratic Empire of the Mughals," *Journal of Asian Studies* 39, 1 (1979), pp. 77–94.
Bosworth, C. Edmund, *The Ghaznavids: Their Empire in Afghanistan and Eastern Iran, 994- 1040*, Edinburgh: Edinburgh University Press, 1963.
Boyle, John Andrew, *The Successors of Genghis Khan*, NY: Columbia University Press, 1971.
Broadbridge, Anne F., *Kingship and Ideology in the Islamic and Mongol Worlds*, NY: Cambridge University Press, 2008.
Buehler, Arthur F., *Sufi Heirs of the Prophet: The Indian Naqshbandiyya and the Rise of The Mediating Sufi Saint*, Columbia: University of South Carolina Press, 1998.
Canby, Sheila, ed., *Humayun's Garden Party: Princes of the House of Timur*, Bombay: Marg Publications, 1994.
Card, Claudia, "Rape as a Weapon of War," *Hypatia*, Vol. 11, No. 4, Women and Violence (Autumn, 1996), pp. 5–18.
Chandra, Satish, *Parties and Politics at the Mughal Court, 1707–1740*, New Delhi: Oxford University Press, 2002–3.
Chatterjee, Prasun, "The Lives of Alcohol in Pre-Colonial India," *The Medieval History Journal*, 8/1 (2005), pp. 189–225.
Conan, Michel (ed.), *Middle East Garden Traditions: Unity and Diversity*, Washington, DC: Dumbarton Oaks, 2007.
Dale, Stephen F., *The Muslim Empires of the Ottomans, Safavids, and Mughals*, Cambridge University Press, 2010.
_____ *The Garden of the Eight Paradises: Babur and the Culture of Empire in Central Asia, Afghanistan and India (1483–1530)*, Leiden: Brill, 2004.
_____ "A Safavid Poet in the Heart of Darkness," *Iranian Studies*, 36/ 2 (June 2003), pp. 197–212.
_____ and Alam Payind, "The Ahrari Waqf in Kabul in the Year 1546 and the Mughal Naqshbandiyyah," *The Journal of Asian Studies* 119, 2 (1999), pp. 210–33.
_____ "The Legacy of the Timurids," *Journal of the Royal Asiatic Society*, Series 3, 8, 7 (1998), pp. 43–58.
_____ "The Poetry and Autobiography of the Baburnama," *The Journal of Asian Studies*, 55, 3 (1996), pp. 635–64.
_____ "Steppe Humanism and the Autobiographical Writings of Zahir al-Din Muhammad Babur, 1483–1530," *International Journal of Middle Eastern Studies* 22 (1990), pp. 37–58.
Dalrymple, William, *The Last Mughal, The Fall of a Dynasty: Delhi, 1857*, NY: Alfred A. Knopf, 2006.
Damrel, David W., "The 'Naqshbandi Reaction' Reconsidered," *Beyond Turk and Hindu: Rethinking Religious Identities in Islamicate South Asia*, David

Guilmartin and Bruce B. Lawrence (eds.), Gainsville, Florida: University Press of Florida (2000), pp. 55–73.

Darling, Linda T., "'Do Justice, For That is Paradise!': Middle Eastern Advice for Indian Muslim Rulers," *Comparative Studies of South Asia, Africa, and the Middle East* XXII 1&2 (2002), pp. 3–19.

Devahuti, D., *Harsha, A Political Study*, Oxford: Clarendon, 1970.

DeWeese, Devin, ed., *Studies on Central Asian History, In Honor of Yuri Bregel*, Bloomington, Indiana: Indiana University, Research Institute for Inner Asian Studies, 2002.

_____ "The Descendants of Sayyid Ata and the Rank of Naqib in Central Asia," *Journal of the American Oriental Society* 115, 4 (1995), pp. 612–34.

Dickie, James, "The Mughal Garden: Gateway to Paradise," *Muqarnas* 3 (1985), pp. 128–137.

Digby, Simon, *Sufis and Soldiers in Awrangzeb's Deccan*, New Delhi: Oxford University Press, 2001.

Dye, Joseph M., III, "Imperial Mughal Painting," *The Magnificent Mughals*, Zeenat Ziad (ed.,) Oxford University Press (2002), pp. 143–182.

Eaton, Richard M. *A Social History of the Deccan, 1300- 1761, Eight Indian Lives*, Cambridge: Cambridge University Press, 2005.

_____ (ed.), *India's Islamic Traditions, 711–1750*, New Delhi: Oxford University Press, 2003.

Eck, Diana L., *Darsan: Seeing the Divine Image in India*, Columbia University Press, 2nd ed., 1996.

Faruqui, Munis, "The Forgotten Prince: Mirza Hakim and the Formation of the Mughal Empire in India," *Journal of the Economic and Social History of the Orient*, 48, 4 (2005), pp. 487–523.

_____ "Princes and Power in the Mughal Empire, 1569–1657," unpublished PhD dissertation, Department of History, Duke University, 2002.

Fleischer, Cornell, *Bureaucrat and Intellectual in the Ottoman Empire: The Historian Mustafa Ali (1541–1600)*, Princeton, NJ: Princeton University Press, 1986.

Fletcher, Joseph, "Turco-Mongolian Monarchic Traditions," *Eucharistion* (Harvard Ukrainian Studies) III-IV (1979–80), pp. 136–51.

Flood, Finbarr, *Objects of Translation: Material Culture and Medieval "Hindu-Muslim" Encounter*, Princeton, NJ: Princeton University Press, 2009.

Friedmann, Johanan, *Shaykh Ahmad Sirhindi, An Outline of His Thought and a Study of His Image in the Eyes of Posterity*, Montreal and London: McGill University Press, 1971.

_____ "Nizami, Naqshbandi Influence on Mughal Rulers and Politics," *Islamic Culture* XXXIX (1965), pp. 40–3.

Foltz, Richard C., *Mughal India and Central Asia*, NY: Oxford University Press, 1998.

Gaborieau, Marc, Alexandre Popovic, Thierry Zarcone (eds.), *Naqshbandis: Cheminements et situation actuelle d'un ordre mystique musulman*, Actes de la table Ronde de Sèvres, Istanbul and Paris: Isis Press, 1985/1990.

Gallop, Annabel Teh, "The Genealogical Seal of the Mughal Emperors of India," *Journal of the Royal Asiatic Society*, 3/9/1 (April 1999), pp. 77–140.

Golden, Peter B., *An Introduction to the History of the Turkic Peoples*, Weisbaden: Harrassowitz, 1992.

Golombek, Lisa and Maria Subtelny (eds.), *Timurid Art and Culture: Iran and Central Asia in the Fifteenth Century*, Leiden, NY, Koln: E.J. Brill, 1992.

Gommens, Jos J. L., *Mughal Warfare: Indian Frontiers and High Roads to Empire, 1500–1700*, NY: Routledge, 2002.

_____ and Dirk H. A. Kolff, *Warfare and Weaponry in South Asia, 1000–1800, A.D.*, Delhi: Oxford University Press, 2001.

Gonda, J., *Ancient Indian Kingship From the Religious Point of View*, Leiden: E. J. Brill, 1969.

Gordon, Stewart, *The Marathas, 1600–1818*, Cambridge University Press, 1993.

Gronke, Monika, "The Persian Court Between Palace and Tent: From Timur to 'Abbas I," *Timurid Art and Culture: Iran and Central Asia in the Fifteenth Century*, Lisa Golombek and Maria Subtelney (eds.), Leiden: E.J. Brill, 1992, pp. 18–22.

Gross, JoAnn, "The Naqshbandiyya Connection: From Central Asia to India and Back (16th-19th Centuries)," *India and Central Asia: Commerce and Culture, 1500–1800*, Scott Levi (ed.), New Delhi: Oxford University Press, 2007.

_____ "Naqshbandi Appeals to the Herat Court: A Preliminary Study of Trade and Property Issues," *Studies on Central Asian History, In Honor of Yuri Bregel*. Devin DeWeese, ed., Bloomington, Indiana: Indiana University Research Institute for Inner Asian Studies (2001), pp. 113–28.

_____ "Multiple Roles and Perceptions of a Sufi Shaikh: Symbolic Statements of Political Power and Religious Authority," *Naqshbandis*, Marc Gaborieau, et al, (eds.), (1990), pp. 109–121.

Grotenhaus, Elizabeth ten, *Japanese Mandalas: Representations of Sacred Geography*, University of Hawai'i Press, 1998.

Guenther, Alan M., "Hanafi *Fiqh* in Mughal India: The *Fatawa-i Alamgiri*," *India's Islamic Traditions, 711–1750*, Richard M. Eaton (ed.), New Delhi: Oxford University Press (2003), pp. 209–33.

Habib, Irfan, ed., *Akbar and His Age*, New Delhi: Oxford University Press, 1997.

_____ "Timur in the Political Tradition and Historiography of Mughal India," *L'Heritage Timouride*, Maria Szuppe (ed.), (1997) pp. 297–312.

Hambly, Gavin R.G., "Armed Women Retainers in the Zenanas of Indo-Muslim Rulers: The Case of Bibi Fatima," *Women in the Medieval Islamic World*, Gavin R.G. Hambly, ed., NY: St. Martin's Press (1998), pp. 429–468.

_____ (ed.), *Women in the Medieval Islamic World*, NY: St. Martin's Press, 1998.

_____ *Cities of Mughal India*, NY: G.P. Putnam's Sons, 1968.

Hobhouse, Penelope, *Gardens of Persia*, Kales Press Inc, 2003.

Hodivala, Shahpurshah Hormasji, *Studies in Indo-Muslim History: A Critical Commentary on Elliot and Dowson's History of India as Told by its Own Historians*, Lahore: Islamic Book Service, 1st ed. 1939; Pakistan reprint 1979.

Howard, Douglas A., "Ottoman Historiography and the Literature of 'Decline' of the Sixteenth and Seventeenth Centuries," *Journal of Asian History* 22 (1988), pp. 52–77.

Imber, Colin, *The Ottoman Empire, 1300–1650*, NY: Palgrave Macmillan, 2002.

Inden, Ronald, "Ritual, Authority and Cyclic Time in Hindu Kingship," *Kingship and Authority in South Asia*, J.F. Richards (ed.), Madison: University of Wisconsin, 1978, pp. 28–73.

Islam, Riazul, *A Calendar of Documents on Indo-Persian Relations*, Tehran, 1982.

Jackson, Peter, *The Delhi Sultanate*, NY: Cambridge University Press, 1999.

_____ and Lawrence Lockhart, eds., *Cambridge History of Iran* VI [*The Timurid and Safavid Periods*], Cambridge: Cambridge University Press, 1986.

Kahn, Paul, *A Secret History of the Mongols: An Adaptation of the Yuan Cha'o Pi Shih*. Francis Woodman Cleaves (trans.), Boston: Cheng & Tsui Company, 1984, 1998.

Keay, John, *India, A History*, NY: Grove Press, 2000.

Keddie, Nickie and Rudi Matthee (eds.), *Iran and the Surrounding World*, Seattle and London: University of Washington Press, 2002.

Khan, Iqtidar Alam, "Akbar's Personality Traits and World Outlook: A Critical Reappraisal," *Akbar and His Age*, Irfan Habib (ed.), New Delhi: Oxford University Press, 1997 and *Social Scientist*, Volume 20, Nos. 232–33, New Delhi, September-October, 1992, pp. 16–30.

_____ *The Political Biography of A Mughal Noble*, New Delhi: Munshiram Manoharlal Publishers, 1973.

Khosla, Ram Prasad, *Mughal Kingship and Nobility*, New Delhi: Idarah-i Adabiyat-i Delli, 1976.

Koch, Ebba, "My Garden is Hindustan: The Mughal Padshah's Realization of a Political Metaphor," *Middle East Garden Traditions: Unity and Diversity*, Michel Conan, (ed.,) Washington, DC: Dumbarton Oaks, 2007, pp. 159–175.

_____ *The Complete Taj Mahal and the Riverfront Gardens of Agra*, London: Thames and Hudson, Ltd., 2006.

_____ "Delhi of the Mughals," *Mughal Art and Imperial Ideology*, Ebba Koch (ed.), New Delhi: Oxford University Press (2002), pp. 163–81.

_____ "The Hierarchical Principles of Shah Jahani Painting," *Mughal Art and Imperial Ideology: Collected Essays*. Ebba Koch (ed.), New Delhi: Oxford University Press, 2002, pp. 130–162.

_____ "The Mughal Waterfront Garden," *Gardens in the Time of the Great Muslim Empires*, Attilio Petruccioli (ed.), Leiden: Brill (1997), pp. 140–160.

_____ *Mughal Architecture: An Outline of its History and Development (1526–1858)*, Munich: Prestel-Verlag, 1991.

Kozlowski, Gregory C., "Private Lives and Public Piety: Women and the Practice of Islam in Mughal India," *Women in the Islamic World*, Gavin Hambly (ed.), New York: St. Martin's Press (1998), pp. 469–88.

Kulke, Hermann, ed., *The State In India, 1000–1700*, Delhi: Oxford University Press, 1995.

Lal, Ruby, *Domesticity and Power in the Early Mughal World*, Cambridge: Cambridge University Press, 2005.
———— "Historicizing the Harem: A History of Early Mughal Domestic Life," unpublished PhD dissertation, Johns Hopkins University, 2004.
Larson, Pier M., "Reconsidering Trauma, Identity and the African Diaspora: Enslavement and Historical Memory in Nineteenth Century Highland Madagascar," *William and Mary Quarterly*, 3rd Series LVI 2 (1999), pp. 335–62.
Lentz, Thomas W., "Memory and Ideology in the Timurid Garden," *Mughal Gardens: Sources, Places, Representations and Prospects*, James L. Westcoat, Jr. and Joachim Wolschke-Bulmahn (eds.), Washington, DC: Dumbarton Oaks (1996), pp. 31–57.
———— "Dynastic Imagery in Early Timurid Wall Painting" *Muqarnas* 10 (1993), pp. 253–265.
———— and Glenn D. Lowry, *Timur and the Princely Vision: Persian Art and Culture in the Fifteenth Century*, Los Angeles and Washington, DC: Los Angeles County Museum of Art and the Arther Sackler Gallery, Smithsonian Institution, 1989.
Levi, Scott (ed.), *India and Central Asia: Commerce and Culture, 1500–1800*, New Delhi: Oxford University Press, 2007.
Mano, Eiji, "The Baburnama and the Tarikh-i Rashidi: Their Mutual Relationship," *Timurid Art and Culture*, Lisa Golombek and Maria Subtelny (eds.), Leiden: E.J. Brill (1992), pp. 44–47.
Manz, Beatrice Forbes, *Power, Politics and Religion in Timurid Iran*, Cambrdge: Cambridge University Press, 2007.
———— "Women in Timurid Dynastic Politics," *Women in Iran from the Rise of Islam to 1800*, Guity Nashat and Lois Beck (eds.), Champagne-Urbana, Illinois: University of Illinois Press (2003), pp. 121–139.
———— "Family and Ruler in Timurid Historiography," *Studies on Central Asian History*, Devin DeWeese (ed.), Bloomington, Indiana: Indiana University Research Institute for Inner Asian Studies (2002), pp. 57–78.
———— "Mongol History rewritten and re-lived," *REMMM* 89- 90 (2002), pp. 129–149.
———— *The Rise and Rule of Tamerlane*, NY: Cambridge University Press, 1999.
———— "Tamerlane's Career and Its Uses," *Journal of World History* 13.1 (2002) pp. 1–25.
———— "Temur and the Problem of a Conqueror's Legacy." *Journal of the Royal Asiatic Society* 3/8/1 (1998), pp. 21–41.
———— "Tamerlane and the Symbolism of Sovereignty," *Iranian Studies* 21, 1–2 (1988), pp. 105–22.
Marshall, D.N., *Mughals in India: A Bibliographical Survey*, NY: Asia Publishing House, 1967.
Matthee, Rudolph P., *The Pursuit of Pleasure: Drugs and Stimulants in Iranian History, 1500–1900*, Princeton, NJ: Princeton University Press, 2005.

McChesney, Robert. *Waqf in Central Asia, 1480- 1889.* Princeton: Princeton University Press, 1991.

Meisami, Julie Scott, *Medieval Persian Court Poetry*, Princeton, NJ: Princeton University Press 1987.

Metcalf, Barbara, ed., *Islam in South Asia in Practice*, Princeton, NJ: Princeton University Press, 2009.

Miller, Barbara Stoler (ed.), *Powers of Art*, Delhi: Oxford University Press, 1992.

Misra, Rekha, *Women in Mughal India (1526–1748),* Delhi: Munshiram Manoharlal, 1967.

Moin, Ahmed Azfar, "Islam and the Millenium: Sacred Kingship and Popular Imagination in Early Modern India and Iran," unpublished dissertation, University of Michigan, 2010.

——— "Challenging the Mughal Emperor: the Islamic Millenium according to 'Abd al-Qadir Badayuni," *Islam in South Asia in Practice*, Barbara Metcalf (ed.), Princeton, NJ: Princeton University Press, 2009.

Morgan, David O., *The Mongols*, Cambridge, MA: Blackwell Publishers,1986; reprint 1994.

——— "The 'Great "yasa" of Chingiz Khan' and Mongol Law in the Ilkhanate," *Bulletin of Oriental and African Studies, In Honor of Ann Lambton* 49:1 (1986), pp. 163–176.

Moynihan, Elizabeth B., "But what a happiness to have known Babur!," *Mughal Gardens*, James Westcoat, et al. (eds.), (1996), pp. 95–126.

——— "The Lotus Garden Palace of Zahir al-Din Muhammad Babur," *Muqarnas*, vol. 5 (1988), pp. 135–152.

Mukherjee, Bharati, *Kautilya's Concept of Diplomacy, A New Interpretation*, Calcutta: Minerva Associates, 1976.

Mukminova, Raziya, "Le role de la femme dans la societe de l'asia central sous les Timourides et les Sheybanides," *L'Heritage Timouride, Iran-Asia Centrale-Inde, XVe- XVIIIe Siecles*, Maria Szuppe (ed.), Tachkent- Aiz-en-Provence, 1997.

Naqvi, H.K., *History of Mughal Government and Administration*, Delhi: Kanishka Publishing House, 1990.

Nashat, Guity and Lois Beck (eds.), *Women in Iran from the Rise of Islam to 1800,* Champagne-Urbana: University of Illinois Press, 2003.

Nasr, Seyyid Hossein, *Sufi Essays*, Albany, NY: State University of NY Press, 1991.

Nasta, Susheila, *Home Truths: Fictions of the South Asian Diaspora in Britain*, New York: Palgrave, 2002.

Necipoğlu, Gülru, "Word and Image: The Serial Portraits of Ottoman Sultans in Comparative Perspective," *The Sultan's Portrait*, Selim Kangal, ed., Istanbul: Işbank, 2000.

——— "Framing the Gaze in Ottoman, Safavid, and Mughal Palaces," Ars Orientalis, Vol. 23, Pre-Modern Islamic Palaces (1993), pp. 303–342.

Nizami, Khaliq Ahmad, *State and Culture in Medieval India*, New Delhi: Adam Publishers and Distributors, 1985.

BIBLIOGRAPHY

_____ "Naqshbandi Influence on Mughal Rulers and Politics," *Islamic Culture* 39 (1965), pp. 41–52.

Paul, Jurgen, *Doctrine and Organization: The Khwajagan/ Naqshbandiya in the first generation after Baha'uddin*, ANOR 1 (1998), pp. 1–79.

_____ "Forming a Faction: The Himayat System of Khwaja Ahrar." *International Journal of Middle Eastern Studies* 23, 4 (1991), pp. 533–548.

Petruccioli, Attilio (ed.), *Gardens in the Time of the Great Muslim Empire: Theory and Design*, Leiden: Brill, 1997.

Pierce, Leslie, *The Imperial Harem: Women and Sovereignty in the Ottoman Imperial Harem*, Oxford University Press, 1993.

Pourafzal, Haleh and Roger Montgomery, *The Spiritual Wisdom of Hafiz*, Rochester, VT: The Spiritual Traditions, 1998.

Quinn, Sholeh, *Historical Writing During the Reign of Shah Abbas, Ideology, Imitation and Legitimacy in Safavid Chronicles*, Salt Lake City, Utah: University of Utah Press, 2000.

Rehman, Abdul, "Garden Types in Mughal Lahore," *Gardens in the Time of the Great Muslim Empires*, Attilio Petruccioli (ed.), Leiden: Brill (1997), pp. 161–172.

Richards, John, "The Formulation of Imperial Authority Under Akbar and Jahangir," *The Mughal State, 1526–1750*, Muzaffar Alam and Sanjay Subrahmanyam (eds.), New Delhi: Oxford University Press (1998), pp. 126–167.

_____ *The New Cambridge History of India: The Mughal Empire*, Cambridge University Press, 1993; repr. 1995.

_____ (ed.), *Kingship and Authority in South Asia*, Madison: University of Wisconsin, 1978.

Rizvi, S.A.A., "Sixteenth Century Naqshbandi Leadership in India," *Naqshbandis*, Marc Gaborieau, Alexandre Popovic, Thierry Zarcone (eds.), Istanbul: Isis Press (1985/1990), pp. 153–165.

Roemer, H.R., "The Safavids," *Cambridge History of Iran*, vol. 6: The Timurid and Safavid Periods, Peter Jackson and Lawrence Lockhart (eds.), Cambridge: Cambridge University Press, 1986.

Rogers, J.M., *Mughal Painting*, London: British Museum Press, 1993.

Ruggles, D. Fairchild, "Humayun's Tomb and Garden: Typologies and Visual Order." *Gardens*, Petrucciolo (ed.) Leiden: Brill (1997), pp. 173–186.

Rypka, Jan, *History of Iranian Literature*, Dordrecht: D. Reidel, 1968.

Saberi, Reza, *A Thousand Years of Persian Rubaiyat*, Bethesda, Maryland: IBEX Publishers, 2000.

Sardesai, G. S. "Shivaji," *The Mughal Empire*, R.C. Majumdar (ed.), Bombay: Bharatiya Vidya Bhavan, 1974.

Said, Edward, "Reflection on Exile," *Granta* 13 (1984), pp. 137–149.

Sarkar, Benoy Kumar, "The Hindu Theory of International Relations," *American Political Science Review*, 1919.

Sarkar, Sir Jadunath, *History of Aurangzib*, London: Orient Longman Limited, 1973.

Savory, Roger, *Iran Under the Safavids*, Cambridge: Cambridge University Press, 1980.

Sax, William S., "Conquering the Quarters: Religion and Politics in Hinduism," *International Journal of Hindu Studies*, 4/1, April 2000, pp. 39–60.

_____ "The Ramnagar Ramlila: Text, Performance, Pilgrimage," *History of Religions*, 30/2, Nov. 1990, pp. 129–153.

Schimmel, Annemarie, *The Empire of the Great Mughals*, London: Reakton Books, LTD, 2004.

Screech, Timon, *The Shogun's Painted Culture: Fear and Creativity in the Japanese States, 1760–1829,* London: Reaktion Books, 2000.

Sharma, Sunil, *Persian Poetry at the Indian Frontier*, Delhi: Permanent Black, 2000.

Shiva, Shahram T., *Rending the Veil: Literal and Poetic Translations of Rumi*, Prescott, AZ: Hohm Press, 1995.

Singh, Ram Charitra Prasad, *Kingship in Northern India (c. 600–1200 AD)*, Delhi/Varanasi/Patna: Motilal Banarsidass, 1968.

Smith, Anthony D., *Myths and Memories of the Nation*, Oxford University Press, 1999.

Soucek, Priscilla, "Timurid Women: A Cultural Perspective," *Women in the Medieval Islamic World*, Gavin Hambly (ed.), NY: St.Martin's Press (1998), pp. 199–226.

Soucek, Svat, *A History of Inner Asia,* Cambridge: Cambridge University Press, 2000.

Soudavar, Abolala, "The Early Safavids and Their Cultural Interactions With Surrounding States," *Iran and the Surrounding World*, Nickie Keddie and Rudi Matthee (eds.), Seattle and London: University of Washington Press (2002), pp. 89–120.

Steingass, F., *Persian-English Dictionary*, New Delhi: Munshiram Manoharlal Publishers, Pvt., 2000.

Streusand, Douglas E., *The Formation of the Mughal Empire*, Delhi: Oxford University Press, 1989.

Subtelny, Maria Eva, "The Timurid Legacy: A Reaffirmation and a Reassessment," *Cahiers D'Asie Centrale* 3–4 (1997), 14.

_____ "The Curriculum of Islamic Higher Learning in Timurid Iran in the Light of the Sunni Revival Under Shahrukh," *Journal of the American Oriental Society* 115, 2 (1995), pp. 210–36.

_____ "Mirak-i Sayyid Ghiyas and the Timurid Tradition of Landscape Architecture," *Studia Iranica* 24 (1995), pp. 19–38.

_____ "Babur's Rival Relations: A Study of Kinship and Conflict in 15th and 16th Century Central Asia," *Der Islam*, 66 (1989), pp. 102–18.

_____ "Scenes From the Literary Life of Timurid Herat," *Logos Islamicos*, Roger M. Savory and Dionisius A. Agius (eds.), Toronto: Pontifical Institute of Medieval Studies (1984), pp. 137–158.

_____ "Arts and Politics in Early Sixteenth-Century Central Asia," *Central Asiatic Journal* 27, 1–2 (1983), pp. 121–48.

Szuppe, Maria (ed.), "Women in Sixteenth Century Safavid Iran," *Women in Iran,* Guity Nashat and Lois Beck (eds.), Champagne-Urbana: University of Illinois Press (2003), pp. 140–169.

_____ *L'Heritage Timouride, Iran-Asie Central-Inde, XVe-XViiie Siecles, Le Cahiers d'Asie Centrale,* Tachkent-Aix-en-Provence, 1997.

Tripathi, Ram Prasad, "The Turko-Mongol Theory of Kingship," *The Mughal State, 1526–1750,* Alam and Subrahmanyam (eds.), New Delhi: Oxford University Press, 1998.

Wade, Bonnie C., *Imaging Sound: An Ethnomusicological Study of Music, Art and Culture in Mughal India,* Chicago: University of Chicago Press, 2005.

Wagoner, Phillip, "Sultan among Hindu Kings: Dress, Titles, and the Islamicization of Hindu Culture at Vijayanagara," *The Journal of Asian Studies,* 55/4 (Nov. 1996) pp. 851–880.

Welch, Anthony, "Gardens That Babur Did Not Like: Landscape, Water and Architecture for the Sultans of Delhi," *Mughal Gardens,* J.L. Westcoat and J. Wolschke-Bulman (eds.), Washington, DC: Dumbarton Oaks, 1993.

Westcoat, James, Jr. and Joachim Wolschke-Bulmahn, eds., *Mughal Gardens,* Washington, DC: Dumbarton Oaks, 1996.

Wheeler, R.E.M., *Five Thousand Years of Pakistan,* London: Royal India and Pakistan Society, 1950.

Woods, John E., *The Aqquyunlu: Clan, Confederation, Empire,* Salt Lake City: University of Utah Press, 1999.

_____ *The Timurid Dynasty,* Bloomington: Indiana University Research Institute for Inner Asian Studies, Papers on Inner Asia, No. 14, 1990.

_____ "The Rise of Timurid Historiography," *Journal of Near Eastern Studies* 46/2 (April 1987), pp. 81–108.

Zarcone, Thierry, "Central Asian Influence on the Early Development of the Chishtiyya Sufi Order in India," *The Making of Indo-Persian Culture,* Muzaffar Alam, Francoise 'Nalini' Delvoye and Marc Gaborieau (eds.), New Delhi: Manohar (2000), pp. 99–116.

INDEX

Abbas I (Safavid Shah): 39, 68–9, 124
Abu al-Fazl Allami (see *Akbarnama* and *A'in-i Akbar*): 54–5, 118, 126 (his murder)
Abd al-Rahim Khan-i Khanan: 59, 118
Abd al-Samad: 63
Abu al-Khayr: 19
accessional fratricide: 124 (Ottoman and Safavid), 129 (Mughal), 132
adalet/'adl (justice): 48, 56 (Jahangir), 92, 94, 118, 144–5, 146–7 (Tusi/Sa'di), 148 (Hafez), 149–50, 150–3 (darshan), 176n, 187n, 190n, 191n
Agra: 3, 5, 23, 26–8 (Timurid conquest), 30–1, 34, 35, 46, 61, 75, 80–1 (gardens), 83, 94–5 (Jahangir's peripatetic court), 98, 112, 114, 132, 135, 151, 176n
Ahmadabad: 135, 152
Ahmedi: 123
A'in-i Akbar: 54, 59
Ajmer: 95, 119, 122, 126, 128, 135, 178n
Akbar (Aurangzeb's son): 134 (rebellion)
Akbar, Jalal al-Din Muhammad: 44 (reconquest of Turan), 49–51 (seal/portrait), 53, 54–5 (history and genealogy), 56, 59, 63 (on painting), 64–6 (imperial atelier), 68, 83–4 (architecture) 86 (Malwa), 90, 91 (opium), 104, 113–4 (appanage and ateke), 116–7 (succession), 117–9 (sons), 123, 125, 126–7 (filial rebellion), 136, 138, 143–4 (divine rule), 149 (Tusi), 150, 170n, 172n, 176n, 178n, 185n, 190n
Akbarnama: 54, 64, 170n
Akhlaq-i Humayun (Ikhtyar al-Husaini): 146
Akhlaq-i Jalali (Jalal al-Din Davvani): 150
Akhlaq-i Nasiri (Nasir al-Din Tusi): 145–6
Alanqua: 14, 37, 54
Ali Shir Nava'i: 58
Akbarabad: 85
Amir Khusraw: 33, 165n
Anushirvan, Khusrau I: 145, 150
appanage (see *ulus*): 13, 19, 105, 107, 108–9, 111 (Timurid), 111 (Babur), 112 (Babur's sons), 113–4 (Humayun and Akbar), 114–7 (Humayun and brothers), 117–20 (Akbar's sons), 121, 123–5 (Ottoman and Safavid), 132 (Shah Jahan's sons), 134–6, 161n

INDEX

Arjun Singh (guru): 127
Askeri: 115–6
ateke/atabeg/ataliq: 106, 109, 112 (Humayun's), 112 (Hindal's), 118 (Akbar's sons), 120, 121, 122, 128, 183–4n, 186n
Aurangzeb (Alamgir/Shah Bulad Iqbal): 50, 57 (chronicles and letter to son), 59, 73, 85 (hunt), 86 (size of hunt/court progress), 98–9 (Deccani campaign), 99 (will), 119–120, 121, 122, 123, 129, 130–3 (succession war, his own), 134 (relations with sons), 134–5 (attempt at appanage system), 138 (divine right), 140, 150, 167n, 171n, 172n, 174n, 176n, 178n, 185n, 186n, 189n
Aziz Koka (Mirza): 118

Babur, Zahir al-Din Muhammad: 2–4; exile and nostalgia: 18, 164n, 168n; in Mawarannahr: 19–21, 44, 111, 164–5n; flight from Mawarannahr: 21–24; female relatives: 22–24, 166n, 167-8n, 186n; in Kabul: 24–26, 44; in India: 26, 36 (Battle of Panipat), 27–32 (exile), 28-31, 34–5 (reaction to India), 31 (abstinence), 45, 46 (India as Timurid territory), 79; ambition and political legitimacy, kingship: 2, 25, 26 (Panipat), 43–4, 47, 107, 108 (shared kingship), 166n, 170n, 172n, 173n; Islam: 41–4 (ghazi), 170n, 178n; gardens: 25 (in Kabul), 35 (Hasht Bihisht), 79–81;
Baburnama: 31–2, 52–5, 59 (translation), 64 (Illustration), 174n, 175n (Zafarnama), 176n (Persian translation); portraiture: 62-3; alcohol: 25, 31, 90, 91 (with Hulhul Anika), 92 (camaraderie of alcohol), 93, 169n; maternal lineage: 102, 172n; inheritance and succession: 111, 112–3 (his sons), 188n
Badakhshan: 24, 25, 26, 111–2, 115–6, 130, 160n, 186n
Bahadur Shah (Azam Shah): 57, 120, 134, 135
Bahadur Shah Zafar (last of the Mughals) : 49, 69–70
Baharistan-i Ghaybi (see Mirza Nathan): 51
Bahmani Sultanate: 40
Balkh: 44, 45, 112, 116, 130, 153
Bayezid (Ottoman Sultan): 61, 77–8, 123
Bayezid Bayat: 53
Bayqara, Sultan Husayn: 20, 23–4, 27, 49, 58, 102–3, 108, 145
Bihzad: 58

Chaghatay (-id): 2, 8, 9, 11, 20–1, 23–4, 47, 52–3, 58–9, 103, 106–7, 110, 125, 157n, 158n, 161n, 162n
Chahar bagh: 75, 76–8 (Timur), 78 (late Timurid), 79 (Babur), 81, 162n
Chakravartin: 97
Chingis Khan (see Chingisid): 1, 2–3, 7, 9–15, 19, 22, 27, 35, 38, 47, 49, 53, 55, 58–9, 105, 108, 111, 138, 157n, 158n, 161n, 168n, 183n
Chingisid (see also Chingis Khan): 22, 39–40, 42, 47, 52, 76, 102–3, 105–6, 107, 141, 158n, 162n, 168n
Chishti sufi order: 42, 66, 140, 174n
Circle of Justice: 145, 151

Danyal: 118–9, 126
Dara Shikoh: 48 (*Sahib Qiran-i Dil*), 122, 129, 130–2 (succession war), 133 (execution), 134, 138
darshan (see *jharoka-i darshan*): 142–4, 151–2, 154

darshaniyya: 144
dawlat khana-i khass: 144
Deccan: 40, 44, 45, 86, 93, 97 (Shivaji), 98–9 (Aurangzeb), 120, 126, 128, 129, 130–1, 135, 167n, 178n, 186n
digvijaya (conquest of the quarters): 97–8
Dildar Begim: 104–5 (divination)
Dost Muhammad: 63
du ashiyana manzil (royal tent): 144

exile; loss; nostalgia (see *ghurbat/ ghariplik*): 2–6, 18–21 (exile), 21–25 (impact on Timurid women), 26–7, 28–9 (exile), 29–30 (studies of refugee and exile/ memory), 30–3 (in India), 34–6 (as cultural bridges), 37, 72, 63 (Humayun), 69–70 (Bahadur Shah), 72, 80, 99 (Aurangzeb), 116 (Humayun), 116 (Kamran), 140–1, 155, 161–2n, 164n

Fatehpur Sikri: 34, 66, 71, 74, 83
Fayzi: 118, 150
Firdaus makani (see Babur): 53, 115
Firdowsi (*Shahnama*): 32, 41, 149, 150

gardens, imperial: 75–81 (Babur's gardens in India), 82, 84
Gawarshad (wife of Shahrukh, daughter-in-law of Timur): 103
genealogy: 3, 5, 6, 9, 14, 37–8, 39–40 (Ottoman), 47, 49–51 (*Silsillahnama*), 50–1 (imperial portraits with genealogical chart), 52, 54–5 (Akbar), 62, 63–6 (genealogical paintings), 69 (inscribed ruby), 83, 100 (women)
Ghazni/Mahmud of Ghazni: 32–3, 41, 113, 115, 116
ghurbat/ghariplik (see exile): 28, 33, 164n
Gujarat: 40,120, 128, 130, 132, 135
Gulbadan Begim (see *Humayunnama*): 3, 26–7 (migration to India), 53 (writing *Humayunnama*), 59, 104–5 (fosterage), 112 (Humayun's governorship), 170n
Guregen: 9, 14, 22, 37, 45, 46, 47, 54, 68, 102
Gur-i Amir (Timur's tomb): 14, 45–46

Habiba Sultan Khanish Dughlat: 23, 182n
Hafez (Shirazi): 92, 93, 147–8, 150
Hasb-i hal: 32–3
Herat: 13, 15, 20–1, 24, 26, 28, 33, 41, 44, 58, 61, 67, 78, 79, 82, 107, 140, 145
Hindal Mirza: 104 (fosterage), 112, 113 (appanage), 115–6
Hindustan: 2–3, 6, 25–6 (Babur's conquest of), 28–32 (Babur on Hindustan), 34–5, 44, 59, 80–1, 114, 141, 162n, 166n
Hissar Firoza: 112, 129
Humayun (*Jannat Ashyani*): 44, 53, 91 (addiction), 104, 107, 112 (governorship of Badakhshan), 113–4 (appanage), 114 (inheritance and fraternal rivalry), 115 (flight and exile), 117, 137
Humayun's tomb: 83

Ibn Arabshah: 77
Ikhtiyar al-Din al-Husayni: 146
Ilkhanid (Empire): 7–8, 11, 49, 52 (histories), 54, 63 (art), 76 (gardens), 147, 176n, 178n
Iqbalnama (see Mu'tamid Khan); 56
Iqbalnama-i Jahangiri: 59
Isan Dawlat Khanim: 104
Ismail (Safavid Shah): 26, 164n
Istanbul: 41, 74

Jahanara: 133
Jahangir (Sultan Salim Nur al-Din): 39, 44–45 (Transoxiana), 45–6, 48 (Sahib Qiran), 50–1(seal and

Index

portrait), 55–6 (*Jahangirnama*), 59 (on reading *Baburnama*), 65 (*Princes of the House of Timur*), 66 (painting), 67–9 (Timurid memorabilia), 82 (gardens of Kabul), 84–6 (the hunt), 85 (Nur Jahan), 88, 91–2 (alcohol and drugs), 93, 94–6 (peripatetic court), 96–8 (*mandala* and cosmology of empire), 98 (death in Kashmir), 104, 118 (princely training), 120, 122, 123, 125, 126 (princely rebellion, his own), 127 (princely rebellion, his son Khusraw), 127–9 (princely rebellion, his son Khurram), 136–37, 138 (divine sanction to rule), 147, 150–3 (justice), 154, 169n, 170n, 171n, 174n, 177n, 179n, 186n, 187n
Jadrup Gosain (Hindu mystic): 147
Jamshid: 126, 185n
Jannat Ashyani (see Humayun): 53
jharoka-i darshan (see *darshan*): 144, 151–2 (Jahangir), 152–3 (Shah Jahan)
Juwayni: 52

Kabul: 5, 44–46, 79, 113, 115, 116
kafes: 124
Kam Baksh 135
Kamran: 44, 63, 81, 107 (inheritance), 112–3 (appanage), 114–6 (fraternal rivalry), 123, 173n, 184n
Kashmir: 82 (gardens), 98, 118, 130
Khadija Sultan Begim: 24, 163n
Khalil Sultan: 111
Khan Azam: 128
Khanzada Begim: 22 (capture and marriage), 115, 162n, 164n
Khanzada Khanim: 23, 24 (Uzbek marriage)
Khurasan: 13, 15, 17, 19, 25, 27, 32 (poetry), 39, 61, 106, 157n, 159–60n, 161n, 178n, 184n

Khurram (see Shah Jahan)
Khusraw (son of Jahangir): 65, 126–7 (rebellion), 129, 138, 174n, 187n
Khusraw (Amir Nasir): 32, 33, 165n
khutba: 114, 115, 131, 133
Khwaja Jalalal-Din Mahmud: 113
Khwaja Kalan: 30, 31, 34–5
Khwandamir, Ghiyas al-Din: 21(Uzbek attack on Herat), 24, 38 (Timur's lineage), 53 (Humayun)

Lahore: 26, 75, 81, 82 (*Shalimar*), 98, 176n, 187n
Lodi dynasty: 2, 26, 28, 46 (Babur), 81 (gardens)

Maham Begim (wife of Babur): 104–5
Majlis: 90 (Timurid), 92 (*majlis-i sharab-i tertib*)
Majun: 164n
Malwa: 40, 86, 130, 135
Mandala: 40, 96 (*raja mandala*)
Maryam Makani (Hamida Banu Begim): 104, 177–8n
Mawarannahr/Transoxiana (Turan): 2, 4–5, 8, 10, 15, 17, 19–21(Uzbek invasion), 26–8 (Timurid flight), 36, 38, 42, 44–6 (ancestral homeland), 61, 76 (gardens), 81, 106, 107, 110–1, 137, 140, 141, 147, 153 (Mughal attemtped re-conquest), 154, 157–8n, 159–60n, 160–1n, 162n, 167n, 183n
Mehmet I (Ottoman Sultan): 123–4
Mehmet II, the Conqueror (Ottoman Sultan): 41, 124
Mihrangaz Begim: 24, 164n
Mihr Nigar Khanim: 22, 25
Mihtar Jauhar Aftabchi: 53
Mir Muzavvar: 63
Mir Sayyid Ali: 63, 65
Mirza Nathan (author of *Baharistan-i Ghaybi*): 51

214 Imperial Identity in the Mughal Empire

Muhammad Hakim: 91 (alcohol), 116–7 (fraternal rivalry)
Muhammad Muazzam: (135)
Muhammad Shah: 58
Muhammad Sultan: 134
Mu'in al-Din Chishti: 186n
Muhr-i muqqadas-i kalan (imperial seal): 49–50
Mulfuzat-i Timuri: 68
Murad I (Ottoman Sultan): 123
Murad Baksh (son of Shah Jahan): 50, 122, 129–30 (assignments), 130–3 (succession war), 153, 186n
Mustafa I (Ottoman Sultan): 124
Mustafa Ali: 39–40

Nomadism/peripatetic court: 5 (Timurid), 71–5
Mu'tamid Khan (see *Iqbalnama*): 56
Nadir Shah: 40, 49, 58
Nazir Beg: 120
Naukar (*noker*): 122
Naqshbandi sufi order: 10, 42, 67 (diplomatic exchange with Jahangir), 140–1
Nizam al-Din Auliya: 174n
Nur Jahan: 85 (huntress)

Ordu-i humayun/urdu-i mu'alla (Mughal imperial camp): 72–5
Ottoman: 1, 6, 13 (Bayezid I), 17, 24, 38–40 (legitimacy and identity), 41, 48, 59, 61–2 (portraiture), 68, 74 (Istanbul), 77–8 (Bayezid's tapestry), 81, 100–1 (women), 104, 123–5 (succession), 132, 135, 176n 177n, 182n, 183–4n

padshah: 24–5, 28, 45, 79, 90, 92, 93, 108
Paira daeza (paradeisos/paradise): 75
Parvez: 65
Payanda Sultan Begim Miranshahi: 25

Princes of the House of Timur (painting): 65, 174n
Pir Muhammad ibn Jahangir: 13, 90, 106–9
  Ruy Gonzales de Clavijo: 77 (gardens), 90–1 (alcohol)

Qaculi Bahadur (Timurid ancestor): 54
Qadiri sufi order: 48
Qamargha (Mongol circle hunt): 86–7, 88
Qandahar: 68–9, 112, 115–16, 130, 161n, 174n
Qutb al-Din Khan: 118

Rashid al-Din: 52, 64
Roe, Sir Thomas: 93, 95, 143, 151–2
Rumi, Jalal al-Din: 147–8, 149

Sa'di: 108, 133, 147–50
Safavid: 1, 6, 17, 24–5, 26, 38–9 (legitimacy and Timur), 44, 49, 61–3 (portraiture/artists), 68 (Qandahar), 89, 92 (alcohol), 123–5 (succession), 135, 164n, 173n, 174n, 183–4n
Sahib Qiran (Lord of the Auspicious Conjunction): 9, 27, 38, 39, 45, 47–8, 50, 54, 143
Sa'id Khan Chaghatay: 118, 185n
Salim (see Jahangir)
Samarqand: 11–3 (Timurid capitol), 14, 20–1, 22–4 (Babur and Timurid flight), 26, 28 33, 34, 36, 40, 41, 44–5 (Mughal nostalgia), 46, 61, 67, 68, 76–7 (late Timurid), 78–9 (gardens), 82, 87, 90, 107, 111, 112, 116, 140, 153, 159n, 159–60n, 164n, 182n
Saray Mulk Khanim: 102
Selim II (Ottoman Sultan): 124
Shah Begim Badakhshi: 25
Shah Buland Iqbal (see Shah Jahan): 132
Shahjahanabad: 71, 99, 130, 165n, 185n
Shah Murad: 118, 120, 126

INDEX

Shahnamah: 41
Shahnawaz Khan Safavi: 121–2
Shah Shuja: 122, 129, 130–32 (succession war), 134
Shams al-Din Khan:118
Shah Begim Badakhshi: 25
Shah Jahan (Khurram/aka Shah Sultan Khurram/aka *Shah Buland Iqbal*/ aka *Bidawlet*): 36, 45, 48 (Sahib Qiran-i Sani), 56–7 (court chronicles), 59, 64–5, 66–7 (imperial atelier), 68 (*Mulfuzat*), 69, 74 (court progress), 82–3 (gardens), 85 (hunt), 93 (alcohol), 98, 104, 120, 122 (sons), 123, 127–9 (princely rebellion, his own), 129 (accessional fratricide), 129–30 (managing sons), 130–2 (succession war, his sons), 132 (attempt to install appanage system), 133, 134, 144 (darshan), 150, 151 (chain of justice), 152 (jharoka), 153, 165n, 167n, 171n, 174n, 176n, 177n, 178n, 184n, 187n
Shahnama (Firdowsi): 41, 149, 150
Shahrukh: 9, 13, 21, 49, 65, 68, 102, 106–9 (Timur's succession), 159n, 161n, 170n, 184n
shari'a: 146
Sharif Khan: 118
Shaykh Salim: 66, 83–4 (Fatehpur Sikri)
Shibani Khan: 19–21 (conquest of Mawarannahr), 21–26 (conquest marriages), 106, 182n
Shaykh Zayn: 58–9
Shir Khan (Shah): 114
Shivaji: 97, 181n
Silsilah-i 'adl/ *bustan zanjir-i 'adl* (chain of justice): 151
succession: 6, 13, 50, 62, 65–6, 74, 80, 100–03 (maternal lineage), 104, 105–114 (tanistry/princely training), 117 (Akbar), 120–122 (atekes), 122, 123–4 (Ottoman and Safavid), 125, 126–9 (sons of Jahangir), 130–133 (sons of Shah Jahan), 134–135(sons of Aurangzeb), 135–7 (re-subjugation) 137–9 (divine sanction), 141, 176n, 182n, 183n, 184–5n, 186n
Suleyman (Ottoman Sultan): 124
Suleiman Shikoh: 133
Sultan Abu Sa'id Mirza: 61, 102, 103, 163n, 186n
Sultan Husayn Bayqara: 20, 24, 49, 58, 90, 102–3 (lineage), 108 (sharing kingship)

Tahmasp (Safavid Shah): 49, 63, 173n
tanistry: 105, 129, 136–7
Timur Barlas (Tamerlane): 2, 3, 4, 8–11 (rise to power), 11–13 (legitimacy and identity), 13 (death), 14 (Guregen), 15–7 (immediate successors), 22, 25–7 (Babur's claims), 34, 37–8 (genealogy), 39–41 (evoked by rival courts), 41–4 (evoked by Babur), 45–6 (tomb), 46, 47–8 (sahib qiran), 49 (silsilahnama), 50 (Mughal imperial seal), 52–60 (history writing), 60–1 (painting and portraiture), 62, 64–5 (genealogical paintings), 66, 68–9 (memorabilia), 71–2, 73, 76–8 (gardens), 87, 90 (alcohol), 102–3 (wives and children), 105–7 (succession), 109–11 (princely training), 114, 121, 123, 138 (heavenly mandate), 141, 143, 149, 157–62n, 169–70n, 177n, 184n
Timurid (see Timur): 2–6, 9–11 (religion), 11 (identity), 13–17 (post-Timur dynastic identity), 18–21 (exile), 21- 25 (impact on Timurid women), 25–6

Timurid (see Timur) (*Cont.*)
    (in Kabul/claims to India), 27
    (migration to India), 28–9 (exile and nostalgia), 29–30 (studies of refugee and memory), 30–33 (in India/*Baburnama*), 34–5, 35–6 (as cultural bridges), 37–8 (lineage), 38–41 (political charisma), 41–3 (legitimacy in India), 44–7 (homeland), 49–50 (genealogy), 51–53, 57, 58, 59–60 (memoirs and texts), 61–3 (painting), 67, 69–70 (Bahadur Shah), 71–3 (nomadism), 75, 76–8 (Timur's gardens), 78–9 (late Timurid gardens), 80–3 (gardens in India), 83–4 (architecture), 84, 89, 90–3 (alcohol), 100, 102 (women/succession), 103–5 (fosterage), 106–13(succession), 108 (appanage), 110 (ateke), 114, 117, 118, 120, 121, 123, 124–5, 129 (accessional fratricide), 132, 134–7, 138–9 (divine sanction), 140–2 (identity), 142–4(kingship), 145–7 (Islamic norms of rule), 147–9 (ethics), 153–5, 156n, 158n, 160–2n, 163n, 164n, 167n, 168n, 169–70n, 172n, 178n
Tukal Khanim: 102, 158n
Tumen Agha: 103
Turco-Mongol: 6, 7,9–11, 13–16, 22, 38, 39, 53, 55, 62, 73, 74, 88, 96, 100, 105, 115, 132, 135–7, 139, 159n, 167n, 183n
Tusi, Khwaja Nasir al-Din: 145–50, 151, 191n

Ulugh Beg: 13, 68 (jade cup), 74, 102 (lineage), 160n, 174n, 184n
ulus (see *appanage*): 6, 8, 103, 108–9, 157n 184n
Umar Shaykh (Babur's father): 45, 65, 90 (drinking),160–1n, 163n
Umar Shaykh (son of Timur): 9, 109, 161n, 184n
Uzbeks: 1, 2, 15, 17, 19–21 (invasion of Mawarannahr), 21–24 (conquest marriages), 24–7 (rout of Timurids), 44 (Humayun), 45, 49, 50, 53, 67 (at Jahangir's court), 72, 79, 98, 106, 107, 111, 112, 135, 137, 140, 146, 161–2n, 163n, 164n, 168n, 182n

Vassaf: 52
Vijayayatra: 97
Vijayanagar: 40

Yasa (Mongol law): 10, 11
Yamuna: 81
Yasavi sufi order: 10
Yusuf Khan, Mirza: 120

Zafarnama: 58–9, 171n